D1590722

THE INNER LIFE OF THE DYING PERSON

END-OF-LIFE CARE: A SERIES

END-OF-LIFE CARE: A SERIES

Series editor: Keith Anderson

We all confront end-of-life issues. As people live longer and suffer from more chronic illnesses, all of us face difficult decisions about death, dying, and terminal care. This series aspires to articulate the issues surrounding end-of-life care in the twenty-first century. It will be a resource for practitioners and scholars who seek information about advance directives, hospice, palliative care, bereavement, and other death-related topics. The interdisciplinary approach makes the series invaluable for social workers, physicians, nurses, attorneys, and pastoral counselors.

The press seeks manuscripts that reflect the interdisiciplinary, biopsychosocial essence of end-of-life care. We welcome manuscripts that address specific topics on ethical dilemmas in end-of-life care, death, and dying among marginalized groups, palliative care, spirituality, and end-of-life care in special medical areas, such as oncology, AIDS, diabetes, and transplantation. While writers should integrate theory and practice, the series is open to diverse methodologies and perspectives. Manuscript submissions should be sent to series editor Keith Anderson at anderson.1630@osu.edu.

Recent titles in the series:

THE INNER LIFE OF THE DYING PERSON

Allan Kellehear

COLUMBIA UNIVERSITY PRESS   NEW YORK

Columbia University Press
Publishers Since 1893
New York   Chichester, West Sussex
cup.columbia.edu
Copyright © 2014 Columbia University Press

Library of Congress Cataloging-in-Publication Data
Kellehear, Allan, 1955–
The inner life of the dying person / Allan Kellehear.
pages cm. — (End-of-life care : a series)
Includes bibliographical references and index.
ISBN 978-0-231-16784-0 (cloth : alk. paper) —
ISBN 978-0-231-16785-7 (pbk. : alk. paper) — ISBN 978-0-231-53693-6 (e-book)
1. Death—Psychological aspects. 2. Terminally ill—Psychology. I. Title.

BF789.D4K45 2014
155.9'37—dc23
2013040487

Columbia University Press books are printed on permanent
and durable acid-free paper.
This book is printed on paper with recycled content.
Printed in the United States of America

c 10 9 8 7 6 5 4 3 2 1
p 10 9 8 7 6 5 4 3 2

COVER IMAGE: *Night Birds*, 2011 (oil on linen), Nicola Bealing/
Private Collection/The Bridgeman Art Library
COVER DESIGN: Lisa Hamm

. . . the light shines in the darkness,
and the darkness did not comprehend it.

—John 1:5

Contents

Preface

This book is about the unusual intersection of personal forces—physical, emotional, social, and spiritual—that predispose dying people to see afresh their old taken-for-granted worlds. Dying people encounter these unique combinations of personal experience and crossroad moments, often for the very first time in their lives. Above all, this book is about how it *feels* to die. But when I say *feels* I do not mean to isolate and describe emotions as if they have no intimate reference to the social, physical, and spiritual forces that create them. In this way I have chosen to write more about the key personal experiences that characterize dying, to describe the inner life of dying as an inseparable mixture of feeling, physical impulses, social interaction, meaning making, and soliloquy.

When I refer to the dying person in this work I am referring to a person who is consciously aware and expectant that death will come soon—often in the next few hours, days, months but almost as commonly within several years. However, irrespective of the calendar of events involved, this saturating awareness, expectation, and acceptance of impending death—sometimes in the foreground, sometimes in the background of the dying person's mind—informs the descriptions, analyses, and reflections in this book. I am not concerned with the increasing number of people who have advanced disease, commonly a spreading cancer, who will not acknowledge to themselves any notions of death or dying. These people are not dying in any sense other than perhaps a medically observed one. Such people often view themselves as people living with serious chronic illness. They are, or aspire to be, survivors to the end. I am also not referring to other people who wish to adopt a type of philosophical pose that suggests all living things are dying things ipso facto. Once we are born, we begin to die. Between these two extreme examples, of sequestering on the one hand and overinclusion on the other, are serious examples of people

who will truly die soon: through accident or by intent, through social and physical circumstances beyond their control, by their own hand, the hand of others
(people on death row, for example), or from a killer disease. This knowledge
changes the way they experience the world—emotionally, socially, spiritually,
and, more often than not, totally. The prospect of dying shortly changes things,
sometimes all things, for dying people. These changes occur right up to the last
minutes and breaths of their organic life. And this book is devoted to the task
of describing these personal changes.

Although dying is commonly portrayed as a dramatic affair, a problematic
thing, a medical experience, it commonly plays out against type. More often
than many like to think, dying is a surprisingly quiet affair, a mixture of both
sad and happy traffic between loved ones and the dying person, and between
the mind and the heart of the dying person as each aspect of one's self strives
to attain some meaningful accord at the end of life.

Most books on dying often simply fail to provide a description of this
handful of usual experiences common to our intimate encounter with death.
Remember that medical observers write most books on dying, and they do so
with an understandable but work-related eye for problems during the dying
process. The emphasis, if not the accent, is on grief and loss, symptom management, and coping or lack thereof. If we put some distance between us and
this kind of academic and clinical writing about death and dying—seeking to
view all conscious experiences near death as a whole—our collection of normal and usual images of dying actually appears to be rather small. Instead,
dominant images of dying tend to have a strong institutional look—fragments
of hospice or hospital life, portrayals of depression and despair, an overattention to the violence of the body.

Absent from most of these snapshots of people facing their own death
are the broader, more typical, less academically scrutinized normal personal
experiences that might balance the human portrait of dying—courage, waiting, hope, reminiscence, love, being alone, or transformation, all of which
might be added to what we know about suffering, fear, anger, or resistance.
In the admirable but overwhelmingly professional focus on solving problems,
we have neglected the more positive, adaptive, side of dying and in the process have given mortality a frightening face that is far beyond what we need.
It is high time we had an introduction to what it typically means to *live* at
the end of life.

To obtain a more balanced portrait of the inner life of dying people, I have included accounts of many other kinds of dying—from death camps, death row, suicides, war and disaster, accidents and trauma, aging and dementia, and many other examples. The recurring elements of personal experience in dying in widely different circumstances alerts us to what we commonly ignore or overlook in the forms of dying that are more familiar—in our hospitals, hospices, or nursing homes. This comparative method invites us to look again at all our recorded experiences of dying. I have attempted to identify the elements common to these different circumstances. To these sources I have added the academic analysis common in such accounts and blended these with insights about dying and death from some of the world's best writers and poets. Sometimes the expression of difficult experiences can use some help from wordsmiths whose trade is frequently in the ineffable.

I would like to add that in my efforts to make this work as accessible as possible to a broad readership, I have dispensed with the defensive academic style of argument: detailed review of every morsel of relevant literature and extensive notes or explanations about my method. I have worked among dying people, and reviewed the literature on this population, for about thirty years now. I have taken the liberty of focusing on a broad range of examples from different settings, ages, social classes, and ethnic and religious background. I have been guided by trends in the current clinical work in this area but also allowed anthropological, historical, and cultural voices found in other literature to influence me.

The existing first-person accounts in the public literature overrepresent those from middle-class backgrounds and those who are highly literate, and my work reflects this dominance. We are at the beginning of our serious exploration of the human encounter with death, and I make no apologies that this book unavoidably reflects the limitations of the present time and state of the art. But whatever those limitations, my hope is that most of my descriptions of that fine balance of dark and positive experiences that characterize the core elements of the journey of dying will be clear to most thoughtful readers, and that, in any case, all readers will value the importance of the attempt for its own sake.

For as we approach a period when the tide of dying is rising, yet another mark of the baby-boom generation, it is more imperative than ever for us to gather up what normal images of dying we can find and attempt to join them up with the other, more problem-based understandings. From here we might see what story or general meaning they have when we combine them, however imperfectly. Let us break away from an increasingly fragmented view of dying as a medical or psychological set of problems and reach for a new, more holistic, portrait of the inner life of the dying person. My aim in this book has been to build a deliberately interdisciplinary work focused on describing and understanding the common and recurring elements of personal experience while facing death.

In self-consciously attempting to create a more holistic portrait of the private experiences of the dying person, by deliberately reviewing and connecting our current rudimentary and unconnected observations, I hope to encourage my academic and clinical colleagues to improve upon what I have done. In any case, we need to make this an ongoing interdisciplinary project. And we need to start somewhere. Dying—the final and normal period of living—is underinvestigated. This is both ironic and dangerous because we now live in a time when new policies about palliative care, aging, intensive care, the determination of death, and euthanasia are being formulated with meager knowledge of the subject at the center of their different attentions.

At the same time, I also hope to offer general readers of this book a sketch of something less than they feared and something more complex, surprising, and wondrous than they might have first imagined. From the stories I have heard from the many who have lived in the shadow of death, and from a review of the literature that has sought to study the voices and the experiences of those who have gone before us, I now introduce the reader to what I believe are the most common personal elements of the journey ahead.

Martins River, Nova Scotia

Acknowledgments

I wrote this book while I was a guest professor in Canada, using the resources and facilities of the Department of Community Health and Epidemiology at Dalhousie University in Halifax, Nova Scotia. I thank my hosts—Adrian Levy, head of my department, and Tom Marrie, dean of medicine—for their hospitality and use of library and IT services. My friend and colleague Aliki Karapliagou at the University of Bath in England was my graduate research assistant. Aliki helped me with the initial groundwork of identifying, searching, and retrieving important lines of literature. She also helped identify fresh lines of writing and research we needed when we regularly reached the limits of the personal accounts of end of life care. My wife and academic colleague, Jan Fook, and I held scores of private conversations and debates about the ideas and perspectives offered in this book, which helped me hone and refine my reflections, as she has so often done in our many years together. My Canadian colleague Margie King and two anonymous reviewers read the manuscript, and each provided encouraging and useful feedback. My old friend and colleague Glennys Howarth read every line of this manuscript, as she has often done for me, providing critical feedback from her perspective as one of Britain's most senior death studies scholars. Keith Anderson, editor of the End-of-Life Care Series for Columbia University Press, was encouraging and enthusiastic about this project from the beginning. I was also lucky to work with Polly Kummel, my wonderful copy editor; meticulous and collegial, she provided deft guidance and mentoring for the final draft of my writing.

In 2003, during his own period of dying from a brain tumor, the British sociologist Ian Craib trenchantly criticized sociology's lack of engagement with the emotional and personal while academically theorizing about the human experience of dying. Those critical comments influenced my own efforts to write a book that would address this all-too-common omission. Whether I have been successful I leave others to judge, but I remain grateful for the truth and timeliness of his criticism. My heartfelt thanks go to all the aforementioned friends and colleagues for their support and inspiration. I also extend my eternal thanks to the many hundreds of dying people with whom I have conversed about their final time, either formally in research interviews or informally in private pastoral contexts. As a long-time witness to this experience, I hope I have been able to provide a worthwhile glimpse of the sadness and pain, as well as the inextinguishable light that, against all odds, seems so often to permeate and rise above both.

Finally, I thank the following authors and publishers for permission to quote from their publications:

Excerpt from *The Diving Bell and the Butterfly* by Jean-Dominique Bauby (London: Fourth Estate, 1997) reprinted by permission of HarperCollins Publishers Ltd. © 1998 Jean-Dominique Bauby.

Excerpt from *This Wild Darkness: The Story of My Death* by Harold Brodkey (New York: New Directions, 1996) reprinted by permission of Henry Holt & Company © 1997 Henry Holt & Company.

Excerpt from *In the Presence of Absence* by Mahmoud Darwish, translated from the Arabic by Sinan Antoon (New York: Archipelago Books, 2011) reprinted by permission of Archipelago Books © 2011 Archipelago Books.

Excerpts from *The Waste Land* in *The Waste Land and Other Poems* by T. S. Eliot (London: Faber & Faber, 1940) reprinted by permission of Faber & Faber Ltd.

Excerpt from *Man's Search for Meaning* by Viktor Frankl (1946; London: Hodder & Stoughton, 1964) reprinted by permission of the Viktor Frankl Institute © 1946 Viktor Frankl.

Excerpts from *Cancer Stories: On Life and Suffering* by David Gregory and Cynthia K. Russell (Montreal: McGill-Queens University Press, 1999) reprinted by permission of McGill-Queens University Press © 1999 David Gregory and Cynthia K. Russell.

Excerpt from the blog *Dying Man's Daily Journal* by Bill Howdle (http://hudds53.wordpress.com/) reprinted by permission of Bill Howdle © 2011 Bill Howdle.

"The Bad Home" in *Openings: Dementia Poems and Photographs* by John Killick and Carl Cordonnier (London: Hawker, 2000) reprinted by permission of Hawker Publications.

Excerpts from *Desperate Journeys, Abandoned Souls* by Edward E. Leslie (London: Macmillan, 1988) reprinted by permission of Houghton Mifflin Harcourt Publishing Company © 1988 Edward E. Leslie.

Excerpt from the poem "Age of Terror" in *Candles in Babylon* by Denise Levertov (New York: New Directions, 1982) reprinted by permission of New Directions Publishing Corp. © 1982 Denise Levertov.

Excerpt from *Six Lives, Six Deaths: Portraits from Modern Japan* by Robert Jay Lifton (New Haven: Yale University Press, 1979) reprinted with permission of Yale University Press © 1979 Robert Jay Lifton.

Excerpts from "The Five Stages of Grief" in *The Five Stages of Grief* by Linda Pastan (New York: W. W. Norton, 1978) reprinted by permission of W. W. Norton & Company © 1978 Linda Pastan.

Excerpts from the poems "Elm," "Death & Co.," and "Lady Lazarus" in *Ariel* by Sylvia Plath (London: Faber & Faber, 1965) reprinted by permission of Faber & Faber Ltd.

Excerpt from *Living in the Lightning: A Cancer Journal* by Natalie Robins (New Brunswick, NJ: Rutgers University Press, 1999) reprinted by permission of Rutgers University Press © 1999 Natalie Robins.

Excerpt from "Do Not Go Gentle Into That Good Night" in *The Poems of Dylan Thomas* by Dylan Thomas (New York: New Directions, 1971) reprinted by permission of New Directions Publishing Corp. and David Higham Associates Limited © 1952 Dylan Thomas.

Excerpt from "The Descent" in *The Collected Poems, Volume II: 1939–1962* by William Carlos Williams (New York: New Directions, 1988) reprinted by permission of New Directions Publishing Corp. and Carcanet Press © 1948, 1962 William Carlos Williams.

Excerpts from "Relationships with Death: The Terminally Ill Talk About Dying" by Kristin Wright in the *Journal of Marital and Family Therapy* 29, no. 4 (2003), reprinted by permission of John Wiley & Sons © 2003 Blackwell Publishing Ltd.

THE INNER LIFE OF THE DYING PERSON

1

In the Beginning...

For dust thou art,
and into dust thou shalt return.
—Genesis 3:19

Dust *n* Old English *dust* (probably about 725 AD), cognate with Old
High German *tunst*, meaning breath.
—*Chambers Dictionary of Etymology*

breath [A.S. *breath*] 1. The respired air. 2. An inspiration
—*Stedman's Medical Dictionary*

Dying has a bad reputation. Most people imagine dying as The End. In
this literal way many people conflate the two ideas, thinking of dying
as death and not the life before it. Either way, dying and death are sad and
bad. In other words, many people believe that nothing good can come of
dying. But this is very much a cultural understanding—and a limited and
narrow one at that. This perspective is not found in the rest of nature. As far
as we can tell, trees and rabbits do not view the threat of death in these ways,
yet they react to the threat of death in similar ways to us. To understand why
a dying human being should have anything in common with a dying tree,
we must start at the beginning of life and not at the end. We must start with
an understanding of our own mortality that links our basic reactions to the
threat of death to what we are made from—organic, cellular life. No holistic
explanation of our inner reactions to the threat of death is possible without
this biological and social context.

Furthermore, because most readers often imagine dying as awful, terri-fying, and self-evidently life extinguishing, we need to reframe this view. This requires understanding how different dying and the threat of death are, depending on one's perspective. The perspective of the participant is not that of the onlooker. The perspective of the dying animal and that of the predator have little overlap. In this way, for both animals and for human beings, dying has unique dimensions of perception and experience that are commonly obscured, even obfuscated, by onlooker attempts to describe it.

Becoming clear about our so-called natural reaction to death, and the role of different perspectives in understanding a personal response to death, is also key to understanding why our academic and clinical literature on death and dying contains so much confusion; why certain dark and pathological myths have risen to explain our experiences of dying—and both fill and terrorize the popular mind; and why the vast majority of people—certainly everyone outside biology and anthropology—think there is not, nor can there ever be, anything good to say about the human experience of dying. For all these dif-ferent reasons we first need to look to the beginning of life and not at the end.

The Nature of Dying and Death

From the beginning of life itself—from the first unicellular organisms to the evolved complex animals—life has recognized and used dying and death as an integral part of its inner workings. Construction and destruction, living and dying, go hand in hand as seamless processes that require each other. To live cells need to destroy smaller chemicals and rearrange them for their sur-vival. Larger animals need to destroy other organisms, usually plants, some-times other animals, and rearrange their cellular material so that they can use them as an energy source and live on. The purpose of this process in the food chain is generally viewed as positive. After all, if you don't eat, you don't live.

However, few people spare a thought for the food—the living things that larger, stronger living things eat. Fortunately for us the biological sci-ences rarely share this blissful denial about dying, so we have a considerable amount of work that examines what organisms do when threatened with death. Most of that literature concerns how animals—bacteria, trees, bees, dolphins, or antelope—defend themselves. Most people understand that the main defense mechanisms center around fight-or-flight responses. Cells harden themselves, develop chemical forms of repelling their threat, later develop specific cells to deal with threat, and later still develop specific physical talents to deal with threat. Humans, at the top of the animal kingdom, even develop technologies and counterideas to deal with threat.

In multicell organisms the two-response fight-or-flight strategy to respond to threat continues to evolve into at least five or six responses. For four billion years we have been coming up with ideas about how to survive, breed, and raise our young. The biologist H. S. Bracha summarizes these as freeze, flight, fight, and then feign or fright.[1] Freezing is the act of not moving—a clever strategy that exploits the evolution of the visual cortex and retinas of many carnivores, which primarily detect movement rather than color. Hiding is also part of this initial response to the detection of a predator, as is fainting. Fainting has been protective even in humans as an adaptive behavior of many noncombatants—females, children, and young men. This leaves an aggressive predator to focus on slow, wounded, and otherwise still moving prey. Flight—running away—and fighting are the best-known responses to threat. Fright or feigning is a response most famously demonstrated by the possum—you act dead so as not to incite the predators to kill you straight away, and as soon as they loosen their grip, you make a crazy run for it.

It is important to remember that these defensive strategies for survival are not either/or responses but can be, and often are, used by all animals at different points of an attack and defense cycle. In fact, many animal watchers believe that these defensive maneuvers occur largely in sequence.[2] The feign/fright response, also commonly called the tonic immobility response—is commonly described as a terminal response—a last reaction when nothing else seems to be working. Each sequence of response is based on "the prey's perceived decreasing distance to the predator."[3] In other words, if you are a long way from the predator, freezing or hiding is a good first response if the predator hasn't noticed you. But if a nearby predator has spotted you, running makes a hell of a lot more sense. If you can't outrun the predator, it makes more sense to at least try to fight it out. Finally, if you are clearly losing, pretending to be dead can slow up or stop the predator from tearing into you, perhaps just long enough for you to dash to safety. This last response is an ancient and useful reaction in the animal world, found in fish and insects as well as in mammals.[4]

These different and sequential tactics are used as defenses across the animal kingdom—in deer, whales, and primates, to mention three random examples.[5] Thus the reaction to the threat of imminent death involves

1. More than fight or flight. Fighting is not the only way to defend—at least five or six defenses are available, and some don't appear to be fighting responses, but that doesn't make them less effective.
2. Different reactions, sorted by order or priority, depending on the perceived distance of the threat.

In the multicell animal world, just as in the single-cell animal world, predation is a primary selective force driving evolution, and much of an organism's biology may represent adaptations to reduce the probability of detection and capture.[6] These range from the complex internal stress response, such as the commonly described cascade of neurotransmitters, hormones, peptides, and cytokines in the blood stream that warn all cells and tissues of the presence of a threat, to the more obvious: inherited colors, running and jumping abilities, hard-shelled and spiny skins, or appalling smells, and surprising behaviors that protect animals and give them their distinctive shape and special presence in the world.[7]

Admiring a desert cactus is difficult without also understanding how the many spines on these plants have evolved to both protect them from being eaten and to help capture the precious little moisture in the desert landscape. Admiring the speed of deer or dolphin is difficult without also appreciating how such sleek maneuvers and shapes have evolved to evade predators in an environment full of carnivorous competitors. Thus fear and the various defensive strategies that we use to counter the threat of death have not only purpose but positive purpose for dying organisms. Fear helps alert an animal to danger. Then fear assists in mobilizing strategies that either save its life, prolong its life, enhance its abilities, or spare the animal from being overwhelmed by terror at the point of death. Fear and defense are positive experiences for organisms threatened by death. Dying and death also play positive and purposeful roles for living in another way.

Cells (like human individuals and groups) will commit suicide for the greater good.[8] There are a lot of examples. Snakeskin, cocoon casings, and autumn leaves are just three of the most obvious organic examples of what is called programmed cell death (PCD).[9] PCD is a way that organisms actually use dying and death as a purposive tool for enhancing an organism's life. Programmed cell death was first observed in amphibians, then insects, and then all life forms. PCD helps sculpt structures (such as the little holes and serrations in leaves),deletes unneeded structures (such as leaves in the dead of winter), controls cell numbers (to make way for fresh energy-producing incumbents), and eliminates abnormal, misplaced, or harmful mistakes (such as cancer cells). Any attempt to stop PCD will is likely to lead to major deformities—or worse—for any animal.[10]

At this point in our discussion we can draw two conclusions from the defensive reactions of animals to the threat of death *and* from the way that cells use dying and death to enhance their lives. First the biology behind experiences of dying and death usually reveals that all living things have a positive purpose. If we move from a predator's point of view and examine how prey defend, we can easily see the life-enhancing reactions within the responses of prey. Dying, up close and personal, displays and embraces a vast array of self-preserving and self-enhancing processes and experiences for the threatened animal. Second, organisms also commonly use dying and death in cellular processes to enhance their life—by being part of self-building and self-designing projects, and in affirming and enhancing their other life functions. But if these positive purposes are so pronounced, so obvious in the biological and social life of small organisms and big animals, and have been around since the beginning of life itself, why is the examination of the dying experience so silent about them in observations of human beings?

Perspective Is Everything

When we look at the emotional picture of dying months before death actually occurs, we often get quite a different impression than when we look at the same situation some minutes before death occurs ("different reactions are sorted by order or by priority depending on the perceived distance of the threat"). In this way we sometimes conflate an onlooker's view of dying (quite distant from the dying) and the dying person's view of dying (near-to-imminent death).

For example, imagine a man who is being attacked by an escaped tiger at the zoo you are visiting. Imagine the horror of seeing that man tossed about in the jaws of the attacking tiger. Imagine your fear—for your own safety and those who happen to be with you. I will wager you cannot avoid imagining the terror that the victim himself must surely be experiencing. Now read how David Livingstone, who survived the ordeal to write about it, experienced being attacked by a tiger:

> Growling horribly close to my ear, he shook me as a terrier does a rat. The shock produced a stupor similar to that which seems to be felt by a mouse after the first shake of the cat. It caused a sort of dreaminess, in which there was no sense of pain nor feeling of terror, though [I was] quite conscious of all that was happening. It was like what patients partially under the influence of chloroform describe who see all the operation but do not feel the knife. This singular condition was not the result of the mental process. The shake annihilated the fear, allowed no sense of horror in looking round the beast. This peculiar state is probably produced in all animals killed by the carnivore; and if so, is a merciful provision by our benevolent Creator for lessening the pain of death.[11]

Raymond Moody, a physician who wrote one of the first modern books on the near-death experience, quotes a man who recollected his experience of a severe head injury. The man's vital signs were apparently undetectable at the time, but the man himself describes something quite transforming and counterintuitive to an observer. "At the point of injury there was a momentary flash of pain, but then all the pain vanished. I had the feeling of floating in a dark space. The day was bitterly cold, yet while I was in that blackness all I felt was warmth and the most extreme comfort I have ever experienced. . . . I remember thinking, 'I must be dead.'"[12]

The feign/fright or tonic immobility response is clearly dominating the responses of both men, who are—at least from their bodies' physiological point of view—clearly in the grip of a serious, close-up, life-threatening situation. No chance to run in these cases, say their bodies, so let's try faking it—and their physiological mechanisms kick in, whereas Livingstone's companions started firing bullets at his attacker and in Moody's case study the bystanders began frantic efforts to resuscitate the man who suffered the severe head injury. Either way the fight has begun on both sides—the observers who are fearful, even panic stricken, and the considerably less anxious victim of the mauling or accident.

Hundreds of cases like the one I have just described exist in the animal and human worlds.[13] Single cell or multicell, dolphin, ape, or human, the body will gear up to save us however it can. However, what makes human beings the most complicated creatures on Earth is that we don't have to wait for an attack or a close threat of death to react to it. Unlike animals and plants, we anticipate death, which means that the number and complexity of potential responses are themselves something of a modern biological and cultural miracle ("fighting is not the only way to defend").

Most writings about dying take the onlooker's perspective. This is the literature we often see from the health-care professions. Some writers do not have even this kind of experience, and their texts are the product of mere speculation about dying, with little or no experience of the process. Many people, for example, have little or no experience of seeing others die and hope that they will live a long life and die quickly at the end. A popular fantasy might be that they will die in their sleep at the age of ninety-seven. Most people do not want a dying that entails conscious experience, even for a few hours. They want their own dying to occur in a dash, preferably when they are ready for it. Or, as Jean-Dominique Bauby so eloquently put it:

> The kangaroo escaped the zoo.
> "Goodbye zoo!" cried Kangaroo. . . .
> Cleared the wall with one clean jump,
> Leapt across with a great big thump.[14]

But with so little prospect of such a clean and quick exit in reality, we have instead become obsessed with a collective picture of prolonged dying that has instead made for grim onlooker-driven reading. For most of us dying *will* take a while, at least a few minutes and probably much longer. In a modern and affluent world where most dying is the outcome of chronic illness—from cancer, circulatory diseases, geriatric diseases, and neurological disorders—dying will take time for most of us. Furthermore, our modern medical technology now ensures that whatever serious life-threatening or life-limiting disease we do have will be discovered sooner rather than later, leaving most of us with having to come to terms with that knowledge well before we are symptomatic. Given the epidemiological and technical aspects of modern death and dying, now is probably an opportune time to ask whether human dying really is so horrible.

What Is Dying?

Although most people think of dying as the final moments of someone who is reclining in bed, perhaps dying from cancer, the experience of dying is both broader and more complex. A number of medical, social, and psychological dimensions of dying need to be considered before we launch into an examination of the dying experience.

First, dying usually takes time. Dying is not only the last few minutes of a person's life. Chronic life-threatening or life-limiting illness gives many people a sense of their own ending some months or even years before their final ending on their deathbed. This means that during this long period a significant amount of their emotional and social conduct and experience will be devoted to thinking, feeling, preparing, and changing their attitude toward life because of this new knowledge. Because of this reorientation, and these changes in their life, the entire length of this experience needs to be considered part of the experience of dying.

Second, people with serious and advanced disease die, as do those with a serious and advanced injury, but these are not the only forms of dying. Other forms of anticipating and acknowledging the imminence of one's death arise from experiences of execution, death camps, or suicide. Being on a sinking ship or a doomed flight, or working in a mine that collapses are other ways that people commonly experience dying.

Third, dying may not be related to events, such as illness, accident, or state decree, at all. The experience of dying may be insipid and gradual, as it often is in advanced aging. Yet this gradual experience of seeing oneself die may follow many of the major social rituals, thoughts, and feelings associated with other forms of dying—will making; financial preparations; physical, social, and psychological defenses and adjustments. Gradual dying may entail the suffering of event-related dying but over a longer period. Aging and dying, for example, can begin to blur into one experience. As a seventy-year-old woman observes about her own predicament:

One doesn't just die all of a sudden. It is a process and one we may be conscious of for the last ten or twenty years of our life, which if you think about it, may be a quarter or more of your lifetime. I find myself wondering why this is not more talked about and why it has not become the common knowledge of our lives. I am self-conscious in writing this. For after all, no one speaks of dying until they have only a few months or weeks or hours to live. This is society's definition of dying. It asks that I deceive myself and others about my daily awareness that my body is using itself up; it prevents me from calling this process by name for myself and others.[15]

In all these ways, dying is not an event, is not to be solely identified with illness, and is nearly always an experience that takes some time. Because it takes time, this personal experience is subject to change and complexity, which leads me to one final point.

To gain a reliable picture of dying staying close to accounts of dying from the dying themselves is essential. If we stray from the dying person's account, we cross quickly into the more unreliable, sometimes confusing, outlook of caregivers, onlookers, rescuers, and the invariably disappointed observers of dying. This we do not want to do because, as we have seen, the current picture of dying provided by these sources looks so grim. We are striving here to explore a somewhat more balanced portrait of dying, one that resembles the more positive purposes of dying conduct we see in the natural world.

Dying should be defined as the personal expectation and acceptance of death as an imminent event. This is substantially different from the philosophical idea that death will come to me one day. Rather, for dying people death is either imminent (on a specific date or time—in the next few minutes, hours, or months) or it is immanent, that is, the date may not be known, but the person is aware that death may come at any time.[16] Immanent death comes from a sense of an ending rooted in the conviction that life is being lived in the end times—as it is for those of advanced aged, the seriously suicidal, and people in death camps.

Of course, readers with a preference for precise theories and definitions will object to this rather relaxed definition of *dying*, arguing that it could fit many other people who may not really be dying. For them I have a couple of replies. First, the identity of dying is a fluctuating and context-dependent one. Just as being a mother is a fluid rather than a fixed identity, so too is dying.

One is a mother when interacting with one's own children, sometimes with other people's children, but not even always in these relationships. Sometimes a mother can be a friend to a child, especially to an adult child. It depends on the circumstances. A mother is rarely in that role or expresses the ways of a mother in the workplace, or in bed with her partner, or she would be widely viewed as acting inappropriately. Identities are context dependent. Sometimes they are in the foreground and at other times in the background of a person's psychology. This is exactly the situation with dying. However it comes to the fore, it is nonetheless always there, and this makes it a quite substantially different psychological experience than a mere intellectual view of mortality.

Second, a broad definition ensures that most eligible people are included. This means that some ineligible people might be included, but this doesn't matter much because some people, at some times in their lives, may find their experience shares some characteristics with the experiences of people who clearly are under mortal threat. Conversely, people have thought that they will die—they feel and act like it for a long while—but then they go on to live long lives. These cases too should not be excluded because we are not embracing the destination of dying (death) to the exclusion of the process we are most interested in (living with dying).

If we define too tightly, we risk excluding people who have significant experience in common with dying people, even for a short while. Thus it is best to acknowledge that all our major understandings about life can be fuzzy at the edges and therefore overinclude rather than insist on conceptual precision. Such fine technical precision seldom exists in real life. Wielding it with passionate academic gusto often results in an equally misleading exclusion of people who have a genuine connection with the experience currently under our gaze.

Rediscovering Positive, Purposeful Behavior in Dying

We, like all organisms, use death and dying, in the form of programmed cell death and the defensive, aggressive, impersonal cycles of a food chain, as part of an affirmation, building, or enhancement of life tasks. Taken together, the physical, psychological, and social processes of dying are life processes and always have been. They are every bit as functional and important as the creation of autumn leaves or the animal need to grow and feed from grasses or algae. How we feel about dying has to do with dying's way of sharply focusing us on our life purposes and living tasks at this new juncture or point in our lives. The prospect of death forces us to think about what role we will play, must play, or have played in life.

The life inside all dying organisms always suggests a specific purpose or meaning for that particular life, for that particular species. Trees use cell death in their leaves to rationalize the effect of drought on their water supply. This is often an evolutionary biological function. The process of programmed cell death in leaves, for example, reflects a set of internal directions—a type of knowing that is embodied in their genetic codes—for what role they will play in the matter of plant design, seasonal changes, and hard times. Skin cells of a snake, for example, know their role when they die—they will help reveal the new life beneath them. The defense reactions of animals to an external threat of death are designed to enhance and affirm their lives, not speed up their extinction, not make it easier for their predators.

For human beings, however, such biologically coded functions are not given, not programmed, not consciously or instinctually inherited, and certainly not easily and consciously understood. Such meanings—like the meaning of *fighting*—are not something we take for granted. Instead, we must discern for ourselves the positive function or meaning in dying.[17] The meaning of our death, like that of our lives, is not preordained by our organic or genetic nature but instead is commonly divined by our conscious effort, reflection, or through review of ideas we inherit from our society and cultures.

We try to make sense not only of biological decline but also the changing inner geography of ourselves, which is forced upon us first by the push of significant suffering, fear, and sorrow and then by the pull of internal reviews of our lives—and our judgments of what we see there. We ask: Who did I become in life? What will I leave for others? What can I, or others, see as the story of my life? Is there a reason for anything here? What's the point of all this trouble? What was it all for? Each of these questions can entail major feats of personal story construction. These stories are about the attainment of a personal truth through the satisfaction of two urgent goals—understanding the purpose and meaning of one's life, and making sense of the ending of that story. As I will attempt to show in the pages that follow, the challenge of understanding our own story is behind every dying moment of every dying person. This understanding is sought by people with months to die, and it can and has been on the lips of those who have taken their last breath—their last inspiration, a phrase true in both literary and medical senses.

These are the experiences and meanings I will attempt to describe and explore in this book. I do not claim to believe that these are the *only* experiences of the inner life of dying people, but they are certainly among the most important and widespread ones within the different types of dying experiences in the modern world today.[18] The personal experiences and meanings I have chosen to highlight in this book are derived from the themes that dominate the concerns of the different literatures about dying across very different fields.

Sadness and loss, for example, are a dominant theme in the palliative care literature but not in the more transformation-focused literature on dying commonly seen in trauma and near-death studies. The theme of courage, to use another example, is strong in military writings about soldiering and dying but not so much in the fear-, hope-, and resistance-dominated literature of cancer and cancer survivorship. Again, waiting is a dominant concern of those about to be executed, just as review and reminiscence feature strongly in the literature on aging. These biases alert one to the omissions, the overlooked, the underdescribed in the overall landscapes of our understanding about how we die. Taken together, all these core experiences provide us with a more complete and balanced understanding of how dying people aspire to self-preservation and how this purpose manifests itself across a diversity of medical, political, and cultural circumstances.

Overall, I will showcase two principles that I have condensed from the biological and cultural approach to death. These are, first, that fear, fighting, and fleeing, although natural initial reactions to approaching death, often give way to a far wider array of more complex self-preserving responses in humans. We frequently cannot escape or control the powerful physical impulses associated with threat or with loss or deteriorating bodies. This surprises many people who die, most especially those who forget or take for granted their physical machinery and its deeply ingrained and ancestral reactions, reactions that go to the very heart of what it biologically means to be alive.

The exact shape of these early reactions, however, and the emergence of other subsequent reactions are best understood as dependent on our perceived distance to the threat of death. This explains the common divergence of reactions found between victim and bystander, or patient and caregiver, or early responses to death by dying people and their later responses. This is why we must stay close to the voices and testimony of the dying themselves in any serious examination of the dying person.

This is also why we need to look at dying over time and not single out any one instance, such as what we might witness or not witness at the deathbed. We need as holistic and as total a view as we can obtain and not be deceived by apparently dreadful or happy time-specific scenes of dying. We need to keep a long view of dying in our minds when we read the chapters that follow, because dying often takes time and we should appreciate the complexities, paradoxes, back-and-forth movements, and surprises embedded in that journey.

Finally, my examination will illustrate one other important characteristic of the widely diverse reactions to dying that human beings display. Despite many similarities and differences in how we and animals defend against threat, the conduct of dying humans mirrors the dying of all other organic life forms in one unshakable and unmistakable way: dying always seems to have a purpose that is surprisingly positive; it is commonly life affirming, life building, and life enhancing. This is not an assertion of New Age or wishful thinking but rather a reasonable interpretation of the voices of the dying themselves.

And although onlookers' experiences of loss or terror, and predators' own experiences of domination and consumption, always seem to dominate the meanings of death, these themes seldom have such singularly negative and narrow meanings for the dying person. Instead, dying people commonly report a diversity of positive themes and meanings. In fact, existing studies of the human dying experience suggest that the road to death tends to erode habit, pretense, preconception, and even fear in one's usual character to reveal deeper and novel experiences in personal direction, positive purpose, and social intimacy.

Whether the dying occurs quickly or more slowly, this orientation is often the result of renewed outlooks and commitments, fresh inspirations, and new experiences within what is commonly a challenging, always strange, and ultimately unknown final journey. Although this brief observation might seem paradoxical at first, even radically counterintuitive to many readers now, my aim is to draw attention to these widespread elements of the inner life of dying that seem to point so unequivocally to these surprising conclusions.

2

Suffering—Enduring the New Reality

I did not know what to say to him.
I felt awkward and blundering.
I did not know how I could reach him,
where I could overtake him
and go on hand in hand with him once more.
It is such a secret place, the land of tears.
— Antoine de Saint-Exupéry, *The Little Prince*

Antoine de Saint-Exupéry was a French aviator, adventurer, and World War II pilot who experienced more than his fair share of plane crashes. He once downed his plane in the middle of a desert in Africa, and, while frantically making emergency repairs during his desperate wait for rescue, he encountered the little prince. Later he would write about this little boy in the now world-famous children's story of the same name. We will never know who the little prince was—an imaginary invention of a little boy from another planet dreamed up as Saint-Exupéry went about his repairs—or perhaps something else, a young spiritual being based on a character the pilot thought he encountered in the desert. Certainly, when one reads *The Little Prince*, Saint-Exupéry gives no clue to the answer. In his autobiographical writings, and his media interviews about his many exploits, he often told strange stories about altered states of consciousness, inexplicable encounters with mirages, dreamlike figures, or conversations with beings unseen by others during their mutual exposure to the terrible heat of the desert, after serious crash events, or in periods of great isolation.

For Antoine de Saint-Exupéry, without doubt, the Land of Tears was a secret place precisely because what suffering brought to his inner life was often unbelievable, that is to say, unbelievable not only to others but even to himself at times. Suffering often is intolerable and has an impact that is both inexplicable and ineffable. This has been a difficult academic area for precisely this reason: human pain and its products are difficult to convey. Yet to attempt to describe the experience of the dying person, we must begin our journey from here—in the secret Land of Tears.

Academic Thoughts on Suffering

We all encounter suffering. As the philosophy and religious studies scholars J. A. Amato and J. W. Bowker observe, this experience is both universal and the starting point for all the great religions.[1] For some religions, such as Christianity and Buddhism, suffering is the basis of its founding philosophies and doctrines. As Bowker argues, "To talk about suffering is to talk not of an academic problem but of the sheer bloody agonies of existence."[2]

In this chapter I am discussing not simply the presence of suffering in the world but that some people will experience exceptional suffering, more specifically the exceptional suffering that comes from being close to your own death. I will refer to this as mortal suffering, described by the poet Levertov as a suffering with two distinct origins:

Between the fear
of the horror of Afterwards
and the despair
in the thought of no Afterwards,
we move abraded,
each gesture scraping us
on the millstones.[3]

Reviewing the literature on human suffering quickly leads to the recognition that suffering is less a single concept than a set of explanations about distress.[4] Such distress can have a primarily physical manifestation, as in physical pain, struggling for breath, constant nausea or vomiting, or paralysis.

Distress can also be primarily psychological as when one experiences severe depression, anguish, or acute anxiety, once or episodically. One's mind can feel so tortured the pain may seem to come from one's very soul. And of course suffering can be social, even political, as when one is the victim of poor state, organizational, or situational circumstances—poverty, torture, imprisonment, social deprivation, stigma, or bullying. This is sometimes called positional suffering—suffering that occurs because of a particular social or political location such as a death camp or abusive nursing home.[5]

In reality, separating out the different dimensions of suffering as it is personally experienced is difficult because people often experience suffering as "total pain," a phrase coined by the British hospice pioneer Dame Cicely Saunders to describe the integrated nature of felt suffering.[6] Suffering is rarely just physical or just psychological or just social. A toothache is rarely a mere physical experience—it causes as much psychological distress to its victim as it does vicarious pain in those who must watch or share the experience with their hapless friend or family member.

Academics who frequently theorize suffering have also observed that at its existential root it is about grief and loss. Suffering is a state of distress that threatens the very intactness of a person.[7] The anthropologist Clifford Geertz supports this view by arguing that serious suffering is a response to the threat of dissolution to a meaningful part of identity or lifestyle.[8] What could be a more serious threat to identity than the threat of death?

Though some believe that deep suffering that threatens the very fabric of our lives cannot really be shared or, if shared by outsiders, commonly becomes trivialized, demeaning, or voyeuristic, many others believe that most of us use our own experiences of personal pain to connect with those who speak or write about their own suffering.[9] This is not total understanding of another, but it is nevertheless the essential meaning of empathy, and this has its own power to make personal, social, and spiritual connections and identifications. The physician-academic Arthur Kleinman doubts this leads to social changes that can help others, yet if personal understanding changes one's perspective, that is a social change in itself.[10] After all, greater understandings come from these small connections and corrections and are themselves prerequisites for broader social, cultural, and political changes in our world. As the writer Vera Schwarcz wisely observes, even if we only have a "path that is no path at all" but simply some "broken words, fragments of metaphor, snippets of survivor testimony," these are and have been enough to help us connect with those who suffer; after all, we live in a world where nothing is certain but our own fragility and mortality.[11] In this spirit I will attempt to convey a modest glimpse of the anguish so often at the core of the dying experience and from which all our major emotional and spiritual responses spring.

This Interminable Suffering, This Architecture of Misery

The physical suffering of those with cancer is well known—people often think of pain and the awful treatments that accompany cancer. However, the diversity of physical suffering is great, depending on the disease one has and the anatomical sites it affects. Weakness and breathlessness commonly affect those with motor neuron disease (ALS), but these also commonly accompany cancer and AIDS. Memory problems dog those living with dementia but also those with brain tumors and strokes. Weakness and tiredness affect not only those with malignancies but also the frail elderly and those with multiple experiences of organ failure. Few symptoms of a fatal disease are exclusive to that disease.

Tom Lubbock, a British journalist dying from a brain tumor, describes the suffering he experienced from trying to communicate with others during that time:

> For me, no word comes without prior thought. No sentence is generated without effort. No formulation is made automatically. I am faced continually with a mystery that other people have no conception of, the mystery of the generation of speech. There is no command situation, it goes back and back and back. Where the self lies at the heart of utterance, the speaker generating the word, is always clouded. This is true for everyone, but for most people this is not something to think about. The generation of words is automatic. For me, that automatic link is broken. Word generation involves strain, guesswork, difficulty, imprecision.[12]

Different people describe their hellish experiences with chemotherapy differently, but what most of them have in common is the nightmare quality of its effects. Yes, some people are only slightly affected by their treatments, but a good many are seriously affected to the point of great distress and despair. Katherine Russell Rich describes her own experiences in the following terms:

> When the fury hit, it hit full force. Objects flew past me in the fractal storm. Remnants of my past life pummeled me into free fall, slamming me off ledges where I had hunkered down. The growl was a roar was a snarl was a squeal that boxed and sliced me. Shapes shifted in the darkness, but by the end that didn't matter because by then I was nearly blind, I was chemo blind. Aureoles obscured figures and the light was no longer an ocean. It stung me. It made me squint. Months in, I spent hours in bed staring at the patterns of the bricks in the building across the street, unable to read, and I almost didn't care. For one thing, I was listless; for another, I'd had enough. By the end, I didn't want to look anymore.[13]

Treatments are commonly worse than the illness itself and induce cries and appeals to die, or apathy toward the idea of dying, simply so as to be free of the misery caused by the treatment to prevent death. Madeline, a woman with breast cancer, recounts:

> He put me on morphine and they found out that didn't agree with me — that worked against me too. We later found out that all the painkillers were causing my nausea. They're giving me painkillers. They're giving me stuff for the nausea and nothing is working. It's just making me feel more nauseated. I lost 20 pounds in a couple of weeks because I just couldn't eat. I couldn't keep anything down. But I just felt, just let me die. Like I don't care anymore. Just let me die. This is enough already. I had no energy. I had nothing. I was just deathly ill. I just looked horrible. I was just white. It is horrible when you have 24-hour nausea. You cannot get rid of it. You try to think about something else and it's just there, it's just there. It doesn't go away.[14]

And Jan Bassett, an Australian historian stricken with breast cancer, says:

> Sometimes during the following six months I wish that I had [died]. I loathed having chemotherapy. Little things to do with the CMF [chemo]

drugs upset me, such as the terrible road-metal taste in my mouth, the seemingly endless mouthwashes to prevent ulcers, and losing lots of my fine blond hair. For days on end, I lay on a sofa, barely able to lift my leaden limbs. As chemicals sloshed about my brain, I could not concentrate, but I stupidly persisted in attempting to read a history of psychiatry, which I would have found heavy going at the best of times. For one of the few times of my life I was bored.[15]

Those on death row, people who are destined and decreed by the state to die, must also undergo a certain social treatment before they die—they must subsist in the physical and social conditions of the death row section of the prison. They often describe being on death row as worse than having to die, a treatment they were not sentenced to but must endure for years before their sentence of death is carried out:

The first thing you notice when stepping inside any prison cell block is the putrid odor. All cell blocks smell, but they do not come close to death row. We all die a little bit each day on the row, and the odor accumulates and builds to an unbelievable level. There are 60 men in this cluster and we cannot escape the stink of fear, anger, rancid sweat, blood, stale urine, wasted semen, feces, and flatulence. . . . There are all kinds of vermin to deal with—families of field mice, scorpions, two-inch sewer roaches, cockroaches, black widow spiders, crickets, water bugs, grasshoppers, flies, moths, gnats, ants, and lots of mosquitos. They come in under the doors, through the bars and the vents, or wiggle up through the sink drains. They are most active at night, so you wake up with bugs in your bed and bites all over your body. . . . Prison noises are haunting . . . it is not hard to go crazy from the din. It invades and pollutes our minds. We become desensitized to everything around us. We decay and rot like unpicked fruit.[16]

Thus the diversity of physical suffering is great depending on the situation of dying and its treatment—not only pain and disability, not only the new physical and social limits to one's new life—but also how these rip dying people away from their usual physical environment and social world. Gradually or suddenly, the dying person loses contact with a taken-for-granted world. We often think that happens inevitably in the minutes and seconds before death, but in fact the process begins much earlier. Our taken-for-granted social world dies early on.

Marion Miller, an eighty-seven-year-old nursing home resident, recalls: "My world closed in gradually. In the last few years that I was at home I could still walk, but the distances gradually shrank. First I had to give up the park. Then I had to give up going to the end of the road. And by two years before I came into the nursing home I could only go out to my letterbox. . . . But then the day came of course when I had the fall."[17]

Frank, a hospice resident, says, "For me the physical and mental are entwined. I've found as I got weaker I've become a lot more apathetic and withdrawn. . . . I've abandoned a lot of my favorite pastimes. A couple of months ago I stopped doing the crossword in the newspaper. Last month I stopped reading the newspaper altogether. I've just lost interest. I suppose that's why so many patients here (in the hospice) spend so much time sleeping. There's so few things we are able to do . . . so you just give up."[18]

Keith Perera speaks about living with ALS: "I just gradually deteriorated from August when they really diagnosed it. I have deteriorated because I find that I can't walk far. I get tired very easily. I can't do much. Can't stand for long near the kitchen sink or anything like that. Ten minutes maximum and my legs are aching and I have to sit down. Sitting down, even, is sometimes not the answer. Sometimes I have to lie down, and that's how it's been for the last six to eight months."[19]

And Oconga Osuwu Omutu writes from death row:

I hated the zoo-like existence of confinement, the regulation of time, and the inability to move at will. I hated being locked inside a cell for twenty-three hours a day and being fed through a "bean-hole." I hated the bunk that owned too much of my nights and days. I hated the inability to escape the cacophony of blaring radios and televisions, hollering prisoners, rattling keys, and clanging doors. I hated the lack of privacy and the tensions that erupted between prisoners who had not chosen to be confined together. I hated being strip-searched, manacled, and shackled. I hated the lack of control over my environment. I hated the pettiness and arbitrariness of prison discipline. And I hated the uncertainty of whether I was going to live or die. It made me feel dehumanized, mortified, and powerless. These feelings left me angry and easily agitated.[20]

The physical trials and being deprived of their usual world quickly lead dying people to catastrophic emotional states. They feel smashed, isolated, torn from their usual assumptions about how the world works or how the world is for them, and anguish, emotional meltdowns, depression and loneliness, grief, and loss of control become strange, sometimes constant, new companions. People who never viewed themselves as emotional become just that. Others, who viewed themselves as people always in control, get a startling new view of themselves in quick order. People who have lived life without regrets suddenly get them. This is because, as Thomas DeBaggio, a fifty-seven-year-old herb farmer living with Alzheimer's disease, reveals: "There is wide emotional difference between knowing you will die one day in the future and living with the knowledge you have a disease that slowly squeezes the life from you in hundreds of unexpected ways, and you have to watch it happen while those who love you stand by unable to help you."[21]

Desperation slips into people's thinking as the realization of being trapped by their new circumstances sink in. Harold Brodkey describes his own anguish in this regard as a paradoxical rise in optimism and hope that seems to run counter to the self-evident facts:

> I do not know at what rate of speed I am moving towards my own death. The doctors cannot tell me — the only hard medical fact with AIDS is death. The hard social fact is suffering. One approaches the end of consciousness — or the end of consciousness approaches one — and strange alterations of the self occur: a hope of cure, a half-belief in treatments that could extend life. (By a year, two years?) Three years or so vast a time, one thinks of life as being extended indefinitely if one can hope to live three more years. The less luck one has, the stronger is one's new conviction in one's luck. This while the doctors back away.[22]

Such experiences of optimism don't last long, or, if they do, they live alongside a darker companion, often depression and loneliness. People feel isolated in the knowledge that they could die soon. Fear and loneliness stoke despair, draining the color from them, from their lives. "Lymphopo" addresses this in her website diary about her disease:

I'll be frank with you: I am going insane. I mean seriously, deep depression, no more will to live type stuff. Cancer is bad enough, but add incarceration, isolation, loss of freedom and autonomy and strength and independence on top of that, and it's too much for me. I'm sorry. Something has got to change. I survived my second treatment just fine on Wednesday; slept all day on Thursday; Friday was brutal, hell on earth; I started to emerge on Saturday and even managed to walk downtown to the bank and back. Sunday was a bit better, yesterday I felt almost normal. Except there I was trapped in the house with no life whatsoever. No one to talk to, no sense of agency or control over my days. I tried to be "a trouper" but all the forced passivity was too much for me. Depression swallowed me alive.[23]

John Diamond describes life with advanced cancer:

Worse, though, was the depression. Every apparent step forward, every signpost on the way to possible recovery seemed to induce in me a massive despondency. The ending of the first radiotherapy sessions had; so had the operation which was due to cut out my cancer. I wouldn't see anybody [for counseling] either personally or—as in the phrase so beloved of doctors "It might help if you *saw* somebody?"—professionally, thus making sure that Nigella continued to get the brunt of my misery. A week or so after I got back I unilaterally declined any further treatment at all: I didn't care what effect it had on my illness, I said, I just couldn't bear the state I was in.[24]

Here Katherine Russell Rich reflects on living with advanced cancer and on other people she has met who are in the same circumstances:

Cancer lies. It tells you there are other reasons why you feel so despondent. And since it likes to piggyback onto other misfortunes, usually there are. "First my lover broke up with me," a woman I met in a support group said. "Then my mother was hit by a truck and killed. I lost my job and I was diagnosed. All in one year. I'm just so fucking lonely," she sighed.

Misfortune can exaggerate the unhappiness a patient feels, but I don't think it creates it. Loneliness is intrinsic to cancer, I believe in more paranoid moments, because loneliness is one of its killing tools. It's useful.

Malignant tumors swell till they cut off nourishment. Malignant despair grows till it weakens and starves the soul. I've seen it happen. After a while some people no longer care.[25]

Sam Johnson, a death row inmate, discusses his reactions to arriving on death row:

I'm still not completely out of that pit of blackness I was in to but I'm at a level now where light shines upon me and I'm able to see. A conglomeration of things helped to take me to the brink of insanity. At that time I withdrew into what I thought was myself but, later, found out that I had withdrawn (or was taken by all I was experiencing) far beyond myself into depths I pray I will never enter into again in my life. Hell, I felt and thought at the time, was a penthouse apartment a thousand stories above me in comparison to where I was.[26]

Between these long periods of physical suffering, deprivation, and depression and loneliness, some people can experience what they describe as "emotional meltdowns"—times when even basic coping seems to desert them and they collapse socially, psychologically, spiritually. Lymphopo addresses this problem:

I opened the door and there stood a large menacing sheriff's deputy, serving me papers to inform me that one of my creditors was suing me. I was sick, I was weak, I was scared, I was alone, I was broke, the debts were mounting, the chemo was kicking my ass real bad, and when that frickin asshole deputy recoiled in disgust at the sight of my shiny bald head for a second before handing me the papers, I totally lost it. At least I managed to stagger back to the kitchen before I collapsed. I spent the next two hours huddled in a ball on the cold hard floor in a corner of the kitchen, clutching the papers and drooling, my teeth chattering violently as I teetered on and off the brink of clinical catatonia.[27]

And Bassett adds:

Roughly halfway through the chemotherapy, I went out for lunch to a local restaurant with an academic friend. I was tired and strained and my friend was obviously surprised and distressed by my appearance. I cut the lunch short, went home, and collapsed into a heap of tears. At my request, Andrew immediately came home from work. I was distraught for the rest of the day. Unwilling to leave me, Andrew called my parents, who drove up the next morning from their house about a hundred and thirty kilometres away. I tried to put on a good front for them, but fell apart when I greeted my mother at the door. They must have been stunned to see their normally composed elder daughter such a blubbering mess, especially as they probably had not seen her cry in her adult life.[28]

Losing control does not always result in tears. Sometimes the loss of control can elicit anger and fear, and interpersonal pain and awkwardness, as John describes living with advanced cancer: "I would go into long rages: I'd imagine myself suddenly able to drink a cup of coffee or eat a soft cheese sandwich and when I found I couldn't—why did I think I could?—hurling the coffee or sandwich across the room. The Gestalt merchants would have said this was just the sort of anger therapy I needed, but it was lousy therapy for Nigella and the children."[29]

Fadia Saba, a seventeen-year-old living with a late stage childhood cancer, reports:

I hold back my thoughts and dreams and say, in a conversation, if someone says, "What do you want to be when you grow up?" I think, "Oh God, I don't know." But really, inside, I just want to say to them, "I want to be this and I want to do that and I want to go there," but because I have cancer I don't say it. Because I just think if something happens to me and I have to get into hospital, or just in case I have to have treatment this week, I don't say anything. It changed me because I was no longer in control of my life. It controlled me—the treatment, or the doctor's appointments.[30]

Now in a new, isolated, and vulnerable place psychologically and spiritually, dying people look at their past and current relationships and often feel grief and sadness, for what they are losing. They also feel powerless to repair the loss that their loved ones will suffer or that others have faced as a result of a dying person's past actions. Anger, fear, anguish, or depression now often combines with the pain of grief and deep feelings of inadequacy and powerlessness. Mary Bosanquet describes this awful combination in a letter to James Casson:

A year ago I was operated on for breast cancer. The surgeon told me that there was an 80% chance of recovery. So I took it for granted that I should recover completely. But nine months later symptoms of the trouble recurred. Now I have been ill for three months. My left arm is crippled, so that I cannot drive the car or ride or work in the house or in the garden. I am often in pain. I rarely sleep through the night. In order to avoid being actually incapacitated by pain I have to live a quiet life with regular rest and exercise and not much else.

Small changes in my condition sometimes make my blood run cold with fear, and often my heart aches almost intolerably at the thought of the grief that may lie ahead for the children, and for Robert, my dear husband, to whom I have been married for almost 22 years.[31]

Christopher Burger, a death row inmate, reflects on his part in causing grief to others:

It took me years for me to find forgiveness for myself for the part I played in R.H.'s death. The day after Tom's execution [the author's partner in crime and fellow death row inmate] there was an article in the paper, in which they spoke to R.H.'s sister (who was six years old in 1977). She said "They should both have been killed over 10 years ago. Not only did they kill R.H., they killed my mother too, because she grieved herself to death." First of all, this shocked me because I had never—in all these years—heard anger like this from R.H.'s family. During my trial in 1977, his mother, auntie and older sister even said they didn't want me to get the death penalty, because it wouldn't bring R.H. back. But his younger sister, the one in the paper who was only six at the time, so this is the first time I've heard anything from her. I could feel her anger and hatred toward me. Even though I understand it, and she has every right to it, it hurt me to feel it—especially at that time.

But, what it all did afterward is, not only did I have to accept and take responsibility for R.H.'s death, suddenly now I feel responsible for playing a part in the lives and deaths of *three* people: R.H.'s, his mother's and Tom's. How am I to deal with this?[32]

As these terrible experiences and turmoil roil the inner lives of these people, one might expect that sleep would bring them some relief. But for many dying people, peace does not come even here, because their fears follow them to bed, as DeBaggio relates about living with Alzheimer's:

In the past, I was a man who did not move in his sleep. Lately I toss and turn on a disheveled bed. Night after night strange dreams inhabit my sleep, nights of lost wandering, terror, fear, and mysterious occurrences. These are dreams of confusion, deep, dreadful dreams I categorize as Alzheimer's experiences. In them the man I see is walking, wandering aimlessly, lost and fearful. I wake up screaming, fearing loss of control, hiccupping with fear, breathless with emotion. I feel myself dying night by night, as I mark off strange wads of wandering scattered in resistant sleep. My mind jumps as if a computer screen scrolled out of control. I am lost and afraid, headed for a hell imagined by a dyspeptic surrealist.[33]

Julia, who was living with advanced breast cancer, told D. M. Gregory and C. K. Russell:

Some time within the last month I woke up screaming one night. Michael shook me and I know he was saying, "Julia, Julia, Julia, wake up!" And I was in the throes of some kind of dream. That was the scariest dream I've had. I was terrified and I was in some kind of situation where I was very, very threatened. I don't remember the details other than being terrified. Feeling very threatened and trying to grasp hold of something to help me or save me or something. And the scary part of it is that, I think that my body is trying to tell me something. Am I dying? And I don't know it yet. My body telling my mind something that isn't physically obvious yet.[34]

Gregory and Russell also interviewed Sarah, who also was living with advanced breast cancer:

I'm not a nightmare person. It was so vivid I couldn't calm down for about four hours after I woke up. I was so afraid that even when I woke up, I was looking around the room, walking around, checking the doors, looking out the windows. It was a dream about a man and the man was everything that was evil. And he was coming to find me no matter where I went and what I did. And this dream went on for quite a while. This man was just slowly, methodically coming after me, looking for me, trying to find me, and finding me and discovering me, and coming towards me, and threatening me. And then I would find another avenue of escape and I would run away and get away and I would be hiding and he would find me . . . slowly, methodically. And he was this grey man. He was wearing a grey shirt, grey pants and grey shoes. I think he represented cancer. I have never had a dream that haunted me so badly. It was just terrifying.[35]

If it isn't tough enough to ride the roller coaster of physical and emotional suffering, some dying people are also forced to tolerate insensitive social treatment by others. These people dole out generous amounts of their own folk wisdom, prejudice, and moral judgments deemed somehow responsible for contracting their disease. People living with HIV/AIDS are regarded as having had a wild sexual or drug-taking lifestyle. Dying is the moral, as well as the public health, consequence of reckless and irresponsible behavior. Just as it is common for some people to link ovarian cancers to early promiscuity and lung cancers to smoking, so it is commonplace for some to think that socializing too closely with those with a terminal illness might leave them vulnerable to catching it. Unfortunately, and tragically for the dying who suffer from these beliefs of others, their death and dying are marked by both superstition and blame. Thus added to the everyday physical and emotional suffering of dying people is the problem of stigma, which haunts like a ghost that walks among them.[36]

Derek Jarman reflected on his own constant battle with stigma and misconceptions after an ignorant and hostile interview by a British journalist:

She defended the foolish *Guardian* article that said a gay man was the end of the line, she seemed unable to understand we had children and families. Had not the slightest interest in the fact that my whole life has been spent under assault. Only those who have lived with HIV can understand the terrible emotional stress. . . . I sensed that behind all this questioning she wanted me to say "Yes I do have unsafe sex" so they could put a tombstone over me and, like the confused, trapped in police custody, I almost falsely confessed so that it could all be over and done with. I pointed out that safer sex was only half a decade old. In 1986 there was no talk of condoms in a list of do's and don'ts in the gay press. By the end of the interview I saw not a chink of understanding and felt either I was mad, or so old I could no longer communicate with those who had grown to adulthood in the 1980s.[37]

Katherine Russell Rich, a young journalist who lived breast cancer that was growing, described her boss's reaction to her continuing to work in an office with often silent and distant coworkers. During a routine staff appraisal she learned her coworkers feared her:

> "I don't know what to say to you," he began, "I can't review your work. You haven't done much this year. I haven't wanted to give you things to do. Partly for humanitarian reasons. But partly because I wanted to be sure that they got done."
>
> But they would have, I assured him. And you can begin now, I said. Smiling, he said he would. "You know," he chortled. "I really felt bad for you. No one here wanted anything to do with you because you reminded them they could die."
>
> He beamed, as if we were finally sharing the joke. My cheeks burned. *That's* what people thought? On the way out, a buzz in my head made me dizzy, as embarrassment gave way to fear. The editor had fired people for lighter infractions than being walking reminders of death. Without insurance I was cooked. I had better shape up, although I wasn't sure how.[38]

However, not all people who experience stigma because of a diagnosis of a life-limiting illness react with their own fear, sadness, or insecurity. Although I think dying people nearly always feel sadness at rejection, that they experience such social episodes as demeaning, many people in these circumstances do rally, find humor, and turn the stigma back on the perpetrators. Katherine Russell Rich, in her own memoir of living with serious cancer, recalls a young friend with an equally serious cancer telling her story of a make-out session with a new male acquaintance that went wrong:

> "So, the first time I was sick, I met this guy at a party," she said, reaching for the butter, not especially concerned about the twenty pounds she'd

gained during treatment. "He's a real Italian stallion, he starts coming on strong. I'm standing there in a wig, no breasts, but the guy doesn't notice. In fact, he wants to go up on the roof, fool around. I thought, Sure. Why not? We go up, we start making out, he runs his hand through my hair. And my hair comes off in his hands."

She was laughing so hard, her eyes squeezed shut. Mine were wide open.

"You know what he did?" she said. "He just stood up slowly and he left. The guy never even said one word." . . . Like a lot of kick-ass patients, she was younger, weaned on feminism, rock and roll, and self-assertion training. She was a tough babe, who'd gotten tougher still since becoming sick. Though twenty-nine and on her second run with the disease, she wasn't going nowhere gently.[39]

Both this and Rich's description of another incident I am about to quote— suggest—and do so in important ways—that private suffering is not always borne with gravitas and despair. Humor, wisdom, and irony do not flee or escape the dying person even in some of their darkest moments. As with all human troubles, most of us retain the ability to transcend our problems. To accomplish this we often use courage, humor, insight, analysis, or a generous spirit, among others. Less acknowledged, even recognized, is that transcendence does not always come to us by our own efforts and that sometimes inexplicable and unusual experiences can relieve us.

Many very ill or lonely and isolated people have reported, when they have surrendered to their darkest hour, unusual experiences of transcendence that seem to have been imposed upon them. The names for these experiences are legion, and their particular application depends on one's ideological or philosophical assumptions—hallucinations, visions, altered states of consciousness, the grace of God, delusions, paranormal states, supernatural contact or deliverance, revelation, mystical experiences. It doesn't much matter, for their taxonomy is more an academic exercise than a meaningful biographical one. These things happen, and they are a common though unexpected part of human suffering and misery, and they form a part of what happens during serious illness. These experiences push the dying person into seeing beyond the obvious misery of their situation. Katherine Russell Rich, diagnosed with breast cancer when she was only thirty-two, describes her despair nearly a year after her initial diagnosis:

In November a curious thing happened. On the night before my thirty-third birthday, I was lying in bed, face to the wall, crying. Despondence had burned off the Scotch I'd drunk, was propelling me into hysteria. Between sobs, I'd go rigid, and it was in one of those moments of silence that I sensed a presence in the room behind me. Startled, I turned my head and saw a diffuse violet light shining through the bedroom door. The light didn't scare me, it soothed me, in fact, and within seconds, I was calm. Puzzled by this sudden well-being — the tears weren't even dry — I tried to work myself back into hysteria, but couldn't. My anguish had vanished, drained by the light. A sense of security overtook me, the first I felt in years, and soon I was asleep. . . . Ten years on, the memory remains indelible, still potent and still inexplicable.[40]

What Use Mortal Suffering?

Though it is difficult for us to think that anything good can be said about suffering in the face of death — that suffering that will end only in death, obliteration, personal extinction could have any use or point — suspending prejudice (prejudgment), stepping back for a moment, and reflecting dispassionately on what suffering does seem to present to us all is essential. It is clear, from a brief perusal of dying people's accounts of anguish and pain, that such suffering presents at least three possibilities to them. Most people, including me, would not like it, but suffering offers us a reality (ontology) check, an emotional (psychological) check, and a moral (existential) check. Let me explain.

Reality Check

Severe suffering at the end of life forces dying people to reexamine their personal theory of how life works. Most of us spend at least half our life, and always the first half, adapting and learning, usually from others, about how life works so that we can obtain an education, friends, a life partner, a career, personal satisfactions from a hobby, and so on. We learn about what pleases or displeases us; what causes pain or offense. We establish, from these diverse sources or experiences, a set of values, and these too undergo several changes while we are growing up and encountering setbacks, failures, and disappointments.

Serious illness and mortal suffering—serious setbacks—challenge us to think again about our assumptions about fairness, love, resilience, and our priorities, and what in our life is real (war, poverty, planets, money, and so on) or not real (God, fairies, Santa Claus, politics, or dreams). Depression, grief, and prolonged periods of pain and isolation, experiences that are extremely difficult for others to share and understand, leave a person feeling distant from others. We are in what Saint-Exupéry called that "secret place, the land of tears." Mortal suffering forces us to take stock of what's important now; we must travel with a new economy of values and priorities, and this gives us a new view of reality. As Rich says of her visit by a diffuse violet light in her room, personal expectations don't always represent the limits of what can happen to you. Being near death can offer many of these new experiences, and the explanations quickly and rashly proffered by the mindless instincts of good health are beside the point.

Mortal suffering challenges the assumptions from which people have slowly constructed their reality over the years. The experience of having these assumptions ripped away can force people into major reflection and questioning. As difficult as it might be to accept, this is the first important way that suffering can be of use to dying people.

Emotional Check

The second important use of mortal suffering is in the journey that such suffering takes us on. Mortal suffering forces the dying person into uncharted psychological territory. Suffering pushes the dying person into new places in mind and spirit. Though all serious suffering has the potential to do this, suffering in the shadow of death is the most unforgiving and most harsh light under which human beings can view themselves. Here, facing death, they have no second chance, no sense that reversing or rationalizing their weaknesses, faults—or strengths—is possible. If anything is false about their sense of personal power and resilience, of their ability to endure or commit to a difficult course, dying will wipe out such delusions or vulnerabilities.

Mortal suffering imposes new experiences—both good and bad—upon the dying person. There is no choice. The dying person cannot choose to avoid nightmares or constant nausea anymore than the guilt or grief at lost love and opportunity. Regrets come unbidden. These experiences wrest them away from the comfortable moorings of their usual rationalizations and supports and places dying people in a new inner place. The mind's eye of the dying person has shifted toward all the anguish, despair, and pain. From here the dying person gains, by force, a new perspective (good or bad).

Dying people question their former views of their value to friends or the workplace. Dying people's view of what is important, what gives them pleasure, now shifts, often dramatically. What they feared yesterday pales into insignificance against today's new fear. Today's barely noticed flower or sky become an object of fresh interest. These thoughts, observations, reflections, and values themselves become objects of curiosity for the dying person. Dying people notice these internal shifts of attention and value. Is this me? What is happening to me? Is this temporary — a sudden weakness and sentimentality because of stress? Each dying person explores the answers to these questions in a naked, undefended way while experiencing the push and pull of suffering and of a self that is increasingly and self-evidently foreign, provocative, and disorienting.

Moral Test

Finally, mortal suffering provides a moral or existential test. In the view of the existential psychoanalyst Victor Frankl, mere biology and environment do not drive and determine the meaning of life.[41] Sex glands, taste buds, or other organs no longer determine the boundaries or limits of our experience. As story-telling animals we inherit and develop a set of values to live by. We are compelled to shape our lives to give that life a meaning.

To shape our lives means that we must behave — act in the world and react to the world. We act in the world by doing things in work, play, worship, and within our intimate relationships with friends, family, and coworkers. But life is more than what we do. Life also does things to us, acts upon us, imposes situations on us that we can do little about, such as being born with a disability or into poverty or without parents to raise us. As adults we may lose our job, our marriage, our health. Things we cannot change remain domains of action nevertheless because we must decide, choose, and live with our own reactions to them. In life, then, we act and react. These two dimensions of life constitute what it means to be responsible — literally to respond to the world. In these precise ways we often forget that our actions have two dimensions: what we do and how we receive. Both test our character, values, and destiny. We often ignore or minimize the importance of our attitudes, but in matters of suffering attitudes are—in fact and in our own stories about ourselves—real and crucial actions we take toward the world.

Most of the time most of us travel along the major highway of life—school, work, marriage, friendships, and so on—without giving major thought to most of the obstacles we encounter; and the more privileged we are in our finances, health, or social position, the less likely we are to give obstacles much thought. Enter terminal illness, major depression leading to suicidal thoughts, or war in your country. These events often lead to crisis and deep suffering, but they do not change the basic human basis of responsibility in life. Unless you believe that life really is only about your personal happiness and pleasure, the need to live life as you, through the exercise of your own values, will remain. You will still need to love and be loved by others who are important to you, to contribute to society in your own way, to leave a unique positive legacy, to embrace dignity or kindness in all you do, and many other possible moral examples. All these remain the central task for you, even though you will die—notwithstanding how: war, terminal illness, or any other terrible event or experience that may befall you.

This means, according to Frankl, that "human life can be fulfilled not only in creating and enjoying, but also in suffering . . . the destiny a person suffers therefore has a twofold meaning: to be shaped where possible, and to be endured where necessary."[42] As Hebbel observes: "Life is not anything; it is only the opportunity for something."[43] Suffering always offers you a moral choice about what to do when nothing can be done, and that is its moral test and use. And therein also lies the mysterious workings and presence of a word that many use but few are able to define—*dignity*.

> The way in which people accept their fate and all the suffering it entails, the way in which they take up their burden, give them ample opportunity— even under the most difficult circumstances—to add a deeper meaning to their life. It may remain brave, dignified, and unselfish. Or in the bitter fight for self-preservation people may forget their human dignity and become no more than an animal. Here lies the chance for people either to make use of or to forgo the opportunities of attaining moral values that a difficult situation may afford them.[44]

3

Fear—A Threat Observed

When two small children,
worried that there might be a wolf at the window,
were asked what did it want to do,
the little boy replied, "Gobble me up."
The little girl said, "Let's go and ask it."
—Darian Leader, *Why Do Women Write More Letters*

So what does death at the window want to do to me, then? Does it want to "gobble me up," take me somewhere, have a quiet word about something? Is it visiting or is it reminding me that I am the one who is visiting? I will reflect here on some key academic arguments and findings about the fear of death. I will also quote a few people who are able to clearly articulate their panic at the sudden presence of death by their window. But I will first interrogate the wolf itself—is it what it appears to be? And then, and only then, will I ask this creature at the window of our lives, What do you want from us?

According to the spiritual teacher Krishnamurti—and a lot of people who don't pretend to that occupation—people fear death because they fear the unknown. We cling to the old and the familiar. We are conservative, meaning that we love to hold and to guard what we have. The roots of fear "begin and end with the desire to be secure . . . with the desire to be certain, to have permanency."[1] This so-called fear of the unknown may be the basis of a fear of death, but, frankly, fearing the unknown is a contradiction in terms. If we don't know what we don't know, fearing it may only be one weak response to, well, nothingness. More likely we fear something, and if we fear that some *thing*, that thing is probably not a good thing. In fact, if we fear it, the likelihood is that the object of the fear is probably quite negative and threatening. Fear of death, however inarticulate we might be when we try to grasp its meaning, is a threat some deep part of our inner self observes.

Fear or Fears of Death?

Hundreds of studies have set out to review what initially appears to be the fear of death, but then this single fear turns out to be a multidimensional array of different fears. The so-called fear of death may in fact be fears about the actual dying process, of not existing, of the moment of death, of pain and suffering, and especially of breathing difficulties and choking, of isolation and abandonment, of a loss of control, of disfigurement, of being a burden, of unwanted dependency, of being unable to complete important tasks and responsibilities, of being dead itself, even of being afraid of the fear that may be apparent in the eyes and conduct of others. Older people have witnessed unpleasant or painful deaths of relatives or friends and may think this is their own fate when dying. In fact, researchers have identified so many different fears of death that we may as well re-label most of them as fears of particular aspects of life itself— exaggerated and sharpened by the threat of finishing up sooner than we anticipated. Fear of death is rarely the content-free image of the unknown. Not too far beneath our initial reactions is a concrete fear linked to something specific and found in this life. A nurse remembered one fearful patient in her care:

> Mrs G was incredibly ill. Everyone expected her to die within 24 hours. A week later she was still holding on. She was incredibly agitated, constantly trying to get out of her bed despite her frailty. One day, her daughter sat down on the bed and said, "Mom, are you afraid of dying?" Despite her delirium, the patient clearly said, "I am terrified of dying. I don't want to meet my relatives." She had had a bad experience early on in life and was really concerned that in the afterlife she would be faced with family members she did not want to reconnect with.[2]

These fears—whether of revolting family members from one's past, of personal extinction, of divine judgment, or of pain or choking are not always easily identified at first. Sometimes it takes a while to acknowledge them, to ourselves or others. Ian Craib, an English sociologist who described the impersonal nature of modern sociologies of death and dying, acknowledged his own fear of death when diagnosed with a life-threatening illness but, again, did not identify the real culprit at his window.

> From the moment that the words "brain tumor" were used by my GP to the confirmation of the diagnosis, I was all but paralyzed by what I would then have called intense anxiety. When the diagnosis was confirmed, the anxiety took off its mask and revealed itself to be abject terror, a fear I had not felt before and which has haunted me ever since, appearing now and again despite my efforts to submerge it in everyday routines. It was a dread for which no words were adequate. I now feel sure that whatever it was in me that changed did so through that experience of fear, which came with a force I had not known before. The furniture of my intellectual and emotional life has been put back together, a lot of it in the same place that it was before, but now it is bathed in a different light and it seems to me in retrospect that the source of this new light was fear. The most vivid expression of the fear I felt has not come from any human but from the screams of a young rabbit as it was caught by my cat.[3]

Kierkegaard further describes the anguish in Craib's description of his fear as a despair, a "sickness unto death." We feel a turning sickness to the stomach. We want to run, run anywhere, preferably back to the time before we heard our horrendous life-changing news. There is a contradiction in this feeling, the feeling of wanting to die—to block out, disappear to nothingness—because we are threatened by death itself, but we cannot die, and because we cannot die we feel another kind of dying deep inside.[4] As Klara Bergman, a hospice patient, once remarked: "I thought I was above being afraid like this, but I am afraid, all the time, and there it is."[5] Or as Thomas DeBaggio described his reaction to his diagnosis of Alzheimer's, "I am breathless, choking with fear."[6] Many people who have been diagnosed with a life-limiting illness, especially advanced dementia or recurrent cancer, feel this way, especially if that diagnosis has come to them in early or midlife.

This kind of fear has a bodily as well as emotional reality to its presence. What does this severe fear of death look like for those with a fatal illness?

Depending on which study we look at, 12 to 28 percent of advanced cancer patients exhibit serious anxiety about death or their dying. Suicidal thoughts are common, as are such symptoms as panic attacks, tachycardia, nausea, gastrointestinal symptoms, diminished libido, restlessness, irritability, depression, insomnia, and occasional nightmares. Thinking styles often display overgeneralization and "catastrophizing," as well as helplessness and hopelessness.[7] As Ian Craib found, the threat that the prospect of dying and death presents seriously impairs people's sense of well-being. They are not only unhappy but deeply anxious all the time. The poet Sylvia Plath offers further comment on the inner experience of death anxiety when she observes:

> I am terrified by this dark thing
> That sleeps in me;
> All day I feel its soft, feathery turnings, its malignity.[8]

The fear begins, as it did for Craib, from such seemingly simple words as *cancer, brain tumor, seropositive,* and *recurrence* of disease—words and phrases that would mean little in a game of Scrabble or an academic essay. Just little words, really. But when applied to your life, they create a low inner voice that seems to say, as T. S. Eliot expressed it, "I will show you fear in a handful of dust."[9]

A life-threatening diagnosis is so often heard as a life-limiting prognosis. Medical reassurances, aggressive treatments, and a thousand social and psychological distractions don't make the news of an advancing disease go away. The words stay. It is, as the Palestinian poet Mahmoud Darwish, put it, "Darkness, darkness, darkness."[10] The news becomes a spiritual stalker in your life, going with you everywhere, however unobtrusively. T. S. Eliot puts it well when he describes the "third who walks beside you":

> Who is the third who walks always beside you?
> When I count, there are only you and I together
> But when I look ahead up the white road
> There is always another one walking beside you
> Gliding wrapt in a brown mantle, hooded
> I do not know whether man or a woman
> —But who is that on the other side of you?[11]

The Existential and Social Context of Fear

What can one honestly say about such fear, such stressful intensity of feeling? First, we know that fear of death is a natural fear built into the cellular fabric of our existence. It's a good thing, making us jump out of the way of a careering vehicle, dodge a punch directed at us, or think creatively about how to outsmart or outrun a predator. For some people a dire diagnosis provokes this natural cascade of ancient neurotransmitters and reactions that usually appears in service for physical threats. This threatening news delivers one unceremoniously to a personal place where the prospect of not existing, of having no future, of leaving everything that has given one emotional and social support in life, suddenly makes the prospect of death real. Now everyone else, it seems, will go on to play golf, get a promotion, write another book, and enjoy their grandchildren forever, but not you. You. Will. Die. You have drawn the short straw. People die, that's true. But it was a queue, and now suddenly no one is in front of you, and it's your time to go—right now!

The second thing to say about this fear is that most people (believe it or not) don't experience this. Either they don't experience the intensity of the fear that I have just described, or they don't experience this kind of fear of death as a major personal experience at all. Reread the prevalence figures—12 to 28 percent of advanced cancer patients experience serious anxiety about dying. In other words, more than 70 percent of advanced cancer patients do not experience this kind of fear. Yes, they probably can feel something that might be described as a disquietude, a little anxiousness about the same things I've just listed, but they have other, greater, more pressing feelings and fears than not being. Sometimes this is because they are older than the middle-aged Ian Craib and have no disease that threatens them directly. The author Thomas Langner ruminates rather calmly about why he is writing a book about dying:

> On January 1, 1994, I turned 70 and it suddenly dawned on me that I would not be around forever. I started to reread Ernest Becker's Pulitzer prize-winning book *The Denial of Death.* I was struck by the fact that Becker focused on killing or wielding power over others as a major mode of coping with the fear of death. Killing others created the illusion of immortality, since the killer had the power of life and death over others. This book

was shortly followed by *Escape from Evil*, which dealt further with man's need to feel powerful and to banish death.

The more I thought about it, the more I felt I should write about the whole gamut of ways in which people cope with the fear of death and dying. These range from the most positive coping modes such as Creativity, Love, Humor, Intellectualization, and Procreation, to the most negative coping modes (those most destructive of the self and others) such as Counterphobic Behavior, Gambling, Dissociation, Repression/Denial, Suicide, Projection, and Killing. Somewhere in the middle lie Obsessional Behavior, Living Life to the Hilt, Living Better or Longer, Group Membership, Religion, and Mementos and Monuments. I call this a moral hierarchy of behavior used in coping with the fear of death and dying.[12]

Langner's tone and observations are quite different, quite calm and academic, compared to Ian Craib's self-reflections. Langner is clearly not viewing himself as a someone who might die at any moment. Nevertheless Langner interprets the main personal experience of confronting mortality as one characterized by fear. He is taking pages out of two different books. The first book from which he seems to draw is the book of psychoanalysis: "Man cannot face his own death. Death is unimaginable so we unconsciously defend against the prospect. Denial, emotional displacement, projection, and a dozen other defense mechanisms that look like creative coping are the order of the day for those dying." At least this would be an engaging view, if fear were indeed everyone's main response to the prospect of death. But it isn't, and if it is initially, it is often overtaken by more important concerns. We must then ask where Langner is getting his particularly urgent idea of fear of death. The source appears to be the other book Langner seems to consulting, the *Dying-as-Dying-from-an-Incurable-Disease Book*. In this book the fear that Ian Craib so ably describes is taken, more or less, as emblematic of all personal experiences of dying. This is also not the case.

An early study by psychologists showed that more than 70 percent of advanced cancer and heart disease patients, as well as healthy controls, acknowledged no fear of death, though further testing of unconscious fears revealed some small but significant differences between the dying groups and the healthy group—but that is hardly surprising. The heart disease and cancer groups showed no difference.[13] More recent studies of advanced cancer patients' anxieties confirm the earlier findings.[14]

Furthermore, the psychologist Stanley Rachman reminds us that "fear of death is of course neither universal nor unchanging" and cites the behavior of suicides and examples of people who anticipate their own death "with composure." Rachman discusses World War II aircrews and combat soldiers as examples of people whose fears were controlled by social pressures and sanctions. People who share the same fear also exhibit substantial individual differences in the presence and absence of certain fears as well as their intensity and expression. And of course there are many individual exceptions.[15]

Finally, although the strong fear of death and dying is present in many people when confronted with a short life expectancy, not only is this not typically the case, but it is important to remember that even many of those whose first reactions might be severe, like Ian's, will find their reactions later evolve into other kinds of emotional responses. Fear and shock when an initial threat—however severe—is observed is natural, but many people's inner life evolves from that point to experience other more complex, indeed sometimes ineffable, kinds of feelings. In the last entry of his memoir documenting an advancing brain tumor that was about to take his ability to talk and write, the British journalist Tom Lubbock writes,

> First of all it was scary; now it's all right; it is still, even now, interesting;
> My true exit may be accompanied by no words at all, all gone.
> The final thing. The illiterate. The dumb.
> Speech?
> Quiet but still something?
> Noises?
> Nothing?
> My body. My tree.
> After that it becomes simply the world.[16]

Perhaps more prosaically we can see that the natural fear of death and any panic about death is less prevalent among the elderly. Like the aircrews and combat soldiers described by Rachman, older people have other pressures and worries that take priority. Moreover, research that privileges voices of the very elderly shows that old people may view death as the lesser evil. The prospect of severe disability and social dependency—the loss of autonomy embodied not just in an inability to go shopping but to perform such intimate tasks as toileting—frequently makes death seem less of a threat and more welcome, if anything.

Maude and Des are the pseudonyms of two people older than eighty who were interviewed for a recent British study; their views are typical of these concerns. Maude observes, "I think we can't live forever. I'm certainly not frightened of dying. The way I die I might be frightened of." Des muses, "The thing that worries me now is, am I going to be a burden to anyone? I would like to be able to sit down and close my eyes and say, 'Goodbye world. I'm gone now.' . . . If I got a stroke, I'd be a vegetable. And I'd have to be nursed and fed. . . . I would rather get a piece of rope (than) let that happen. But, you can't say, 'There's a stroke coming next Christmas Eve, so you better get a bit of rope out.' It doesn't work like that."[17]

I interviewed an eighty-seven-year-old Australian woman who lived in a nursing home. Marion Miller had been a journalist and served on a local government council. Her growing frailty and failed hips left her no choice but to live in a wheelchair and eventually place herself in institutional care. When I interviewed her, she was a cheery and opinionated woman who took a passionate interest in everything around her, from the residents and staff of the nursing home to world news and affairs. Her education, experience, and sociological imagination made her seem more like one of my colleagues than many of my colleagues do. Nevertheless, when the conversation turned to her attitude toward her own death, she spoke matter-of-factly:

Every day I hope that I won't wake up in the morning. I want to die. Sorry, but I do. This will be the end. And I don't expect anything beyond "the end" either. I'm not religious. They have a very nice woman here, not Church of England, which I was brought up in, of course. It's Uniting Church. She comes to check on me and have a bit of a conversation, but I have convinced her that it's too late but she still comes to see me for a general chat. But my views about death have not changed.[18]

Miller's interview was part of a popular book that I edited with a colleague who wanted to enter the field of palliative care as a researcher. We decided to put together a book of seven Australians who would tell the reader what it was like to die. These seven people were dying from an assortment of diseases, and all illustrated different concerns and feelings, depending on their age, gender, and social circumstances. The one striking theme that did not emerge was the fear of their coming death. My colleague and coeditor David Ritchie recalls:

> The sadness I had expected to be there is coupled with frustration— frustration expressed, for example, at what Marion refers to as "shedding." This is not just the shedding of life, but of what formerly gave living significance: Marion's personal space, her independence, her privacy; Iain's looks, career status, mobility; Fadia's educational opportunities and her health; Alexander's ministry project for his people; Keith's parental involvement with the growth of his daughters. *The sadness, however, is not the tearful fear of venturing into the unknown that I had expected* but, as Iain perhaps best puts it, sadness about what their dying is doing to their loved ones, the sadness of saying goodbye, of worrying about how those left behind will cope.[19]

So we have now closed the circle—from terror to equanimity. Fear seems not far from all our meditations and night terrors about our own mortality, yet the meaning of this fear—whether strong and strangling, or muted and deflected—remains a question to be addressed. How are we to understand this fear when its expression and power differ so much from person to person? My opening question remains: What does fear—muted or not—want to do to us? One of the first major meditations on the fear of death in the medical sciences was by the psychiatrist Elizabeth Kübler-Ross. Although her work remains to some extent emblematic, both of most psychologies of our personal reactions to dying and the problems associated with such formulations, she does raise cultural matters that have received less attention.

Modernity and Fear

In her famous 1969 book, *On Death and Dying*, Kübler-Ross first argues what most psychiatrists influenced by psychoanalysis argue—that the fear of death is universal and that we can never conceive of the death of our self as we might the death of others. This is, as I mentioned earlier, a stock belief of the psychoanalytic mafia from Freud to the philosopher Norman O. Brown to the Pulitzer Prize–winning anthropologist Ernst Becker. Nevertheless, the method used to interpret a denial can equally serve to deliver an interpretation of acceptance. My religious beliefs in an afterlife can be substituted for your equally compelling psychoanalytic beliefs about my projections. The only academic mileage in this methodology takes us to the doors of our respective churches.

Therefore, if you suspend a tendency to apply your cultural beliefs as the criteria for judging mine (or vice versa)—called ethnocentrism in anthropology and egocentrism in psychology—and we accept what people say about themselves and why they do things, we quickly conclude that many societies, groups of people, and individuals are not gripped by fear of death when they know they are to die soon. Though all living creatures might be expected to fear death, fear does not characterize or dominate their approach to death unless there are clear reasons for that special kind of fear. In other words, an exaggerated fear of death is linked to specific cultures, specific circumstances, and specific developmental contexts in human life. Fear of death is most likely when the prospect of death itself—as a personal or cultural image—represents a clear and solitary threat (i.e., not compounded by other competing fears or desires). And fear, in that context, will be a natural response to that clear threat. At this point we can meet up with Kübler-Ross once more.

Kübler-Ross at least concedes that the apparent modern *increase* in the fear of death is linked to the problem of unfamiliarity, and she means this in at least two ways. First, modern populations simply have less actual experience with seeing people die. In the past, for example, people who had reached maturity often had witnessed some death in the immediate or extended family. Today we have the opposite situation: few adults have witnessed a dying or seen a dead body. In this way lack of familiarity breeds ignorance and, as everyone knows, ignorance can breed fear or compound it. But Kübler-Ross also meant that dying in unfamiliar surroundings could also breed fear—unfamiliar environments brought their own sense of threat, and this might be confused with fear of death or exaggerate its presence. Too often people are plucked from the familiar surroundings of their own home, among family and friends, and suddenly rushed off to emergency rooms or placed in nursing homes, where even such things as their favorite foods or music are suddenly and permanently gone. In these contexts of modern end-of-life care, the many little deaths herald the big one to come. Fear is the result. In a broader cultural sense, for many people today finding a sense of the familiar also is increasingly difficult. International migration, work-related migration, as well as the push to institutionalize at the end of life, make dying in so-called familiar surroundings increasingly unlikely.

According to Kübler-Ross, then, even in 1969 the march of medical science did not necessarily step to a heroic and welcoming tune but one that sounds more like a melancholy, even menacing, piece that grows louder and more threatening as we get older and more frail. The fear that Kübler-Ross spent her opening chapter describing was in fact the fear of dying out of place—that is, away from home—and out of reach—away from our usual loves and connections. In a postmodern world of change and uncertainty this is the real and enduring foundation for the contemporary fear of death, one that stimulates and exacerbates the basic natural cellular, animal, mammalian, and human response to any grievous threat. Death in such a context really is the solid, genuine, and common basis for fear of death. Nothing is unconscious about these processes; these social conditions common to modern dying are real and legitimate sources for our personal fears. There is enough here to cope with without having to speculate about unconscious defense mechanisms that may or may not exist. As Walter Lippmann wryly observes about contemporary life:

> We are unsettled to the very roots of our being.
> There isn't a human relation,
> whether of parent or child,
> husband and wife, worker and employer,
> that doesn't move in a strange situation.
> We are not used to a complicated civilization,
> we don't know how to behave
> when personal contact and eternal authority
> have disappeared.
> There are no precedents to guide us,
> no wisdom that wasn't made for a simpler age.
> We have changed our environment more quickly
> than we know how to change ourselves.[20]

We live in an age of fear. Imagine dying in such an age. In this modern context the wolf is not outside the window, he's already inside the house. Our fears about dying, then, are inexorably linked to our fears about modern life. The fear of death means to do for us, more powerfully, more shockingly, perhaps more urgently, what our fears about living in an uncertain age have been whispering to us all along. We must act to understand the purpose in our individual life. Like any animal facing its predator in the forest, fear demands to know what we are going to do in its presence. What are the choices?

Our Potential Allies Against Fear

The historian Joanna Bourke reminds us that fear is not simply a report about our inner states but rather both a product of power relations and a change agent within those power relations. Fear often characterizes and creates specific social groups such as victims, the powerless, the subordinated, the oppressed and the chased, but fear can also be the impetus for uprising, conflict, retaliation, defense, and attack. The incitement of fear in individuals and groups undoubtedly signals the power of another, but its presence in these powerful Others may also be the engine room for their ultimate undoing by their so-called victims.[21] In every context, however unequal, potential to turn the tables exists.

In fact, most dying people do not simply give in to the powerful image of their own death projected to them by a predator. Few people choose the option of suicide in the face of the advancing wolf—the advancing age or cancer that grows inside them, for example. Some do, of course, but not the vast majority. Most stand their ground and attempt to create a coalition of support against the threat. In broad cultural terms, most people seem to call on two major social institutions in combating their fears. The first is religion. Some writers believe that religious belief is declining in the West, particularly among the professional classes. Researchers report a steady decline in belief in God and falling numbers of church attendance, full-time professional clergy, and use of the sacraments in most Western countries since the 1950s.[22] Of course, these are very public types of social indicators and do not tell us the more elusive story about the rising interest in spirituality, new religions, or more private ways modern people tend to create and sustain a relationship with the divine, however, they might define that relationship.

Nevertheless, the question remains: Can religion effectively help protect you against the fear of death? Apparently it might but not if you are ambivalent or half-hearted. If you are convinced God and an afterlife do not exist or are convinced that they do, and you consistently believe this, such certainties can bring a certain comfort in the face of death. But mere religious practice or the specific content of the belief system itself are not by themselves protective in this way.[23] For the majority of people, then, religious belief does not afford any major protection against a fear of death, although we should remember that both the dogma and spiritual traditions within many religions can be an important part of making meaning or sense of your life and dying.

The other main support against the fear of death, indeed the most popular choice for those with an advancing disease, though not necessarily for those with advancing age, is aggressive medical help. As Alice Stewart Trillin, a cancer patient, argues, our attachment to doctors is at least partly a psychological talisman: "First of all, we believe in the magic of doctors and medicine. The purpose of a talisman is to give us control over the things we are afraid of."[24] And indeed people turn to Medicine—the hospitals, the treatments, and the countless drugs and technological wonders associated with modern medicine—not only for hope against premature death but also in their parallel battle against their different fears of dying and death. Joanne Bourke recounts the 1913 Mary Entwistle account of Livingstone's arrival in an African village being terrorized by "big lions." This story provides a rather handy metaphor for the role of modern medicine in the lives of people at the end of life.

This story is told in a manner that implies the inherent superiority of the "white man" (read: medical help), but it also tells us more about how the economy of fear is mediated by such factors as experience, equipment, alliances, and personal courage:

> The black men started out with their spears to hunt the lions. "We will kill them all," they said, and they looked very fierce. But when the lions roared at them, how quickly they ran home again! Then David Livingstone helped them. He took his big gun, and the black men took their spears. They kept very close to Dr Livingstone, for he made them feel very

strong. He shot one of the lions and it sprang upon him. It knocked him down and bit his arm very badly. It was such a strong, fierce lion that the Doctor felt like a mouse. The black men then thought that he was killed, and all but two of them ran away. But the two who stayed behind were brave, and helped Dr Livingstone to kill the fierce, growling lion. Then the poor frightened ones came back, when they saw the lion was dead.[25]

How often in the matter of serious life-threatening illness do we place our trust in those in the community who have medical knowledge and specialist expertise and with them shake the "big guns" against the lions of mortality? We bring our own personal courage to these scenarios, sometimes one or two other helpers will assist us—the counselors, chaplains, therapists, some close friends, and lovers. But the battle is always a scary one for everyone, even the ones who wield the powerful equipment and who have witnessed as many victories as failures. Medical rescue, as the anthropologist Sharon Kaufman documents in her study of dying in American hospitals is a modern adventure full of hope as well as its own unexpected dangers.[26] But as Ian Craib also remarks in his final article about his own experience with these cultures and professions, these modern helpers are not with you at night, when you are alone in your bed with your own thoughts, doubts, and fears.

There is little doubt that for many people the company of doctors and clergy can be an important comfort, can make a serious difference in the dying person's morale, can lift dying people to drink more easily from the chalice of hope. However, the modern absence of an eternal or unquestionable authority provides little or no comfort for other people, and the loneliness of modern relationships, especially in very old age, leaves them regularly to depend on their own resources. Many individuals do die surrounded by the love and intimacy of family and friends whatever their place of death. But increasingly this is not the case. Increasingly people do die alone, and some people experience this aloneness even in the presence of others. Even so, few of those who receive all the emotional support one could reasonably expect of life in the modern world will not acknowledge moments of self-doubt and fear during their dying, and these moments can seem like an eternity in their own terms. In these ways the personal and spiritual question pointed at the wolf, first at the window, now inside the house, remains: What does it want of me? Although the biological and sociological contexts and debates about the fear of death provide a basis for understanding how we feel about the prospect of death, they do not provide a deeper personal answer to the exchange of looks between death and the dying person. That, of course, was the original criticism of the sociologist Ian Craib. Let us return once more to his extreme situation of fear and dying.

The Fear in My Heart

Ian Craib lived with his fear day by day. He played a cat-and-mouse game with his feelings, attempting to regain some sense of normality during his remission, yet he always felt that the prospect of dying was not far away. The paradox for Craib was that, although this feeling of fear often seemed subterranean in his life, it also seemed somehow to dominate it. He feared death, and he feared the fear of it: "Occasionally people would say I was brave, but that seemed meaningless. I felt very strongly that I did not want to die and I would have done anything to avoid it. Perhaps I was embracing the coward's role, clinging on to life for as long as possible, whatever the cost to myself or others. This would follow the script offered by the last two generations of my own family, but not . . . contemporary media and research reports" that emphasize heroic fights by those living with cancer.[27]

At first impression Craib's personal experience of the fear of death is radically different from that of Marion Miller—the former journalist and politician who at eighty-seven welcomed the prospect of death because her natural fear of death was well and truly out-competed by a greater set of fears about dependency and loss. Are they so different? If we accept the academic insight that fear of death is not a fear of the so-called unknown but a signature phrase for a set of our most deeply held personal fears at the end of life, then we may be talking about the same thing in both Craib's and Miller's cases. In this way both view the prospect of their end as a final threat to their most deeply held and cherished values about their individual selves. In other words, the realization of the end of their lives brought with it a set of unwelcome challenges—a serious, apparently unresolvable, threat that created a deep fear inside them.

For Craib that threat might have been "not existing," or at least facing the prospect of not existing, before he was ready to deal with it. For Craib, being ready might have been in very old age or not at all. Dying toward the latter half of his work life was not what he had bargained on. Craib may have also felt a despair at the loss of a work legacy; anger at his own sense of personal inadequacy or inability to draw on some social or professional guidance in what he clearly felt were the grossly uncharted waters in which he was now sailing. The idea of a good death or of heroically battling a brain tumor or of "moving through a set of psychological stages" toward personal acceptance seemed trite, sanitized, and one-dimensional when his personal experience was one of constant turmoil of "powerful feelings, contradictions and horrors."[28]

This was also Miller's experience. Miller would have days when she wanted dearly to die, feeling so keenly her social deprivation of her old friends still living in their own homes, the limitations of her physical disabilities, the daily invasion of her personal and bodily privacy. Yet Miller often would present a cheerful face and feel cheery toward her daily companions of other residents and staff of the nursing home. Most days Miller looked outwardly with a keen interest in her daily affairs and with great enjoyment of and curiosity for worldly affairs. Her experience was not to be understood as a one-dimensional psychological experience of loss and depression. Her social role was not to be understood narrowly as a singular response to institutionalization and incarceration—though all these things were true at different times. Miller's fear and Craib's fear intersected precisely at the point where they were unable to sustain their old sense of self. Their experiences of the end of life—uncertainty and fear—were characterized by a personal struggle against deprivation. Their fears focused on losing a cherished part of the self they did not want to give up—ever.

In most animals the fear of death when faced with a predator is a fear based on self-preservation. Self-preservation is an important evolutionary organic goal designed to enable an animal to live long enough to reproduce itself. In a human being with a life expectancy commonly well past the reproduction age, self-preservation is more broadly about preserving a lifelong self-creation and design of attitudes, values, and sentimental attachments related to family, work, and play. Although these differ vastly from person to person, the end of life produces challenges that can threaten these creations in major ways. Because most of us so cherish our self-designs, an early unexpected death or a prolonged expected one can be a major disaster. To many people, then, the wolf at the window, or inside our house, does seem at times to want to gobble us up. However, the outcomes are rarely determined by anyone's first impressions—Craib's, Miller's, or anyone else's. The wolf in our story does not determine how we die, never mind that it should come as no surprise to anyone that the wolf must eventually come. The question, then, is not about the (inevitable) arrival of the wolf but rather what we do when it does arrive.

People in the Melanesian Islands of the New Hebrides use an ancient initiation rite that incorporates an equally ancient myth.[29] Every young man must undergo a trial in which he is required to walk into a long dark cave. Its entrance is symbolic of the meeting place of life and death. At some point deep in the cave, the initiate is told, he will meet a devouring female ghost-monster who will block his way. Her name is Le-Hev-Hev. As the ghost-monster waits for the initiate to approach her, she will draw a geometric design in the sand. At first the young man will feel confused and hesitant because of his own fear and uncertainty. He will have heard all about Le-Hev-Hev throughout his young life, but now he will finally meet her. As he approaches the ghost, Le-Hev-Hev rubs out half the design. Now the initiate, who is also known as the "dead man," must redraw the figure or be destroyed by Le-Hev-Hev. The geometric figure in the sand is in fact a metaphor for the life of the initiate. The part Le-Hev-Hev rubs out is the initiate's future. Can he redraw this?

The ghost-monster of the New Hebrides is a wonderful anthropological story for what happens to us when faced with our own monsters, one of the biggest of which is the prospect of death itself. Le-Hev-Hev is the wolf in our house or at the window. This can be enormously frightening, for sure, but the Le-Hev-Hev test is not one of simple graphic design—she does not care what you draw. The questions here are: Can you redraw the pattern of your life at all, especially under these fearful conditions? And should you try to do so as a mirror image of the existing pattern or should you redraw it differently? Fear can immobilize us or spur us to action. Immobilization is a bad, nonmove when faced with a predator in the forest, a wolf at the window, or a monster in a dark cave. In this way fear can turn to panic and immobilize. But more often, after a brief time fear can make us act.

Ian Craib was frightened, but he did not freeze to the spot where he stood. He walked with his fear. He tried to understand what was happening to him, so much so that he put his thoughts on paper for us to read, so that we could share in his dilemmas and trials in some small way, so that he might help us in our own time of future academic or personal need. If he embraced "the coward's role" it is because in these situations we are all cowards but cowards who are compelled to move forward with our fears. His life and Marion Miller's life would never be the same because of the new turn in that life, a turn of events that was neither sought nor invited but one that came anyway. In time something must be done, and each of us will try, in often-difficult circumstances, to do something that tells a new story about who we are or who we might become at the end of our lives.

Ian Craib begins his academic article, and Marion Miller agrees to be interviewed for our book, because, as he said, this was "part of an attempt to make sense of traumatic events." Although life can seem to be a series of random, sometimes cruel, events, most of us cannot leave it at that. We need to try to make sense of it, to tell a final story to ourselves, even to those we love, about how our story ends, how the story of me ends. This may not be a heroic or tragic story in some grand sociological narrative that can easily be theorized but rather a more personalized story of individuality linked to who we think we are and wish to remain.

In her book *Monsters of Our Own Making* the cultural historian Marina Warner reminds us that not only is fear a painful thing to experience but it can and has been, rather ironically, a traditional source of *pleasure*. When we read about death, dying, and fear, we too easily forget that fear—and especially the fear of death and dying—has been used as a major cultural source of pleasure from children's traditional fairy tales to contemporary horror films. Warner argues that we have three main ways of coping "with anxieties grounded in common experience": We scare ourselves (to inoculate, to harden, to strengthen a sense of being alive, and to gain a certain mastery over these feelings); we lull ourselves with words, images, and song (to create a protective, magical barrier against fear, to create a peace and sense of security through a strong sense of the presence of a protective Other); and finally we mock, laugh, and make comedy out of our fears (to rechannel energies we feel could destroy us and send these packing—transformed and defused, now deflected as so much harmless confetti embodied in laughter, screams, and squeals.[30]

Although more than three main ways to cope with fear are available—she acknowledges forms of resistance far less than I believe she should—Warner does remind us that fear of our end does more than produce angst. Our fears do suggest humor as well as dread and sorrow, and we do see this complexity in people who face their own death. And it is not simply gallows humor but, as Warner observes, a way to take the intensity out of our powerful companion so we are not blinded by fear, so that we can make some personal space for the forging of some new story or the reinforcing of an old story about ourselves, forged from the darkest, most difficult, fires so often found at the end of our mysterious lives. Lymphopo puts it better than I ever could, so she gets the last word in this chapter:

> I had always believed that people dying of cancer were doomed to lie awake every night with their eyelids paralyzed wide open, trembling in terror as they spent hour after sleepless hour staring straight up into the rosy pink asshole of Mortality.
>
> But that's not actually the way it works.
>
> When I wake at 3 am, the Hemorrhoids of Death are just about the last thing on my mind. No, my very first thought is always this: . . . *fuck*, my goddamn scalp is cold. Where the hell is that fluffy warm terrycloth sleep turban I was wearing when I fell asleep?[31]

4

Courage—Facing the Overwhelming

I am not bound to win
But I am bound to be true.
I am not bound to succeed,
But I am bound
to live up to what light I have.
—Abraham Lincoln

Courage is not fearlessness. If you were fearless, you would not need courage. Rather paradoxically, fear gives birth to courage. Courage lives alongside fear—it tempers fear, it reasons and counsels with fear, it restrains fear, and courage transcends or helps go beyond fear. Fear and courage are, if you will, unlikely buddies but perhaps not mismatched buddies. People admire the one and denigrate or stigmatize the other, rarely recognizing that, like it or not, they are an existential double act. Their unequal treatment in the literature on death and dying is worth noting at the outset. Fear gets most of the academic publicity. Whole chapters in books on death and dying, and sometimes even whole books, are devoted to the fear of death.

Courage, on the other hand, is the conceptual wallflower in the academic world of death studies. Yet other academic writings show us that courage has been a core reaction and behavior in people who face their own death and know it—in military histories, histories and sociologies of martyrdom and of executions, and in trauma and disaster studies.

Throughout history men, women, and children have knowingly gone to their deaths displaying courage and dignity as martyrs, soldiers, prisoners of war, victims of extermination camps, and castaways or in sinking ships, as emergency service personnel, and even as airline passengers about to die. Although courage is observed and noted in the clinical annals of cancer and palliative care, these are often passing observations, commonly eclipsed by our rush to document the awful—the grief, loss, and suffering of dying. But courage is an essential and mainstay element of the inner life of dying people. If fear is the dark twin, then courage is the light one, often tempering and holding its troublesome sidekick to account.

What Is This Thing Called Courage?

Psychologists frequently like to divide the idea of courage into types. Physical courage is the courage of people in overcoming their fear of probable death such as by diving into a burning building to save another person or when a soldier begins or resumes fighting the battle. Moral courage is the bravery shown by individuals and all great leaders when they need to stand up for noble values despite disapproval or ostracism, ridicule, or rejection by the main group. This type of courage often goes under the rubric of another phrase, "the courage of one's convictions." Psychological courage describes the inner strength of people battling their fears about letting go of familiar habits, ideas, and attachments. For some people this could be the courage people use to change jobs or career after twenty years or the strength to quit a domestic relationship that just isn't working but one in which they are highly dependent.[1] To this might be added vital courage, a variant of psychological courage, as demonstrated by persistence and determination in a course of action even when the outcome is uncertain—as it is for treatments for serious illnesses or diseases.[2]

In all cases people face their fears—of not being alive, not being with others, not being true to themselves, or not being able to act at all in times of desperate need. Courage confronts a difficult task, one that often evokes fear and risk; people push forward or against, perhaps endure, a physical, psychological, moral, or spiritual trial. It often takes determination, conviction, perseverance, sometimes even what some individuals might describe as a superhuman effort. Courage can entail a struggle in the moment, in the hour, in the day, or sometimes for a year or more, but it is always a struggle because one always confronts this fear of not being. In this way, as the philosopher Paul Tillich would remind us, the root of all human courage is the effort to be, to preserve what we are.[3] What does "being what we are" actually mean in this context?

Philosophers like Tillich, and more recently Douglas Walton and Geoffrey Scarre, have reviewed the concept of courage in all its finer details and complexity.[4] Courage has traditionally been thought of, at least initially, as a physical virtue and commonly identified with soldiers' work in war or heroic people during emergencies, especially the sacrifice that both often make for their brave efforts. However, more recently the identification and discussion of moral courage has democratized the idea of courage as a virtue that exists in most people's everyday lives. Courage goes beyond the instances of exceptional valor often exemplified by the soldier. And the existentialists, like Tillich, have gone even further, emphasizing the psychological and spiritual courage that exists at the core of being human itself. In other words, courage is not simply a virtue but the leading question of human existence itself, for to be courageous is to consciously or intuitively ask what things in the world are worth affirming about oneself and the world and what things are not. In other words, courage is about the courage to be what you most value, understanding that you are what you most value. This must mean that people often encounter resistance to their own goals and values and that it takes effort, persistence, and endurance to protect them and prevent them and one's self from being eroded and literally de-moralized, so to speak. To choose to continue to live out one's life, come what may, as the person one is or aspires to be, is to dig deep for the courage to be that person or ideal. This is the "courage to be" of which Tillich speaks.

However, the English philosopher Geoffrey Scarre reminds us that all courage is not necessarily good courage, at least from other people's point of view. For example, we do not often admire, less admit, the courage of suicide bombers, of the boss who has to fire us, or of the big company that stands by its political and economic convictions against striking workers. These examples highlight the debates about whether there must be something noble in one's goals for a boldness or bravery to count as courageous. Scarre emphasizes the Aristotelian principle that courage is courage only when it aspires to the highest ethical ideal.[5] Thus Aristotle might not view the courage to rob a bank as courage but boldness. But what if the motive behind the robbery was to secure money to save others' lives—to procure money for a life-saving surgery for the robber's young daughter, or to secure her release from kidnappers who will kill her if the father does not rob a bank, for example? Anthropologists and political historians might also argue that the highest ideal changes with culture, historical circumstances, and national perspectives.

Yet the Canadian philosopher Douglas Walton persists in arguing that any understanding of courage that does not include a positive or good aim, and involves some experience of danger or difficulty, would simply open the flood gates to related ideas of courage that could include all bold, reckless, fearless, careless, and impulsive acts and make the idea of human courage rather meaningless.[6] But other philosophical commentators might accept and sweep these related ideas together under an even more culture-specific label, "bad courage." Maybe the courage of which you do not approve might be banished with this sleight-of-hand?[7]

According to Walton, to avoid a relativist and meaningless use of the term, courage must not be related to fear, or at least not always be about fear. Rather, it must always be about self-control in overcoming an obstacle or difficulty, with a noble or ethically positive end as the aim. Persisting with a difficult task—such as a key that will not open a door despite being the correct key—does not qualify as courageous.[8] But doing so when a bomb may go off at any time and the person with the key persists, because she is trying to free someone trapped in the office behind the door, does make this a courageous act. How do any of these qualifications and reservations shed light on courage in the face of death?

At the end of the day, as the sun sets on bickering philosophers seeking precise definitions of human courage, it is best to step away from detail. The portrait of a person as a whole, and not every detail of his clothing, is what we use to identify the sitter. For people who face their deaths in the short while, one of the first difficult tasks or obstacles that they must confront is fear. Not always, and not always initially. Sometimes fear comes early and sometimes fear comes late in the course of dying. At other times fear comes and goes like a regular visitor. But fear is a major factor in the experience of courage for dying people.

It is true that many difficult tasks commonly lie ahead of those about to die soon and that some of these tasks are done mindlessly, as if in a dream, or sometimes as if they seem to be the only things that people can do, so they do them, without a sense of personal control or conscious choice. Yet even here dreams and the control of others are not without some relief or opportunity for reflection and choice in act or attitude. We are rarely simply canvas on which the world paints its will. We can, and we often do, choose a position to take, and at the end of our world some choose not to play, choosing to take their own lives physically or psychologically to another place where their captors, torturers, healers, or even their own families would refuse their passage if they could. Even a change of attitude can be an act of great courage when that change risks all. It takes courage to choose death because, apart from other influences, doing so requires us to fight against 4 billion years of organic ancestry and instinct. And it takes courage to endure going to one's death because it is always truly, madly, deeply difficult to leave the things and people you love.

Finally, although the positive good or ethical ideal inherent in most philosophical definitions of courage enjoys an infinite variety of possibilities, the history of dying conduct shows that most of what dying people aspire to involves the good of those they love, the protection of the values that they cherish, and the desire to stay, as long as they are able — to be part of that life-affirming and life-defining circle of social relationships. Dying people display courage in all its physical, moral, psychological, and vital dimensions because they know they will lose those attachments even as they attempt to embrace and affirm them. Their embrace or affirmation of these important relationships and values is futile in the face of an always uncertain future, whatever their personal spiritual beliefs, and therefore always signifies the courage of the lone rider on a one-way road. The ability to face that journey alone, aware of the imminent loss of their precious relationships or values but with dignity, strength, and endurance and without falling into the oblivion of personal despair, is the exact meaning of courage. In this way, most dying people courageously attempt to live up to what light they have.

Examples of Dying and the Courage Within

During a long terminal illness dying people often have alternating experiences of fear and courage. This is because illness itself and the treatments for a long illness can vary widely — with sufferers commonly reporting good days and bad days. For carers and other onlookers courage is less discernable because its manifestation is quieter and less obtrusive than its absence, such as during emotional meltdowns or public displays of panic. Panic and grief are more memorable to carers, who often overlook the thousands of hours and the hundreds of days of calm, control, and selflessness that are more common. In some ways carers' perceptions skew the clinical and academic literature toward fear and grief and away from courage, toward the dying of an illness and away from the many other causes of dying.

Among the dying are those without disease who face the prospect of death at the hands of others or in circumstances that can be all too sudden. Their oscillating experiences of fear and courage are often compressed into a short, dramatic, and rather public form. Apart from having to deal with their own fears about the prospect of death, these dying people must deal with onlookers who are either jeering and celebrating or are panicking themselves. The most prominent examples of this kind of courage in dying are those who are about to be executed and those who are about to die at sea.

Edward Leslie, historian and journalist of people who have been cast away and other perils of seagoing, documents the courage of sea captains who went down with their sinking ships as well as buccaneers and pirates hung at the gallows for their crimes at sea. Both types of men were often recorded as facing their dying and death with great courage:

> The *Earl* sank with great loss of life. . . . The captain, John Wordsworth, was among those who drowned. He was warned that the waters were rising, "that all exertions were now in vain," and he had better get off, but he declined to do so. Instead he turned to Mr. Baggot, the man who had warned him, and looking at him steadily with the expression of "a heart-broken man," softly whispered, "Let her go! God's will be done!" They were his last words. He stood stock-still as the water rose around him and made no effort to save himself. Some of his crewmen did try to rescue him from the sea, but they could not, and so he went down with the ship.[9]

Leslie also described the hanging of ten English pirates in the eighteenth century, and most of them died bravely, often spending their time between sentencing and execution reading the Bible or praying, even comforting others. Some sang psalms on the gallows before they died, whereas one man gave a speech: "That drew tears to the eyes of many who heard it. He ended with a prayer and died with such dignity that of the ten pirates executed that day, he was accounted as having shown 'the greatest courage.'"[10] Both examples show great psychological courage because these people had to cope not only with their own fears of death and dying but also do so in front of a public and often unsympathetic audience.

Such psychological courage, however, is more than a custom but an occupational expectation for those enlisted in the military. Soldiers have been and remain an occupational group of men and women who are required, if circumstances demand it, to make the ultimate sacrifice. In other words, dying is part of the job description of the traditional soldier. The historian Drew Gilpin Faust, in her record of death and dying in the American Civil War, documents that soldiers on both sides saw their task more in terms of dying for God and country than in killing. As dying people in this respect, many made wills and placed farewell letters among their belongings, to be found after their deaths. If they lay dying in a field hospital after fatal injury, these soldiers would surround themselves with pictures of their family and do their best to "die well." These men showed a courage in dying that displayed endurance for great suffering as well as thought for God and family under physical conditions of great trial. Faust writes:

> L. L. Jones anticipated that he would be killed in the fighting in Missouri in the summer of 1861 and so provided his wife with his dying sentiments before he went into combat. "I wish you to have my last words and thoughts," he wrote. "Remember me as one who always showed his worst side and who was perhaps better than he seemed. I shall hope to survive and meet you again . . . but it may not be so, and so I have expressed myself in the possible view of a fatal result." He was killed in his first battle.[11]

And:

> Bloodstains cover James Robert Montgomery's 1864 letter from Spotsylvania to his father in Camden, Mississippi. A private in the Confederate signal corps, twenty-six-year-old Montgomery reported that a piece of shell had "horribly mangled" his right shoulder. "Death," he wrote, "is inevitable." But if the stained paper makes his wounds seem almost tangible, his assumptions about death emphasize the years that distance him

from our time. "This is my last letter to you," he explains. "I write to you because I know you would be delighted to read a word from your dying son." His choice of the word "delight" here—a term that seems strikingly inappropriate within our modern understanding—underlines the importance accorded the words of the dying.

A witness four days later described Montgomery's death as "an exhibition of fortitude and Christian resignation."[12]

Even these military contexts of dying and death, however, contain an acknowledgment that fear and courage do not exist separately and that their particular combination is an unsteady balancing act, with courage largely, if precariously, dominating fear. Lord Moran, the personal physician to Winston Churchill, wrote a book about his personal experiences as a medic on the western front during World War I. He believed most soldiers felt fear in the face of their own death—and either they did not show it, they showed it but did their job whatever that job was, or they showed fear and were paralyzed by it, at least for a time. Those who seemed to have no fear died more quickly, for they lacked the caution that having fear might bestow. Courage was not the opposite of fear but its transcendence, helping those in fear to move backward and forward across the different experiences of fear and not be destroyed by it. In this way, most men showed courage when faced with death in war.[13]

Physical courage in the face of death is manifested in many ways, and there are differences in those who show courage in anticipation and those who face death with little or no time to reflect on what is happening. Sometimes soldiers must decide if they should save their own lives or stay and do the right thing, and this will mean that they will die in the next few minutes. A classic example of such physical courage can be seen in the actions of Michael Monsoor.

The Medal of Honor is awarded for an act of such courage that no one could rightly be expected to undertake it. Yet those who knew Michael Monsoor were not surprised when he did. . . . On Saint Michael's Day— September 19, 2006—Michael Monsoor would make the ultimate sacrifice. Mike and two teammates had taken position on the outcropping of a rooftop when an insurgent grenade bounced off Mike's chest and landed on the roof. Mike had a clear chance to escape, but he realized that the other two [Navy] SEALs did not. In that terrible moment, he had two options — to save himself, or to save his friends. For Mike, this was no choice at all. He threw himself on the grenade and absorbed the blast with his body. One of the survivors puts it this way: "Mikey looked death in the face that day and said, 'You cannot take my brothers. I will go in their stead.'"[14]

This example of military valor and noble ideals so often colors the general public's attitudes about courage that such physical courage is viewed as the benchmark for all other types. This leads most people to think of courage in military terms (bravery in the face of death) and patriotically (our troops and not those of the enemy) and not to identify their own daily struggles with such a word as *courage* and furthermore to think that they are, in any case, unworthy of such descriptions. However, it is useful to remember that most courage in soldiering is a daily courage in fighting on the battlefield away from other people's gaze (because all people on that battlefield are focused on their own life-and-death battle with the enemy and their own fears).

However, some soldiers stand out because their task is not only to risk dying but to embrace dying as their particular soldiering act. I refer here specifically to the act of suicide in a military context. Suicide bombers, kamikaze, or martyrs for religious and political causes have a long history in Christianity, Islam, Hinduism, and Shinto, among other religions. These people declare themselves willing to die for a cause and in so doing begin to act and feel everything familiar to those who are dying of cancer — they prepare for death by making their wills and last testaments, and they feel grief and sadness, isolation and loneliness, as well as deep suffering and stress before their death.[15] Here a Japanese kamikaze addresses that particular mix of emotions:

No one but myself will be aware of this act [his dying]. My will, written last night in the underground shelter, and full of heart-rending words, will remain on this earth, either in my parents' keeping or in the library of my university. But only I can know what is passing through my mind now, during the time since I climbed into the suicide-plane. And I have no longer have any means to communicate with others.

Suddenly, a feeling of terrifying solitude freezes my blood. Who is my companion at the last moment? A soulless metal object — the control column! At this thought I grasp it more tightly in my gloved right hand as if it were a living thing. Yes, this is my last companion-in-eternity. . . . In spite of my efforts, I am suffering cruelly, as if from a sly dagger thrust. It stems, not from fear of death or the desire to flee, but from the realization that I shall have no one near me at that final moment. . . . The important thing is to know how to die. And this, too, causes me to suffer.[16]

In modern times Islamic suicide bombers or Japanese kamikaze have often come from well-educated, middle-class families. They are rarely the stereotypical fanatics so often described hysterically by the popular press. A personal and national sense of powerlessness often has produced a class of men (and sometimes women) who have turned this sense of powerlessness into a personal and personalized power against their oppressors. They have used their life as a weapon.[17]

And as Susan Sontag herself once wrote after 9/11, "in the matter of courage (a morally neutral virtue): whatever may be said of the perpetrators of Tuesday's slaughter, they were not cowards."[18] Courage and bravery to take your own life, even for those you do not hate, is as great in the perpetrators of terror and war as it is in their defenders and victims. Both types of dying people — as aggressors and martyrs and as defenders and victims — show what can only be described as extraordinary courage in the face of their own death — whatever side you identify with in these wars.

One of the best recent examples of courage by victims faced with death as a result of a military terrorist action were aboard one of the hijacked planes on 9/11. On United Airlines Flight 93, the fourth plane to be hijacked that day, the hijackers killed or disabled the pilots and took control over the cockpit of the plane within forty-five minutes of its takeoff.

To keep discontent down, they encouraged passengers and crew to contact their families by cell phone. Passengers made more than two dozen phone calls. This relaxed style came back to haunt the hijackers, for passengers who contacted family members learned that three other aircraft had been hijacked and had been turned into flying bombs.

As passengers began to realize there was no possibility of survival, plans circulated among some of the more aggressive men on board to attack the hijackers and regain control of the aircraft. . . . They were under no illusion about their probable fate, and showed extraordinary courage and compassion for others by waiting for the aircraft to fly over a rural area. . . . Sometime around 10:00 a.m. the passengers attacked the hijackers using a food tray container to smash into the cockpit area. Earlier the hijackers had all retreated into the cockpit area. A voice recording from the black box (cockpit data recorder) indicated the fierce nature of the struggle. For the next seven minutes the outcome was in doubt.

Jarrah was the pilot, and his contingency plan was to crash the aircraft if it seemed as though the hijackers would lose control of the plane. Evidently this is what happened.[19]

However, once again, such popular stories of valor in the face of certain death tend to eclipse, cloud, even negate the equally inspiring courage of those who — in the face of terrifying, quick-moving events that can easily be recognized as leading to death — are able to find the presence and strength of mind and heart to take an action that focuses only on others: their family and other loved ones. As unlikely as it might sound to some, in circumstances of sudden calamity, even chaos, many ordinary people about to die can draw upon such strength in themselves to think of others and their future needs. The *Wall Street Journal* columnist Peggy Noonan describes some of the last-minute telephone calls made by victims of the 9/11 tragedy, and she ends with final observations about their courage in this terrible and rapidly changing context:

Flight 93 flight attendant Ceecee Lyles, 33 years old, in an answering-machine message to her husband: "Please tell my children that I love them very much. I'm sorry, baby. I wish I could see your face again." Thirty-one-year-old Melissa Harrington, a California-based trade consultant at a meeting in the towers, called her father to say she loved him. Minutes later she left a message on the answering machine as her new husband slept in their San Francisco home. "Sean, it's me," she said. "I just wanted to let you know I love you." Capt. Walter Hynes of the New York Fire Department's Ladder 13 dialed home that morning as his rig left the firehouse at 85th Street and Lexington Avenue. He was on his way downtown, he said in his message, and things were bad. "I don't know if we'll make it out. I want to tell you that I love you and I love the kids."

Firemen don't become firemen because they're pessimists. Imagine being a guy who feels in his gut he's going to his death, and he calls on the way to say goodbye and make things clear. His widow later told the Associated Press she'd played his message hundreds of times and made copies for their kids. "He was thinking about us in those final moments."

Elizabeth Rivas saw it that way too. When her husband left for the World Trade Center that morning, she went to a laundry, where she heard the news. She couldn't reach him by cell and rushed home. He'd called at 9:02 and reached her daughter. The child reported, "He say, mommy, he say he love you no matter what happens, he loves you." He never called again.[20]

Such selflessness in the face of one's own death is extraordinary because their jobs and usual occupations do not include a requirement that they die if circumstances call for it; rather they are simply ordinary and everyday people expecting, and expected by others, to be home that evening. This is a more common situation of dying than many people think. In August 1985, twelve minutes into JAL flight 123 from Tokyo to Osaka, the Boeing 747 suffered a catastrophic loss of all hydraulics. It was airborne for about thirty minutes before crashing into a remote mountainous area of central Japan's highlands—long enough for many passengers to write letters of farewell to their families to be found after they died.[21] This is exactly the type of conduct described by Drew Gilpin Faust in dying soldiers in the Civil War.

Describing some telephone messages left by people atop the World Trade Center on that fateful day, Noonan reflects, "People are often stronger than they know, bigger, more gallant than they'd guess."[22] And she is right. People do frequently underestimate how strong they are. They are more likely to ascribe courage to others than themselves. People do frequently exaggerate or emphasize the dramatic, public, and conscious nature of brave acts and ignore or downplay the everyday, private, and unconscious nature of courageous attitudes and acts they take and choices they make. This bias in popular culture makes other dying people question their own courage in the face of death.

The journalist John Diamond did not think he was brave because courage, in his terms, is a choice. For him courage meant making the difficult choice for some greater good. He thought that living with cancer didn't give him that kind of choice. In his book, *C: Because Cowards Get Cancer Too*, Diamond muses:

> I am not brave. Indeed, when I say I am the world's least brave person it isn't false modesty speaking: I know me and you almost certainly don't, and I can't think of a single moderately brave thing I've done in my life. If I could have gone through those first post-diagnosis months more successfully by sucking my thumb or lashing about me I would probably have done so. It just so happened that sucking, crying or lashing weren't my natural reactions to the diagnosis. . . . If I had become ill because I had chosen to take my daughter's illness to save her from it, that might have been brave. But I had no choice. I had cancer and this was the way I was reacting to it.[23]

Diamond demonstrates the all-too-common downplaying or misunderstanding of the role of courage in everyday life and certainly the everyday life of those living with a life-threatening or life-limiting illness. Defying fear on a moment-to-moment basis, struggling to resist despair and fighting for life with medical treatments, or making difficult treatment decisions that give loved ones more hope than the patient does require courage. Diamond also fails to acknowledge that "sucking, crying or lashing" are not natural reactions (we don't see this decompensating behavior in animals) but rather are cultural attitudes and behavior. His decision not to engage in these behaviors is about his own socialization: about how he has adopted values and attitudes that have in their turn molded him against other choices and conduct throughout his life. People do make courageous decisions about how they will face their deadly illness and their own risk of death from it. But such decisions can be so unobtrusive, so subtle, and so gradual that they may not be able to easily identify all the physical and psychological events behind their own courage. The journalist Katherine Russell Rich describes this change:

> Emotional exhaustion put me into a stupor. I was apathetic, dimmed. Now that I'd learned to cry, I couldn't stop. "You sound like you're on the edge," Joe said, and he was right. I was; on the edge of nothing. I didn't like to leave the apartment. I was scared of people, scared to have them

look at me. Shrouded in unhappiness, unemployed, I slipped back into the old mantra. Divorce, cancer, pariah-hood on the job—I replayed my tragedies till I was tired of them, till I felt like I had taken them up the nose. I was sick of being indebted to tragedy for definition, of regarding it as predictive. I decided to become my own psychic, make my own forecasts. Wouldn't it be funny, I thought, if I actually kept on going? They'd be amazed. I wasn't sure who "they" were. But one Monday in June, I felt something sing within me, some universal harmony. It occurred to me that I was glad to be alive, glad to be who and where I was. I began spending less time in the chair.[24]

The psychotherapist Marilyn Rawnsley identifies another clear case of courage with no clear articulation or awareness of it by the person at the center of her suffering. Once again we see the incremental nature of courage in those who live daily with the emotional, social, spiritual, and physical erosion that dying can sometimes bring. Here Gracie explains what happened after a second mastectomy that required radiation treatment:

Something went wrong, they burned my arm and my lungs too. I had such pain, and they gave me more drugs. I was drugged most of the time. Finally, they had to amputate my arm, right to the shoulder. When it was all over I was very depressed. My poor husband retired to take care of me. Then they wanted to give me drugs for the depression. I don't know how, but I came out of it after that. I didn't want to spend whatever life I had left drugged up. Now here I am going to Florida to visit my girlfriend. We've been friends for over 40 years, but I haven't seen her in a long, long time. It was hard to do, but I talked to my son and daughter and they encouraged me. They'll visit my husband until I get back in two weeks.

I feel bad about leaving him, he's in a VA hospital. Eight months after I came out of depression, he had a stroke. Only retired a year, then paralyzed on one side. The worst part is he can't talk to me. I bring him home a week each month. . . . Sometimes, when I don't understand what he wants, he pushes me. I tell him, "Don't do that or I can't take you home." Then he cries and I sit and cry with him. Then I say, "Okay, we've had a good cry and we feel better" and then I give him something to eat.[25]

As Rawnsley correctly observes, Gracie describes her suffering at the end of life "without self-pity, without despair, profound in its simplicity" and with a quiet courage to be, to sit in the presence of her suffering world, that coveys both profound patience and dignity.[26] This is the courage described in the Bible story of Job—a man sent all kinds of terrible physical, social, emotional, and spiritual woe but who maintained courage, patience, and dignity in the face of the many deaths that he faced.

Equally relevant and crucial are the observations of the unobtrusive presence of courage in people residing in internment/death camps. The physician John Hinton, in his own book about the medical and psychological situation of dying people, quotes observations by the psychiatrist J. E. Nardini of about 30,000 men under guard by the Japanese during World War II; only about 40 percent survived the appalling prison conditions: "The determination to survive was normally bolstered by their ignoring some hardships, resorting to fantasy, retaining a sense of individuality, and directing humor and surreptitious acts against the captors. By these means the courageous were better able to resist not only the sense of defeat, but illness and death."[27]

Such qualities associated with the courage of prisoners of war also have been observed of those in death camps and are similar to the techniques adopted by others—people facing their death in cancer wards and nursing homes the world over.[28] In these harrowing circumstances of death and dying, the courage to be is synonymous with the courage to endure with patience, humor, and an ability to disassociate within one's mind and spirit. In this way the courage to endure is also the courage to resist while accepting one's suffering and describes the courage to be when doing so is difficult. One lives at the center of yet another storm sent by life, sitting as Job did among the afflictions sent by his testing God—and transcending them. The poet George Herbert describes this quality of human courage and endurance well when he writes,

Who, when great trials come,
Nor seeks, nor shuns them; but doth calmly stay,
Till he the thing and the example weigh;
All being brought into a summe,
What place or person calls for, he doth pay.[29]

This is also the quiet courage described by the great U.S. clergyman, ambassador, and author Henry van Dyke (1852–1933): "An everyday virtue. It includes the possibility of daring, if it be called for; but from hour to hour, in the long, steady run of life, courage manifests itself in quieter, humbler forms, — in patience under little trials, in perseverance in distasteful labors, in endurance of suffering, in resistance of continual and familiar temptations, in hope and cheerfulness and activity and fidelity and truthfulness and kindness, and such sweet, homely virtues as may find a place in the narrowest and most uneventful life."[30]

Both modern and traditional ideas of courage frequently overlook the everyday and the private in favor of the more glamorous and spectacular examples of military and public spectacle. Sometimes, as the philosopher Geoffrey Scarre complains, courage can be an abused and misapplied term, a bit like its kindred term *hero* — also a commonly misapplied, but in this case overused, term.[31] Courage is a core element in the everyday experience of the dying person. It is commonly acknowledged in people living and dying with a life-threatening illness, but it is also equally dismissed or downplayed by the people to whom it is often applied.

Dying people are shy about the application of the term *courage* to them. But notwithstanding its prestige, courage does describe a constructive resurrection of spirit crucial for the defense against the real "predators of the human spirit" — despair, pain, disappointment, loss, and tenacious fear. In this way courage is so often an essential counterbalancing element of the inner life of the dying person.

What Use Is Courage in the Face of Death?

Sometimes it appears that courage hastens death. In the examples of those who face death when going to war, for instance, courage seems to put men and women in the front line of vulnerability when others might run away or hide. Courage might be admirable, but it is also commonly fatal in its consequences and can give the cynical observer reason to believe that courage, not war, is the dangerous pastime. In fact and in spirit the observation that courage is dangerous to life is a misunderstanding of the nature of courage itself. As I have described, the spiritual and social meaning of courage is never about the valuing and protection of one's own life but rather the preservation and protection of those things and people one cherishes—foundational personal values, friends, family, country—and the dignity, social bonds, cherished reciprocity, and self-identity that are embedded in these crucial relationships. People face death with courage—in war or in serious illness—not to avoid death itself but rather to protect others from harm, and to protect from harm those personal values so important a part of the self that their destruction would be a death to self anyway. The question of the survival value of courage must be viewed primarily as sociological rather than physical, if courage is not to be trivialized as self-endangering.

However, courage does seem to have some physical survival value. As Nardini and Frankl observed, courage actually helped keep people alive in internment camps, where humor, passive aggression, and fantasy against captives preserved and maintained morale, even hope. Hope is of equal practical value in staying morally, spiritually, and physically afloat in dying from cancer and living in internment camps. Courage—born of fear—seeks to dominate, transcend, control the enemy—to link up with hope and give its bearer time to find meaning and sense in this new and however short life.

Courage is useful because, in maintaining hope and encouragement for self and others, it can buy time. That time can be used, with a presence of mind bought by courage, to do the things that a mind and heart paralyzed by fear could not think to do—to write farewell letters to loved ones, to phone home and offer a lasting positive memory for survivors, even to plan a counterattack against one's assailants.

Courage is useful because, in providing a mental space in which to distance oneself from fear, it can create a social and spiritual space in which to do more, be more, and think more, thereby enhancing the quality of one's remaining life. Courage is, in this way, essential to quality of life in circumstances of dying. Without courage fear is in control and diminishes and subtracts from an ability to be one's self and to reaffirm the values and goals that one cherishes in life.

Finally, courage is useful to dying people because the decision to mentally shun fear and despair is a decision to fight both—even in the private reaches of one's own mind, and this provides the crucial difference, a spiritual and mental truce, as it were, between hope and encouragement on the one hand and complete demoralization and personal defeat on the other. In this way dying people can remain surprisingly defiant.

5

Resistance—Facing the Choices

I am red meat. His beak
Claps sideways; I am not his yet
— Sylvia Plath, "Death & Co."

S ylvia Plath was a young American poet who took her own life at the age of thirty. By all accounts Plath suffered from long-term depression, perhaps linked to the early death of her father, perhaps exacerbated by a marital separation some months before, or the antidepressants designed to help but that might have also deepened her melancholy. In any event it was at least her second known attempt to take her own life. Her struggle to live was a journey she was conscious of—writing about it in direct and indirect ways:

Dying
is an art, like everything else.
I do it exceptionally well.
I do it so it feels like hell.
I do it so it feels real.
I guess you could say I've got a call.[1]

Al Alvarez, Plath's friend and fellow poet, described his own view of her suicide as an unanswered cry for help. He was convinced that she thought she would be found. In fact, Plath—who put her head in the oven in her kitchen and turned the gas on—left a note with the name and contact number for her doctor for those she anticipated would find her. Alvarez argues, "Suicide, in short, was not a swoon into death, an attempt 'to cease upon the midnight with no pain'; it was something to be felt in the nerve ends and fought against, an initiation rite qualifying her for a *life* of her own."[2]

Yielding or Resisting?

I commence this chapter with reflections on a suicide because, even here, in this example of dying conduct that people commonly think of as escapist—dying people are found to resist. It is true that most people don't think of suicide as a form of resistance. We often think of suicide as an attempt to escape from troubles or personal responsibility. Sometimes suicide is medicalized, viewed as an act beyond responsibility, an outcome caused by a disturbed mind, much as fevers are caused by infection and not personal intent. Although I do not wish to argue here that all suicides can be understood to have just a handful of causes—they do not; they probably have hundreds of reasons—it is important to note that among these numerous reasons, a big one is resistance.[3]

People who wish to die may be resisting losing parts of themselves that are important to them—dignity, independence, an old but cherished way of life, for example—and suicide is also a form of outright military resistance, as we have seen in suicide bombers from Japan to the Middle East. Furthermore, suicide itself—particularly when it becomes a strong inner drive, as it was for Sylvia Plath—is also a form of dying *to be resisted by the self.* As Alvarez has suggested, this might be a resistance against the inner forces that would compel one to endlessly replay past suffering, conflict, and emotional bondage. Resistance in these ways can be a "rite qualifying (one) for a life of one's own." In the case of Plath, resistance gave way to defeat. However, the purpose of any resistance to dying is not to defeat death itself—impossible and widely understood to be impossible—but rather to buy time, to self-consciously earn the right to live, day by day, week by week, month by month. That was Sylvia Plath's form of resistance, one she shared, perhaps counterintuitively, with most other people who face imminent death. People often appear to resist the unresistable because we mistakenly believe they are resisting only death itself and not other demons.

In another consideration about suicide, some who write about palliative medicine view the desire for euthanasia as a flight response to the prospect of death or dying.[4] But to characterize the request to die as a way to avoid death or dying is a bit of an oxymoron, if there ever was one. I can certainly understand the desire to flee to an isolated beach in the Hawaiian Islands or to a ski shack in the Pyrenees so one can try to forget, as a flight from the idea of death or dying, but a desire to die as a way to avoid dying? I think not. Again, we need to remind ourselves of what people commonly fear about the process of dying—being a burden to others, being vulnerable, being abandoned, dying in great suffering, or losing dignity at the end.[5] A desire for a quick and sure death makes more sense when these desires are reframed as a flight from these life-oriented, interpersonal terrors. Running away from these terrors (flight) is an understandable response to the prospect of suffering.

Most of us would not choose death to avoid suffering, but the choice itself is nevertheless part of a list of possibilities on the run-and-hide menu from which all animals—including humans—are free to choose. However, even this run-and-hide option is a serious and useful form of resistance. It is neither a denial of death nor evidence of surrender. It is in fact part of a wider menu of active resistance that in the popular imagination is eclipsed by an all-too-common public image that privileges a more exaggerated, more outwardly aggressive, fight response. This is the response that attracts the lion's share of media and academic attention. Fighting has become *the* cultural signature in relation to modern death. No one is encouraged to "go gentle into that good night."

War, Fighting, and Death

In the United States the so-called war against cancer announced by President Richard Nixon in 1971 gave voice to both a cultural mood and a social attitude toward life-threatening disease that had been in place for many years.[6] Since then a preponderance of academic literature in the social and health sciences has described how personal struggles with life-threatening diseases, especially cancer, are replete with militaristic language such as *fight, war, battle,* and so on. Susan Sontag's famous book, *Illness as Metaphor,* is the landmark work describing the cultural basis of such language and metaphor.[7]

The resistance against the prospect of dying and death is often great, and it is part of contemporary medical culture. Medical systems are geared to postpone death, to fight its eventuality. As the surgeon Sherwin Nuland observes, "We live today in the era not of the art of dying, but of the art of saving life."[8] Hospitals recognize the coming of death only so they can throw as many technological barriers against it as possible, no matter what the age, diagnosis, or life expectancy of the patient.[9] Dr. Kent K. Hu, an internist at the University of Pennsylvania, exemplifies the concern of many Americans when he fought with his family and medical colleagues to allow his grandmother to die a peaceful death after she endured a massive stroke. He writes:

> I am glad that I was able to advocate for her without reservation. It continues to upset me that the aggressive "do everything" approach is the default position. If there had been no one to advocate for YaYa's peaceful death, the standard of care would have been to fight against death with all the technology and money available. In that fight to keep her alive, the treatments for pain, anxiety, nausea and air hunger could not have been done well. Then we would have failed her. In acknowledging the process of her death we were able to focus the treatments on providing comfort. With YaYa at peace, we were able to view her death as a final bonding and affirming process.[10]

But fighting a life-threatening illness is not a tendency (with both good and harmful aspects) emanating solely from the medical profession. People outside the medical profession who have often been personally affected by these diseases are keen to lead the fight, too. For example, both governments and ordinary citizens raise billions of dollars for more research into new treatments that might help them or those they love. Some of these funds are raised in the general fight against cancer. But about 6,000 rare cancers affect small groups of people and do not therefore attract major funding. Called orphan diseases, these cancers affect fewer than 200,000 Americans every year and do not attract the big dollars for research into new treatments. Such diseases rely on groups of experiencers and their carers to band together to create new philanthropic organizations to raise money and awareness of their diseases. Many of these organizations have been successful in their mission, and therefore their fight, to gain new resources to stop their particular disease from killing more people, or at least slow its progress in those who live with it.[11]

Such political, cultural, and organizational values and attitudes not only set the social stage for national policies and social movements; they also create and shape personal experience. Moreover, as social observers such as Sontag have observed, these influences provide a language for experience. When people use such terms as *fighting, war,* or *combat,* they are using metaphorical language that allows them to tell a story about what is happening to them in terms that others can identify or connect with. These words provide a basis for expressing their vulnerability and fears, making their experience intelligible to those with little or no medical or biological knowledge about diseases and their treatment or the effects of both on personal experience. In this important cultural way, the language of resistance is about both describing the personal experience of resistance and creating metaphors that allow individuals to connect their experience to the wider collective experience.[12] Ethan Helm, a young man diagnosed with Hodgkin's disease, describes a classic stance of resistance couched in terms of fighting:

> Cancer is not only a war; it is a civil war, in which a person's cells revolt. These rebel cells want to take over. . . . The war is multifaceted. Emotional as well as physical, the soldier feels the effects of the war. The beeping of the IV line reminds the patient of the brutality of the war like the firing of distant shells. Physically and emotionally exhausted, the soldier fears death. The shrapnel takes its toll as the soldier places his head over the toilet and hurls. Perpetually tired, the marching becomes tedious but the choice is to continue or die, and death increasingly seems the better option. Fellow soldiers pass away at an alarming rate, and the support cards from friends and family seem almost trivial. They claim to understand, but they do not. The have no clue what the war is like. The officers have no answers as to when the war will be over, and slowly the dread which comes from the war becomes normal, and the soldier ponders, "When will I return home?" I cannot think of a better metaphor for cancer than war. It echoes my experience perfectly.[13]

However, the mood and the language of fighting as a form of resistance are not the sole purview of those with cancer and dying of cancer. Nor is it reserved for those dying of an illness and the effort to halt the process with pharmacotherapies. In fact, when the process of dying is more gradual, insidious, and developmental—as in growing old—resistance can become a crusade of fights on several fronts. People in their seventies, eighties, and older commonly resist social and physical forms of dying. Most people in these age groups do not feel their age; they often feel much younger. This theme has long been a mainstay of both autobiographical and research literatures. The British author J. B. Priestley famously describes his own experience of being old: "It is though walking down Shaftesbury Avenue as a fairly young man, I was suddenly kidnapped, rushed into a theatre and made to don the grey hair, the wrinkles and other attributes of old age, then wheeled on stage. Behind the appearance of age I am the same person, with the same thoughts as when I was younger."[14]

Ros, the pseudonym for a respondent in a social research project, describes it in similar terms: "As you get older, your body gets older, and you look older. But, if you had no mirrors and no clocks you would never know that you are getting older, because the inside of your brain is still exactly the same. It doesn't get any less. You think exactly as you thought . . . fifty years ago." And Hettie from the same research adds: "The thing is that bits of your body wear out, but inside, the essential me is still the same. The physical me is the envelope in which the letter is, and the envelope gets worn out."[15]

The wider society reads basic identity information off our bodies and concludes that who we are is what people see. What you see is what you get. In fact, according to most older people, the truth is exactly the opposite. However, both the appearance of gradual aging and physical decline, reinforced by age-related employment laws and health policies in some countries, encourage people in many parts of the world to see and experience aging as a slow social death—an incremental denial of the basic rights to work, increasingly unequal access to certain medical treatments, and a slow decline of financial, social, sexual, and political support.

In a modern culture in which youth dominates financial and cosmetic priorities, resistance to growing old is manifested in political movements, such as gray power and pensioner rights, all over the modern world as well as the smaller more personal attempts to forestall aging—dying one's hair, cosmetic surgery, or dressing in the fashions of younger cohorts. Such priorities and social movements illustrate Dylan Thomas's exhortation that we

Do not go gentle into that good night,
Old age should burn and rave at close of day;
Rage, rage against the dying of the light.[16]

Although growing awareness of their mortality and frailty does lead many older people to suicide and despair (the highest rates of suicide are among people older than eighty) most older people respond to their gradual physical deterioration with a stronger and more focused desire to contribute in more social and spiritual ways to their social circle and themselves.[17] As Tennyson wrote:

Death closes all; but something ere the end,
Some work of noble note, may yet be done . . .
Tho' much is taken, much abides; and tho'
We are not now that strength which in old days
Moved earth and heaven; that which we are, we are;
One equal temper of heroic hearts,
Made weak by time and fate, but strong in will
To strive, to seek, to find, and not to yield.[18]

Fleeing and Hiding as Forms of Resistance

But fighting is not all there is to the desire to resist dying before we are ready. The animal world has more ways to resist a predator than mere fighting. Sometimes prey know they cannot outrun their chaser. What else can they do? If prey see predator first, prey can hide. This hiding response is sometimes viewed as an alternative to the fight-or-flight response of animals or sometimes as merely a novel extension of the flight response itself.[19]

The physicians Henry J. Carson and Richard Fiester, in a letter to the *Canadian Journal of Psychiatry*, recall the response of one woman to a tumor growing in her breast. The authors describe the woman's response as a case of "denial and avoidance," but her conduct could just as easily be described as hiding from her wolf at the window:

The patient, aged 48 years and white, lived at home with her husband and 2 young children. For 4 to 6 weeks preceding her death, she isolated herself from her family in the basement, explaining that she had personal issues that she was handling alone. She continued to work at her job, where her co-workers noted that she had become withdrawn. She was later found dead in her basement, surrounded by blood-soaked, foul-smelling clothing and gauze. There was a penetrating injury of the right breast and chest wall. An autopsy revealed that the injury was from a large ulcerated breast carcinoma, which eroded the chest wall and opened a large artery.[20]

Denial is commonly a transitory reaction to a threat or shocking news and soon transforms into other emotions and reactions such as anger, sorrow, despair, or thirst for further information. When *denial* is used to describe a prolonged response to bad news, it seems more likely to be a misnomer — that is, the person is instead dealing with a conscious choice or decision about how to deal with the threat. *Denial* would suggest a tendency to continue as if nothing had happened or that the new and shocking news was simply not true. In the case of the woman with breast cancer, she seems to have undergone a marked change of behavior based on some recognition that she had a problem to deal with. She explained to her family that she "had personal issues that she was handling alone." That's not a comment from someone denying something. This is notifying her family of a new arrival in her emotional life that needs attention and that her plan is to deal with it alone — for whatever reason. What her story suggests is not denial but recognition. The response is unusual, divergent from most people's response in a similar situation, and as such subject to psychiatric scrutiny and labeling, but that doesn't necessarily mean that the labels and the diagnosis are correct.

The woman spends her time in the basement hiding from any social prying by others — her family and any health-care professional. She has found a large lump in her breast. She may be assuming that the lump, if diagnosed by a medical practitioner, will be cancer — a big cancer that may not be curable. To avoid the diagnosis may be to avoid the fate. In other words, hide from the medical gaze and the bad news one expects and one just might escape the fate itself. Maybe the lump will go away in time. Maybe she needs time to review her options. But the tumor wreaked its havoc before she could decide another course of action. Hiding, in this case, killed her, probably earlier than if she had sought appropriate medical attention. A lot of people do the same with their chest pain symptoms, with other symptoms of unusual bleeding, of increasing breathlessness, or a niggling pain they have in their back or chest that later, on autopsy, appears to be a malignancy or advanced arterial disease. How many people have ignored a small bout of dizziness or headache, thinking it was something else and rationalizing, until suffering a major stroke or heart attack?

Denial may be the psychiatric label for hiding, but hiding works well for the millions who ignore their daily aches and pains and who are not found to have a malignancy or cardiovascular problem as the underlying cause. *Denial* is the term reserved for the unfortunate few whose personal guess about what is happening to them or their hiding strategy turns out to be wrong or the wrong strategy. This poor subgroup of hiders gets the psychiatric label. But hiding *has* proved to be a good strategy in the animal and human kingdoms, and if it weren't, our medical services would be flooded with people seeking attention for every ache and pain that afflicts them every day. That is often called *hypochondriasis*, another psychiatric label for those with hyperawareness of what could go wrong with them. A difficult choice of psychiatric diagnoses for those of us who hide and those of us who don't!

On the other hand, a group of clinicians in the United Kingdom analyzed communication patterns between doctors and patients with serious cancer and found that for most patients fighting actually meant concealing emotional distress to protect family and clinicians.[21] This would actually mean that encouraging people to fight or be positive actually may encourage them to conceal—or, to use, another phrase, engage in hiding conduct—not as a way to avoid death but rather to avoid distress in others. For many dying people this form of resistance may paradoxically be a form of resistance to any social or emotional erosion of relationships resulting from the news of their life-threatening illness. Like most forms of resistance, this is less a fight against death than a fight to preserve a way of life.

Some studies of dying people who feel they are a burden to others have described the different strategies these people use to cope with this threat to their way of life. Before their illness most of these people experienced the autonomy and independence that most of us take for granted. Most of us believe we earn respect and love from each other through a reciprocity of positive relations and support. Serious long-term illness disturbs that balance, tilting toward friends and family who become carers. The balance in relationships becomes skewed in our favor. We feel that we are incapable of giving back as much as we receive. Our efforts at resistance, to this dimension of our dying experience, is also shaped by fighting to right this imbalance (by being active in our own care); hiding (forgoing or cloaking our needs so as not to further burden others); tending and befriending (managing others' needs, especially by encouraging them to take respite from their care responsibilities), and so on.[22]

In all these ways, resistance is, again, not about a denial of death but a positive, though difficult (and much misunderstood), attempt to support current relations in one's life. Hiding is life affirming rather than death denying. It is a form of resistance, for sure, but resistance to yielding to a lesser quality of emotional life for all, including themselves.

When it comes to strategies of resistance, though, people often ask: Does a fighting spirit aid survival? We do not have studies of how this form of resistance might affect those faced with death in combat, in incarceration, in intensive care, or in the very old. Most studies of this attitude toward death have been conducted with cancer patients, and there the answer appears to be negative. In other words, a fighting spirit is not associated with longer survival rates. However, attitudes of helplessness and hopelessness are associated with relapse and early death.[23] If a fighting spirit doesn't help, what about resistance in general? Why fight at all, why run and hide, why tend and befriend, if extending our lives is not the end result but rather what some people might see as the lesser prize of simply avoiding likely relapse and early death?

Why Do We Resist?

Since the meaning of fear is ultimately about self-preservation—about preserving the self—it is entirely understandable that resistance will often be our first-line response in servicing that fear. We will resist a threat to take the self away, even to alter that self in any major way. We want what we know. We like the self we have created, or remade throughout our life. Others may not find their selves all that likeable, but it is all they have and they're very attached to the only thing they know in this way. Sometimes we resist because the project that is our identity is unfinished—as it often is when we are young.

However, for some people becoming the self we want is a lifelong project with no expected end. Either way, the message and meaning are the same — we resist being derailed or losing this precious self, this identity that we take for granted as me. The time one may gain by avoiding relapse and early death may be just enough time to apply ourselves to finishing our selves in the way we want. It may also be the time we need to take stock of what remains in the pile of ashes left by advanced or recurrent disease and/or very old age.

Sometimes, however, at some point in the vigorous — and often cruel — treatments for serious illness, after a period of watching the years take their toll on their aging body, people realize that their self has changed. In this context, we have often been too busy with the business of resisting to realize what we have lost and what is new. At this point we notice first what we have already lost. And then the long shadows of sadness and sorrow catch up with us. Like it or not, acknowledge it or not, parts of our old self have already died. Although a sense of loss is natural upon these realizations, resistance to the prospect of death itself may yet continue because, as Santayana observes:

A candle wasting itself before an image
will prevent no misfortune,
but it may bear witness to some silent hope
or relieve some sorrow by expressing it;
it may soften a little the bitter sense
of impotence which would consume
a mind aware of physical dependence
but not of spiritual dominion.[24]

To resist, to be able to feel the ability to meaningfully resist, is an important part of maintaining personal morale. Resistance is also an important foundation and cornerstone of the building of personal hope. To feel unable to fight, run away, or hide from the threat to one's self is to court serious sorrow and depression. Several studies have demonstrated that people who are unable to feel they can fight, who feel trapped by their circumstance (living with a fatal illness or waiting on death row, for example) or trapped by their painful thoughts and moods, are more likely to feel depression, defeat, hopelessness, and the urge to commit suicide. The feeling of being trapped by circumstances is itself a kind of emotional dying and death. Resistance may be difficult, may often even feel futile, but its expression provides both a sense of purpose and hope as well as a real and powerful tool against self-destruction of the spirit.[25]

All that said, some find resistance difficult, even impossible. People with an early history of feeling powerless in their lives, of feeling little relationship between their personal efforts to resist and an outcome of some success, feel helpless again when faced with feeling trapped by life. In the case of such circumstances as living with a life-threatening illness, or advanced aging, people who feel little ability to deal successfully with troubles in their world may fall in a heap when confronted with death. The wonderful early review of animal studies by the psychologist Martin Seligman remains instructive. When rats held in a closed fist until they stop struggling are released into water, they drown within about thirty minutes. Rats not exposed to this experience of futile struggle can swim for sixty hours before drowning. If the experimenter holds the rat, then lets it go, then repeats this several times, it also does not suffer sudden death or drown quickly. The early experience of uncontrollable and ineffective personal action can drain the confidence and hope out of animals—rats, cats, dogs, fish, mice, and even human beings.[26]

Sometimes when parents, siblings, friends, or lovers begin to speak and act as if they are accepting the inevitable, speaking about their coming death with candor and openness, and acting and planning accordingly, their loved ones may think they are giving in to helplessness. They may appear to us as people who may feel defeated and powerless, and we—we who take our own health and energies for granted—feel that they must not give up. But fight-or-flight forms of resistance usually don't last. Sometimes people have the opportunity to openly accommodate the knowledge that they will die quite soon. People find both peace and personal wisdom in accepting a time to "be dying"; to look ahead at what might come, what might be, in the mystery of their own ending. In the wider culture of resistance, whose main theme is "let us fight the great fight till the end," this attitude is largely misunderstood by family and professionals who care for those who are seriously ill and dying. I have seen and talked to many older people, as well as other people with advanced terminal illness, who wanted to decide for themselves when the time to resist dying should give way to another form of resistance—a time to resist the pressure to stay.

Another (and Unpopular) Kind of Resistance

Resistance to the pressure, self-imposed and from or others, to stay a while longer eventually arises in most people who are dying. Sometimes this form of resistance can come too early for their families and doctors; sometimes this resistance comes only in the last few hours of life. It is nearly always difficult to witness the dying person's decision to make this final push away from us and toward something new and unknown.

Elizabeth Kübler-Ross liked to call this form of resistance *acceptance.* But the term has created a lot of theoretical angst, debate, and criticism. Acceptance sounded a lot like "giving up" to many people, or it sounded like putting an artificially positive spin on something indisputably negative. Although Kübler-Ross was careful to point out that "acceptance should not be mistaken for a happy stage [because] it is almost void of feelings," many health professionals clearly resist the idea that such a time should come, or they believe it should come only at the last possible minute.[27] But in my experience Kübler-Ross is right to speak of a time when "the pain has gone, the struggle is over, and there comes a time for 'the final rest before the long journey,' as one patient phrased it." This also usually is a time when the family needs more help, understanding, and support than the dying person does.[28]

If only because the idea of acceptance of death runs so strongly against the cultural life-celebrating mores of the day, this time in a dying person's life, this aspect of the inner life of dying, might more usefully be viewed as a controlled change in focus — away from resisting our demise and toward resisting those who would take our attention away from the inevitable. This change in attitude — from the work that has been done to the work that is before us — is the essential turning point. Our normal and usual habit in dealing with all of life's numerous tasks is to draw a line through today's demands and — for better or worse, in eagerness or trepidation — to look toward our next tasks or journeys. When the new process of resistance commences is, of course, different for each dying person. For some it can begin quite early.

For example, M. A. Cowan and R. P. McQuellon, who are researchers in pastoral care, tell the following story:

When Mary's physician told her that her breast cancer had returned and spread to her lungs and liver, her reaction took him by surprise. He requested a consultation with the psychosocial oncology service, indicating that she didn't seem to understand the seriousness of her predicament. When one of the authors spoke to Mary in consultation she was sitting at the bedside in some discomfort but managing her pain reasonably well. She understood that her cancer had now moved to her liver and lungs and that it was not curable. She stated that she trusted her doctors and relied on their input, but her main physician was the "man upstairs." She was dignified, humble, and unafraid of talking about what may lie ahead for her. She had buried her father, and cared for a brother disabled by a stroke within the past year. She had grown familiar with the possibility of dying. Her caring physician-in-training was not sure that she fully understood the gravity of her situation. He was not critical of her, but puzzled by what seemed to be her "denial" of her situation. She was prepared to discuss the limits to her life but hopeful that God would touch her with a miracle.[29]

Here again is the most overworked word in health care — *denial* — now commonly and widely used by both professional and lay publics to describe any person's reactions to death or dying that the observer or listener cannot accept. Mary has clearly come to a certain understanding about her future that is tightly tied to her faith in God, her immediate past experience with the recent death and disability of close family members, and the additional time to consider her own imminent prospects of death. After who-knows-how-many evenings and nights when she contemplated these issues, Mary now takes philosophically the not-unexpected news of the cancer spread. She reacts, as many cancer patients do — not all cancer patients but many — calmly, reflectively, as a person who has an ability to gaze at the worst news without flinching. This is highly disturbing to many onlookers, perhaps because it is not a common reaction. Nevertheless, many people in this emotional and intellectual space now must resist often-increased pressure from their physicians and family for aggressive treatments. Bad news frequently prompts supporters to encourage dying people to redouble their efforts, not to get philosophical, as Kent Hu found when advocating for a peaceful palliative care solution for his grandmother, YaYa.

As Iain Gardner, who was dying from AIDS, once told me and a colleague while we were interviewing him about his own acceptance of his imminent death:

Patrick's [Iain's partner] only just starting to face it. He finds it very difficult. I'm an extrovert, I don't find it all that difficult. I also find it reasonably OK to connect with my emotions. He finds it more difficult. A breakthrough really was that conversation I was mentioning earlier, where he said he was just starting to think what his life would be without me. And the counselor that I'm going to see does a lot of work with couples in grief and anticipatory loss so I suspect that I will be able to drag Patrick into some of those sessions, which might give him an opportunity and a probe rather than it always being me. But I can't imagine what it must be like for him, or the others. It's a bit arrogant in a way, isn't it? Like they all manage in their own ways. I'm going off and I have a sense that I'm going off to something safe and secure, whereas they will always have that loss. And that's delightfully selfish in a way.[30]

Both Mary and Iain Gardner are dying people who, in Kübler-Ross's terms, have accepted their dying but now find themselves surrounded by those who have not. For this group of ill and dying people the task is often to resist the well-meaning attempts for them to keep trying to hold on to life — from the loving family and friends who are cheering them on to the social and medical labeling, referrals, and attitudes heaped on those no longer singing a fight song. Many dying people reach a point at which their goals and story lines have little to do with the next treatment possibilities or platitudes about control, remissions, prognoses, or well-being. As Gillian Rose once observed about turning away from a medical view of her remaining life, "Medicine and I have dismissed each other. We do not have enough command of each other's language for the exchange to be fruitful."[31]

This form of resistance is also not confined to dying from an illness but is also found among the very old and dying. A study by the U.K. Centre for Policy on Ageing identifies a sample of what neighbors described as hermits and loners and what the report also described as "service refusers." These were negatively described as people who kept to themselves, refused to open doors, or receive social or health-care workers. Even individuals who displayed clarity of mind and purpose, such as a ninety-three-year-old woman discharging herself to her home after a heart attack ("She *insisted* on discharge," reads this report), is labeled as a service refusers.[32]

Holding On and Letting Go

The fight-or-flight response to death as a threat is now redirected. Sometimes dying people must exert great effort to resist efforts to keep them alive, at almost any cost. Sometimes dying people must exert great effort to resist stigmatizing and labeling by people who poorly understand or misunderstand the dying person's end-of-life decisions or when these are delayed by a caregiver's deep attachments and grief for the dying person. Often this leads people to delay their dying, for need of permission to go. Because both carers and the dying person care for each other, the decision by one to emotionally proceed with dying can lead to relationship tensions. Many dying people experience resistance and conflict—surprisingly and unexpectedly, not from the threat of death but from its opposite, from the threatening demands that life itself can make when one chooses the seemingly unimaginable. This too is often the basis of the turmoil, anger, and grief so often experienced by the family and friends of a suicide.

Finally, as dying proceeds into the last months, days, or hours of life, many more dying people focus on what is to come for them. But here still, they meet and must resist protests and challenges to their leaving. Recently I completed a study of family care of dying people in eastern Europe, where I interviewed more than one hundred families.[33] In the Republic of Moldova most people die at home under the care of their families. Here, as elsewhere, family and friends resist the idea that dying people will accept their coming death, even when they are seriously ill, or as in the examples that follow, when the dying experience what they believe are spiritual or mystical premonitions of their death.

> About a month before she died she told me she had dreamt her [deceased] husband was calling her. She woke up one morning and said, "[He] is calling me, my turn has now come." To which I replied that she shouldn't take dreams seriously.
>
> He dreamed about my mother, who had already died and whom he missed, he had been extraordinarily fond of her. He also dreamed about my brother [a son of the dying man], who died suddenly at the age of 32; he had a heart attack and died within half an hour. Father dreamed about both of them, they seemed to be dancing happily at a wedding and they

called him. He then told me, "They will take me away with them." I tried to console him, told him it would not happen, that he would get well . . . but he said he would die, that I had done everything for him. . . . He had that dream about one month before he died.[34]

It is entirely understandable that family and friends should resist losing someone they love. Often the affections that they feel is shared by health-care providers, too. And since most health-care institutions and professions are geared toward cure or the hope of longevity, a dying person's candor and acceptance of death is not welcome news for all these interested parties. Resistance in the face of death is not always entirely about death but can often arise from a mixture of threats that originate in a conflict between the dying person's changing priorities and the often more-singular priority of caregivers, who want to keep the dying person with them for as long as they can. Ironically, and often sadly, this means that sometimes resistance to death can suddenly change into detachment as the needs of dying people and their loved ones diverge.

In summary, then, few people wish to die, even among those who commit suicide. Fear of and resistance to death is natural. But as with the general fear of death, resistance to the prospect of death is often revealed to be resistance to other, more important, aspects of life itself. The most common target of resistance for dying people is to having their lives changed in unwelcome ways—from seeing the distress of their friends and family to seeing their friends and family burdened by both the news and the care of the person facing death. The reciprocity that most of us take for granted in our loving relationships is a precious thing to be saved for as long as possible. The resistance we so often see among those who grow very old, who live with advanced disease, is a social resistance to the passing of an old way of life. In these specific ways the resistance to any erosion of our relationships or to increasing distress among those we love becomes integral to the broader aim of staying alive for as long as they can. Resistance is not death denying but life affirming. As the late Palestinian poet Mahmoud Darwish writes in his final collection "The road rises and falls, undulates, zigzags, extends, and branches off into countless roads that meet back at the beginning. How many times must we start at the beginning? We survived much death. We defeated forgetfulness and you said to me: We survive, but do not triumph. I said to you: Survival is the prey's potential triumph over the hunter. Steadfastness is survival and survival is the beginning of existence."[35]

But it is important to record that resistance also commonly evolves—the targets of resistance frequently change or can group together, competing for equal attention from the dying person. Yes, in the early stages of aging or advanced illness we frequently observe a resistance to the idea of death itself, and we even observe this in suicide—mainly an abhorrence toward ideas of extinction, separation, or loss—but these quickly merge with or evolve into other concerns for those around us.

Eventually, as we physically weaken, treatments fail, diseases progress, or religious or spiritual ideas take greater priority, we refocus on the future— whatever that idea might mean for each dying person. For the suicidal person an interpersonal or political situation may tip the balance or their psychological ability to tolerate any more of whatever plagues them psychologically or culturally becomes too frayed. From any of these crucial turning points the dying person may begin to resist the pressure to stay. After an interminable period of thinking that death is no future at all, or no acceptable future, curiosity, fatigue, faith restored, or fear of worse—any of these late influences can bring revision and reorientation to the dying person. The dying person in the last minutes, hours, days, or even months before death can accept, or begin to accept, a new or old view of what lies ahead—relief from a long battle, a dreamless sleep, a final end, or a new beginning, reunion, and a new world to explore.

Many dying people resist these vistas and remain, at least in their public presentation of themselves, as people clinging tightly to life and their old ways, friends, and family. But many others do not, and for this latter group of dying people, the final period of their dying experience will attract new targets of resistance, and these may well be loved ones who do not share the dying person's latest insight into personal mortality. Resistance in all these ways takes the dying person on a common journey—from attachments that have deep roots in old love to another point in that journey, where tired necessity begins to loosen their grasp. At this time of divided attention and a new horizon, the dying person begins to understand that the new goal of letting go must be a joint effort. As is so often the case in life, resistance is a story told by new pressures about old ties. Without the cooperation of one's old loves and attachments, going can be difficult. In these new terms resistance is a common personal experience for the dying, right up to the end of their lives. Emily Brontë illustrates this spirit of resistance in adversity when she writes,

> The night is darkening round me,
> The wild winds coldly blow;
> But a tyrant spell has bound me
> And I cannot, cannot go.
> The giant trees are bending
> Their bare boughs weighed with snow.
> And the storm is fast descending,
> And yet I cannot go.
> Clouds beyond clouds above me,
> Wastes beyond waste below;
> But nothing drear can move me;
> I will not, cannot go.[36]

6

Sadness and Anger—Facing Loss

The dog walked off to play with a black beetle. The beetle was hard
at work trying to roll home a great ball of dung it had been collect-
ing all morning; but Doss broke the ball, and ate the beetle's hind
legs, and then bit off its head. And it was all play, and no one could
tell what it had lived and worked for. A striving, and a striving, and
an ending in nothing.

—Oliver Schreiner, "The Story of an African Farm"

The realization that you will die soon—not abstractly in some far-off
future—but soon, perhaps next week or next month, perhaps at the
end of the year, brings existential questions about the meaning of life quickly
and suddenly to the fore. An abrupt revision of one's future, from something
to nearly nothing, forces us to ask what life is for, particularly if we feel cut
short in life as a young person or someone in the middle age. The loss of a
personal future and every dream and hope associated with that future makes
you not only sad but angry. What was my life supposed to mean if I am not
even allowed to finish it properly? Never mind that most animals and people
have never been able to see out an optimal life expectancy; people today
experience the benefits of modern public health as if it were a right. In this
modern context people commonly feel sad—and a bit cheated: as if life were
not fair to them, as if the dog in the epigraph had torn off our legs and head
before we completed our important work and put it where we and all those
we loved could receive and appreciate our legacy.

The Australian historian Jan Bassett speaks about just this seamless mixture of feeling when she reflects on her professional work given her own
mortal predicament. During chemotherapy for breast cancer that is getting

worse, Bassett reflects on the confrontation with death of an Antarctic explorer whose life she had studied:

> Phillip Law writes about his feelings during a dangerous voyage from Antarctica to Australia: "I recall quite clearly my emotion when confronting what then seemed like certain death. It was one of intense anger and resentment. Here I was, the successful expedition leader, returning with a story of accomplishment and a load of scientific records and photographs. Was all this to be lost? Was all our work to be wasted? And no one would ever know exactly what had happened to us." This statement seemed horribly close to home.
>
> My feelings were closer to Law's than to those of joy, which poets sometimes attribute to dying explorers, but they differed from his in some ways. I felt, and still feel, profound sadness rather than anger at the loss of my old life and hoped-for future.[1]

In this chapter I discuss the experiences of sadness and anger because these feelings often coexist or run a tandem race together. Their targets are not always the same, to be sure, but they are companions born of loss and fed by the abruptly changed circumstances that imminent death can force upon people. I am not saying that sadness and anger are the same emotions or experiences, but they are often inexorably linked; they are clearly family. Sadness and anger come from the same place—loss, pain, frustration, and a sense of personal or spiritual insult or injury. Their bilingual expression, so to speak, can be confusing to others because a single act can mean either or both emotions may be at play—we weep in anger or sorrow; we appear downcast, whether we are in despair or suffering fist-pounding frustration. The public displays of both underline the internal predicament of loneliness for the person momentarily reeling from another emotional blow. Let me begin the discussion with why it is necessary to emphasize the word *sadness* rather than *grief* or *depression*.

Sadness or Depression?

Since the 1960s the natural occurrence of sadness in our lives has come under increasing scrutiny. In fact, the slide away from viewing the human experience of sadness as a normal expression of sorrow and grief that is understandably proportional to the size of the loss has been noted since the 1980s.[2] Even then researchers were warning of a gradual inclusion of a normal emotion such as sadness in a disease model of grief.

Sadness is a natural reaction, in fact a natural biological reaction, to loss in our social environment. Separation causes biological reactions that make higher animals—especially primates—experience severe anguish, a condition to be avoided. This has evolutionary advantages, promoting cohesion and group life, that protect individuals from the vulnerability of isolation. This biological reaction is cross-cultural, although its prevalence varies considerably depending on the level of context-specific losses that characterize a particular environment. Depressed mood, loss of appetite, insomnia, oversleeping or trouble staying asleep, weepiness, and tiredness and lack of energy are entirely normal and usual. These have always been normal reactions to losses external to the self—breakups in important personal attachments, bereavements, threats to important life goals, dreams, or identity. But since the 1980s the DSM—the *Diagnostic and Statistical Manual of the American Psychiatric Association*—has actively turned sadness into depression. If all the major signs of sadness, now called symptoms of depression, last longer than two weeks, they are classified as an MDD—a major depressive disorder (with the exception of experiences of bereavement). Because the DSM focuses on symptoms and not contexts of sadness, the current definitions of depression encompass most people's sadness.[3] In fact, sadness is a normal, self-limiting, proportional reaction to loss that commonly lasts far more than two weeks.

The modern and dominant professional trend to classify sadness without understanding its context or proportional relationship to a loss means that depression is becoming quite an epidemic. This is good news for pharmaceutical companies and for clinicians who feel inadequate in the face of the tide of despair, misery, and loss brought to them on a daily basis in the private practices of medicine and psychology around the modern world. And whatever one thinks of the debate about whether more people are experiencing serious "clinical depression" or more people are simply being overclassified as such, in fact 15 to 25 percent of cancer patients are classified as experiencing serious depression, depending on whose study you read.[4]

Sorting through the different meanings that different writers—both clinical and academic—have to say about the experience of depression is difficult.

Sometimes authors appear to be clear about a serious depression that uses a clinical set of criteria linked to existing psychiatric guides (such as the DSM). Other authors at other times are referring to spiritual pain or suffering, existential suffering, or even sadness as a symptom while facing death. The psychological literature commonly uses synonyms, as well as vague and overlapping definitions, and is based mainly on cancer patient populations. To make matters worse, academics have reached no general agreement about what constitutes "clinically significant depression" or indeed even its different subtypes. This is a problem regardless of the age group examined by clinical studies.[5]

The literature rarely explores the sadness of other populations facing death. Extensive reviews or theoretical explorations of the distinctions in and meanings of *depression* and the common experience of sadness when facing death are impossible to find. The few clear statements about sadness, such as those by the eminent British psychiatrist John Bowlby, for example, are rare. Usually the author quickly folds words like *sadness* into larger discussions about depression. Both the direction and the mood of the writing in this area are decidedly biased toward seeking out the dysfunctional aspect of human sadness. But even when psychiatrists such as Bowlby write about sadness, the reader is left with the strongest impression that reflecting on sadness is merely a pause in his rush to ogle the animal called depression.

In a 472-page book entitled *Loss: Sadness and Depression* Bowlby devotes a single page to the topic of sadness. That's the bad news. The good news is that he at least says important things on that one page. The most important point he makes is that he considers sadness a normal, healthy response to "any misfortune" and that the reaction is nearly always a response to some kind of loss or expected loss. People experiencing or anticipating a loss will sometimes feel a little depressed—meaning they will suffer from some physical symptoms of depression such as loss of appetite or sleeplessness and even psychic features such as thoughts of suicide or complete but temporary despair. Usually, however, sad people use their network of family and friends to cope, keep a certain level of hope for their own future, and are able to maintain a personal sense of worth most of the time. Although sadness can be painful, even bewildering, it can also in the long run be adaptive. This is absolutely all Bowlby has to say about sadness. Rather strangely, the normality of human sadness, although it is the major response to loss, is not Bowlby's focus. He is more interested in the disordered and "more intense" examples of helplessness and hopelessness and devotes the rest of the book to these kinds of unusual cases.[6]

The Experience of Sadness

Since *sadness* is a word so frequently identified with professional-problem terms such as *depression* or *grief*, and because the wider discussion of sorrow is also commonly subsumed or co-opted into broader and murkier debates and theories about existential or spiritual suffering, going back to basics and checking the etymology can be more useful—and clarifying. According to the *Chambers Dictionary of Etymology*, the original meaning of the word *sad* was sated, satisfied, to have grown weary or tired of something. But for reasons unknown this meaning evolved into the current meaning of *sorrowful* around the fourteenth century. Perhaps the earlier expressions about growing tired or weary of something also contained a sense of regret about an ending, and this finer aspect of the earlier meaning eventually gave way to a larger dimension of loss and sorrow in the evolving definition of the word *sad*.

Parallel to these etymological developments, *sorrow* emerged around the twelfth century and focused specifically on the experience of emotional distress, regret, and "troubled care." These different developments subsequently converged so that today, for example, the *Oxford English Dictionary* describes *sad* as referring to *sorrow* or being mournful. *Roget's Thesaurus* deepens the idea of sadness by describing it as an affliction, especially "to the heart," a sense that echoes cognate meanings from the Old Irish and Slavic meanings of *sad* as a kind of sickness, presumably of feeling and attitude. Such origins make it easy to see that the basic long-standing character of human sadness is a distressing feeling of regret, sorrow, and longing for something or someone lost.[7]

Bill Worden, a counseling psychologist, makes the observation that although sadness is not necessarily manifested by crying behavior, it commonly is. Crying is a common expression of the experience of sadness, because deep experiences of sorrow at a loss are painful, that is to say, are experienced as physically and mentally breaking, ripping, or crushing. Crying is an emotional response to the realization of loss, but it can also be a reaction to feeling altogether dreadful in one's whole self—tiredness, lack of motivation and interest, obsession about the lost object, gastrointestinal upset, cardiac arrhythmias, feelings of anxiety, too much sleep or lost sleep, and headaches. On the other hand, sadness or crying can also occur suddenly and with little warning, as when someone experiences a spike of strong emotion that erupts from an ache or hollowness in the chest, a choking or tightness in the throat that overwhelms the social moment and/ or task at hand.

The experience of sadness in these ways is anguishing, a suffering that is both emotional and physical, and over which few have any inner control, no matter how stoic their public face. The feeling may be temporary, or it may last a long time. For the dying person the sources of sadness are in the past, especially in memories the good and/or the regrets at past loss; the present, especially in cherished social and personal relationships and experiences that are now changed forever; and in the future, especially the felt loss of what might have been.[8] Regrets and sadness often come unbidden, often prompted by the little experiences of daily endings such as nightfall or bedtime, as the poet Linda Pastan reminds us:

In the evening
my griefs come to me
one by one.
They tell me what I had hoped to forget.
They perch on my shoulders
like mourning doves.
They are the color
of light fading.[9]

For younger people who are dying, the losses, and the deep sadness that springs from them, are commonly about the future and even about how their present predicament might change how they are regarded by the people they love. They fear being left out, being left behind, becoming something they don't want to be in the minds of others. Sometimes they feel or anticipate the loss others experience.

Ulla-Carin Lindquist, a middle-aged Swedish TV producer with ALS, laments:

I grieve a lot now. Alone.

Will the sum of my life be this illness?

Will the images of me as a healthy mother, woman, wife and friend crumble away?

Will Gustaf, the youngest, ever remember a living mummy?

Will sorrow stand in the way of everything that has been good?

It is when melancholy wants to root itself in the December darkness, when the smell of mulled wine wafts up to me, in bed with my nutrition tube, that I feel bitterness creeping up.[10]

Natalie Robins, a middle-aged woman with cancer, reflects on her sadness in these ways:

Last night Christopher and I went to Ikea in New Jersey to buy a rug for our living room. We found just the right one, as I knew we would — a Southwest design in muted pinks, blues, and greens. Afterward we sat in the store's café having a snack (a bag of Swedish fish for me). I became very weepy over the thought that some other woman might live in my house after I died. Christopher just listened to me, of course, and then quietly told me that if I died before he did, he'd live in the house alone, and if he remarried, he'd buy a new house. I like hearing this — not only because it seemed real — but because such truth-telling heals.

. . .

With great clarity I soon realized that this fear of being left behind is the real fear of dying. It's not the physical act of dying; no, it's not that at all; it's this other fear that is so dreadful: the fear of not only being left behind but being left out of the future. That is the pain, the misery, the sorrow.[11]

And Fadia Saba, a seventeen-year-old high school student with dreadlocks, described to me the anguish she felt in anticipating her family's loss when she dies: "I'm not the only one going through it. They're also going to be in a bit of pain and will be upset by it. I've said it to them a million times: 'I don't mind dying.' But when I die I don't want my mum to cry, or my family to be upset. I just don't want to have *that* bit. And what hurts me the most is just my missing them . . . and knowing that they're going to be missing me. That's what hurts the most."[12]

Kübler-Ross describes a man whose sadness grew as his illness progressed. She described two kinds of sadness or, rather, two different targets for his sorrow.

He expressed many regrets for his "failures" when he was well, for lost opportunities while there was still time to be with his family, and sorrow at being unable to provide more for them. His depression paralleled his increasing weakness and inability to function as a man and provider. A chance for additional promising treatment did not cheer him up. Our interviews revealed his readiness to separate himself from this life. *He was sad that he was forced to struggle for life when he was ready to prepare himself to die.* It is this discrepancy between the patient's wishes and readiness (to die) and the expectation of those in his environment (to live) which causes the greatest grief and turmoil in our patients.[13]

These examples of sadness are not stages that each person experiences. On the contrary, these experiences coexist with other experiences and feelings, are companions on the journey of dying, which *takes dying people away from the social bonds and values they cherish yet must relinquish.* As the American poet Linda Pastan writes in her satirically titled book *The Five Stages of Grief:*

Acceptance. I finally
reach it.
But something is wrong.
Grief is a circular staircase.[14]

In each of these examples of sadness we can make the rather abstract observation that these feelings flow from a sense of loss, or that each person feels sad because of the sense that valued things—dreams, relationships, hopes, supports, or comforts—are or will be taken away from them. From that blunt recognition of the details of loss, we can see that the sensation of losing something and the sensation of having something taken away or stolen from you brings us close to the emotional territory of being the victim of a crime—in the case of the dying, an existential theft, if you will. From this point of view it is easy to see how anger might not be far from the feeling of sadness. "Follow the trail of anger inward," observes the psychologist Carol Tavris, "and there you will find the small, still voice of pain."[15]

Anger as Disappointment

Tavris argues that many people persist in the childhood belief that if they follow the rules, life should go as expected or, at the very least, be fair. When events in their lives don't turn out well—they divorce, fail to be promoted, have a parent who deserts, or are diagnosed with a serious illness—the first comment such people make is that these things are unfair. "Why me—it isn't fair" emerges from such self-observations as "I'm not responsible for how things turned out, look at all these horrible things that have happened. If anyone has a right to be angry, it's me." Tavris describes this as the "the victim's" stance. However, this passive view often is a transition to a more realistic, active one. Survivors of tragedy often get past this initial anger by developing a healing ritual of some kind, helping others, confessing, or seeking ways to break out of an angry and self-consuming cycle of resentment. Dying is no different in that anger can be expressed as episodic expressions of great sadness and frustration and also is a reaction that some people become chained to. Because anger frightens others easily, partly because a bark is often mistaken for a bite, people caring for dying people rarely attempt to explore the anger.[16] Yet anger is a common problem in hospice and palliative care and generates a significant literature not only because addressing anger helps the patient but also because this is a significant problem for health-care staff.[17]

The palliative care physician Michael Barbato lists the many different sources of anger—usually as an understandable reaction to losses of control, independence, and hopes, and the frustration that such disappointments bring. The targets of anger may be real or imagined, major or minor. But the anger is nearly always a reaction to loss and when submerged appears as sadness. According to Barbato, then, anger is the second face of sadness. This is the emotional reaction that screams no and enough when the other emotional arm, sadness, is for whatever personal reason restrained and unable to freely express itself.[18]

Although loss clearly is the source of both sadness and anger, the mere presence of loss does not explain the expression of one instead of the other or even their coexistence. Some people who are sad are rarely angry, and others are quick to anger, depending on their changed circumstances. Although sadness may convey such messages as "I feel sorrow," "I feel anguish," "I feel deprived," or "I feel a piece of me has gone missing," anger, on the other hand, sends slightly different and distinct messages—"Pay attention to me. I don't like what you're doing. Restore my pride. You're in my way. Danger. Give me justice."[19] Some psychologists believe that anger is part of a fight response to threat where that threat might come from blocked goals or hopes, or threats to personal integrity or dignity.[20]

In these ways, anger is not to be understood glibly as solely a matter of loss but rather as a deeper, perhaps parallel, response to pain, frustration, and particularly to insult or offense. People in pain—from cancer and chest pain to chronic pain and spinal cord injury—regularly report anger, with themselves as much as others.[21] So although many palliative care commentators believe that anger is nearly always a reaction to loss, we must acknowledge other factors that temper this single explanation. Despite popular views that suggests anger is simply another expression of sadness, anger in fact is also commonly a response to pain. Accidently hammering your thumb, running into a door, or bumping your knee while rounding a corner of furniture also commonly produces anger. Anyone who doubts how anger can be a physical reaction to pain should be careful approaching and placing their hands on an injured animal.

Furthermore, theorists of anger are quick to point out that anger is widely (though not always and necessarily) associated with some kind of negative appraisal of experience or events, something or someone—people become angry when they perceive offense or injustice and then feel an urge to injure and blame some target. People typically become angry when they are frustrated in their expectations of attaining an important goal. When Thomas DeBaggio was diagnosed with Alzheimer's disease at the age of fifty-seven, for example, he observed, "I am forced into old age against my will and I am full of rage."[22] Anger can be felt in a number of nuanced ways, such as irritation, annoyance, exasperation, disgust, and hate, to name only a few linguistic members of the anger family. It may or may not be associated with feelings about whether the offense or treatment directed at the person was justified. The mere presence of unpleasant environmental, biological, and social stressors will lower a personal resistance to anger even in infants, let alone reluctant residents of an nursing home or a hospice. Overall, then, anger can be about loss, but it can also be about frustration, pain, and a sense of offense or injustice. In these ways anger is not simply or merely displaced sadness and loss but also separately and distinctly about frustration, with or without justification, and furthermore it can also convey legitimate criticism. As the psychiatrist Victor Frankl found in his own experiences inside a Nazi concentration camp, indignation and anger can arise—even in the most downtrodden prisoner—not simply from cruelty or pain but from the insult connected with it.[23]

Forgetting that anger can be the emotional backwash of unresolved problems in a dying person's environment is a common way that carers often—consciously or unconsciously—personalize anger as a personality or psychological matter when in fact it may well be a legitimate criticism of poor social relations. Psychological reductionism—reducing everything about a person's reactions to the individual's psychology—is an annoying modern habit of people who refuse to understand social and cultural differences or who refuse to accept criticism from others as a form of social exchange.

Although anger can be part of a general feeling of helplessness, and in this sense a part of despair and an expression of personal losses, it can also give or fill the anger-aroused person with a sense of power and self-assurance. In other words, anger can have some personal benefits, too. Some studies have shown that experimental subjects have experienced both anger and sadness when faced with irretrievable loss. On the one hand, angry people faced with irretrievable loss feel grief but also rage at their deprivation. In some this may be a deep reaction to the psychological experience of loss as pain; for others this may be a reaction to some sense of unfairness about their situation; and for still others an increase in both their pain and their parallel anger lead them to seek out targets for blame. As H. G. Wells said of his last months of life, "I have one foot in the grave and the other kicking out at everything."[24] Anger can *simply be*—a state of being that reflects a general annoyance about how short life and possibility has suddenly become, at any age, from any disease, for anyone, but especially now, and particularly for me.

The writer Patricia Boston, a professor and registered nurse, tells this story: "Victor had metastatic disease throughout his pelvis now, and it had made it difficult to urinate, among other symptoms. 'It's no good. Just leave me alone!' he would sometimes snap at his wife. 'Why doesn't everyone just leave me?' he said to me during one of my visits in the spring. 'Can't they see there's nothing to be done?'"[25]

Finally, the lower threshold that many people experience while in physical, social, or psychological pain may make these people sensitive to the insensitive treatment of them by others while enduring their new circumstances of living with dying. Dying people and their carers have widely reported unhelpful or incompetent treatments at hospitals, nursing homes, or even at the hands of their own friends and family. As Lois Jaffe, a writer dying from acute leukemia, explains: "The bulk of my anger became displaced on my hospital environment, particularly those aspects that threatened my sense of control. These aspects included having to endure endless waiting in the X-ray department when I was racked with chills and fever; experiencing the traumatic loss of my hair that became symbolic of all my potential losses; seeing my body waste away and having no appetite to combat it; vomiting perpetually and continually; feeling trapped in a bleak grey room that over-looked the barren rooftops of the city."[26]

The surprising, irritating, and unnecessary or premature experiences of role reversals, infantilization, and patronizing experiences in health-care institutions often compound the losses one expects to experience at the hands of a perceived short life expectancy. The following poem by an anonymous nursing home resident displays just this sort of anger as criticism:

The Bad Home

God so loved the world
but he did not love this place.
All I want to do is die.
So why can't I be let to do so?
Why can't you just lay down your head?
I walk and walk and walk
but there is no God,
not in this place.
This is the Bad Home — He has forgotten its existence.
I get up and walk till I fall.

Sinful though I be
I'll ask God for his mercy.
I'm too old to do anything.
I'm just a dustbin.
It's all the same here.
Some of the girls grasp you
as if you're a cat or a dog.
They're too young. They can't
understand the problems of age.
It's all the same here.
They're so busy, they'll help you into anything,
even rags. You're not a person
when you come in here.
Nothing to do, nothing to say.
It's all blackness in front of me.
Another thing, they just sit there
and turn their thoughts inward.
That's why we'll never get better.
God so loved the world
But he doesn't love me.
I used to be happy,
but now I'm angry with Him
because I'm still here.[27]

Anger can also emerge as an equally understandable result of stigma, rejection, poor information flow, role theft, and other experiences of inter-personal inequality directed at the dying when others assume the afflicted person is inadequate simply because of advanced age or disease, even in the absence of obvious social, psychological, or physical decline. Lindquist, the TV producer with ALS, recalls her own anger at the pain of losing her posi-tion as a mother sought out by her children with any small trouble — a role she understandably valued as a parent:

I receive a visit from a conversational therapist.
   "I recognize your anger so well from other sick people. It is such a dis-appointment to be crippled as you are. Many people, even those who can

speak, react like that. But it is hard for those who are close to you. And to be cared for by a friend can be tricky. Are you seriously angry with her?"

"No," I reply, and start to sob.

"Why are you upset?"

It tears me apart and wears me down, but in the end I manage to say it.

"Because Pontus asked her, not me, for sticking-plaster and sympathy when he hurt himself."

"You feel that others are taking over?"

"Yes."

This was clearly a reaction that welled up in the reptilian part of my brain. Not worth analyzing really. But normal for someone who has lost her grip on something she is used to holding on to.

Accordingly, I forgive myself.[28]

The pain of loss, the feeling that things are unfair, can lead to a combative attitude toward the problems of everyday life. In the absence of a viable, visible, physical adversary such as death, we can instead choose something more banal to punch, any small issue or person, releasing a pent-up anger at the seemingly bottomless injury of premature death in younger people, or the infuriating wait for death in unpleasant circumstances for older people. Robins, the middle-aged woman dying of cancer, reports, "I'm in a crying rage over the smallest things. I bought the wrong kitty litter. The kitchen floor is overwaxed. The outside of the house needs painting. And I'm in a frenzy over the cost of my cancer treatments, even though my health benefits are excellent. But all that money spent to curb a disease that will kill me anyway, unless of course something else does first. Like my high blood pressure. The silent killer."[29]

A. S. Trillin, a woman being treated for lung cancer, reflects on her anger with a close friend also diagnosed with cancer: "I was also angry with my friend who died of cancer. I felt that she had let me down, that perhaps she hadn't fought hard enough. It was important for me to find reasons for her death, to find things that she might have done to cause it, as a way of separating myself from her and as a way of thinking that I would somehow have behaved differently, that I would somehow have been able to stay alive."[30]

Finally, some people may deal with their guilt at feelings of anger by atoning with pain. They more self-consciously feel their pain at their anger toward the world, an anger they may also feel is shameful.[31] On the other hand, some people carry guilt and remorse at wrongs they believe they or others have committed, and their anger may simmer and boil in their last days when they realize they can do little to atone, be forgiven, or to receive restitution from others. Hope, as the saying goes, folds her wings, looks backward, and becomes regret.[32] Barbato, the palliative care physician, remembers just such an angry patient:

> Mick . . . was admitted to the hospice with a diagnosis of end stage AIDS and at the time his major complaint was constipation. Well, that is what the referring letter said, but, when asked, Mick's response was, "I am full of shit." I was taken aback by his descriptive language but assumed this meant that he was indeed constipated. Mick proved to be a real challenge. He was a very angry man and frequently abused staff. Despite his manner I persisted in my efforts to befriend him and did everything possible to fix his "constipation." Each day I would ask Mick "how things were" and always got the same reply—"I am full of shit."
>
> In time I realized that Mick was not constipated. So when I next visited, I pulled up a chair, sat beside him and said, "Mick, tell me what you mean when you say you are full of shit." A long silence followed. . . . All of a sudden Mick started to sob and managed to blurt out, "I am full of shit because I raped my younger sister before I left home." I was stunned and did not know what to say. Silence reigned as he continued to cry. I stayed with him for quite a while and, although few words were said, there was no lack of communication.[33]

Behind and Beyond Sadness and Anger

The most interesting sociological fact behind the public display of any emotion, but especially the ones people fear the most such as sadness and anger, is that it hides a host of questions, fears, sorrow, injury, insult, self-doubt, self-recrimination, social criticism, anxiety, anguish, frustration, and, above all, pain. These elements erect a wall of complexity and assemble a diverse array of energies behind such deceptively simple words as *sad* or *angry*. We are in deep waters here, and they are dark ones as well, making seeing and traveling through them difficult for both swimmer and observer. But these feelings — better couched in terms of experiences because of their seamless links with social interactions and problems, personal values, goals, and dreams rather than mere emotion — are the sparks flung from the human struggle with leaving what you value most. The prospect of dying forces people to make some kind of emotional, spiritual, and social sense of loss on a time scale not of their choosing, in a context of suffering not of their making. They control nothing but must ask themselves the most difficult questions while being required to leave their most cherished relationships and hopes. After fear and initial resistance, sadness and anger are the major responses to personal loss, disappointment, and injury. Dying people are at some point or at every turn struggling to express these struggles to themselves or anyone who might listen.

The psychologist Tavris tells the following story about anger and conflict:

A mother and her three-year-old son argue every night about bedtime. "Won't go!" says the boy. "Yes, you will!" says the mother. This tug-of-war makes bedtime miserable for both of them, but the mother can't see a way out of it. A psychotherapist suggests that she stop quarreling with her son, acknowledging his feelings, and see what happens. The mother tries this. When her son, as usual, digs in his heels and refuses to go to bed, she says: "I can see that bedtime makes you very unhappy."

Long pause. "It's the ghosts," the boy whispers.

"Ghosts? Where are the ghosts?"

"In the tree outside my window."

Instead she went to the window, opened it, and ordered the ghosts to get lost. Then she said to her son: "Tell you what. I'll sit here until you fall asleep, and make sure that not a single ghost gets in here." The boy went to sleep like a baby, which of course he was.

Consider all the "ghosts" behind the problems of anger: *I'm hurt. I'm worried. I don't know how to express myself effectively. I don't know how to talk to her about my feelings. No one will ever love me again if he leaves me. I don't know how to get my way. No one listens to me. I can't forgive.*[34]

All of us have a sense — however primitive — of function and direction, of having tasks and roles to perform for and inside our worlds. We are designed and meant to fulfill these plans, usually with others. All animals know this and we are no different. Sadness and anger have primal origins, as indeed do all human emotions. Ethological studies recognize animal emotion as a result of hours of field observation but is less eager to attribute emotions to laboratory animals for self-serving reasons: to admit this dimension of animal experience would undermine justifications for experimenting with animals. Nevertheless, our long history of associating with animals has given us information beyond simply understanding how we, as part of the animal kingdom, react to threats such as death brought by predators. The animal kingdom is also the basis of our other emotions — including sadness and anger. In the animal kingdom, as Jeffrey Moussaieff Masson and Susan McCarthy observe, "Animals cry. At least, they vocalize pain or distress, and in many cases seem to call for help. Most people believe, therefore, that animals can be unhappy and also that they have such primal feelings as happiness, anger, and fear."[35] In the preface to her book *Ape Language*, E. Sue Savage-Rumbaugh, formerly the ape ethologist at Yerkes Primate Center in Atlanta, observes: "There are few feelings that apes do not share with us, except perhaps self-hatred. They certainly experience and express exuberance, joy, guilt, remorse, disdain, disbelief, awe, sadness, wonder, tenderness, loyalty, anger, distrust, and love. Someday, perhaps, we will be able to demonstrate the existence of such emotions at a neurological level. Until then, only those who live and interact with apes as closely as they do with members of their own species will be able to understand the immense depth of the behavioral similarities between ape and man."[36]

Sadness and anger in the face of death are intrinsic to life itself and are as natural as fear and resistance, and hope and love. These personal experiences are hardwired into our biology as much as they are intrinsic to our personal values and social relationships. They are not abnormal negative emotions, nor are they to be avoided by dying people or those who care for them. Sadness and anger — this Janus of feeling — these two sides of the human experience of loss, propel us to search and to polish the final tasks required of all reflective animals — to love, to hope, to make sense, to forgive, to reconcile, to accept, to summon our final message. The feelings of sadness and anger lead us to our most difficult, final, but frequently rewarding last tasks.

We all hope to fulfill our desires and goals — as animals or human beings — and the prospect of dying curtails and thwarts many of these, perhaps all. Those of us who expect to die, are resigned to die, or feel the time is right to die can experience other frustrations, hopelessness, or injuries to our dignity and hopes at the end of life. A common part of hopelessness is sadness — not necessarily the absence of hope itself, according to the psychiatrist Mark Sullivan, but more often an "attachment to a form of hope that is lost."[37] Hopelessness has a predictive value in both suicidal thinking and acting. As one dimension of both sadness and depression, hopelessness is what best predicts a suicide even in those who have been successfully treated for depression. Often what prevents suicide in those with high levels of hopelessness are the ties and responsibilities toward others, fear of social disapproval or moral objections, other fears or better coping skills.

Hope for those who are dying is often mistakenly viewed as a quality confined to prognosis — the only hope worth hoping for is not dying. But this is not true, for according to Sullivan, hope can and often is meaningfully redirected toward effective symptom control; the assurance of quality relationships in a deteriorating social context — a felt sense of committed presence by others; life review in the context of a sense of one's ending; and the fostering of reconciliation or affirmation with friends, family, and community.

These experiences of hope and love are commonly forgotten in the thousands of examples of discussions in academic journals about sadness, anger, and depression, yet without this recognition of the presence of hope and love alongside experiences of sadness or anger, the inner life of dying people can be viewed as moody, overly dark, and morbid. But sadness and anger rarely exist alone, because emotions so rarely exist as purely inner categories of experience anymore than conflict and sorrow exist as purely social categories. Sad experiences — their inner and outward elements — often exist in a wider and commonly more positive context, one that is seldom described. Lindquist describes this well when she observes:

> "Halfway" through my life I have been invaded by a rare disease, amyotrophic lateral sclerosis, ALS. It has a fast and aggressive course. There is only one end: death. No cure. No recovery.
>
> What happens to a person in this situation?
>
> A year ago I was a full-time TV reporter. Today I cannot eat without help, walk or wash myself.
>
> I feel profound sorrow about everything I am not going to experience. I am devastated that soon I will leave my four children.

And then Lindquist adds:

> At the same time I feel great joy and happiness about everything I am experiencing at the moment. Several times a day my house is filled with laughter.
>
> Does that sound strange?[38]

Sadness and anger push many dying people to reassess and realign their existing social relationships and values, often toward a new understanding of themselves and the role they have played and continue to play in other people's lives. These new insights and relations are frequently both positive and meaningful. The voices and criticism of those who experience dying as being marginalized and forgotten express both surprising power and autonomy. This is a personal power that repeatedly denies "a striving, and a striving, and an ending in nothing" but rather expresses a striving, and a striving, and an ending in something important to them and, just as commonly, for others.

7

Hope and Love—Connection

Love, like meaning, is out on the open road,
but like poetry, it is difficult
—Mahmoud Darwish, *In the Presence of Absence*

What happens to hope when you are faced with imminent death?
What exactly is there to hope for in these circumstances? Does life
in the shadow of death become hopeless? Rather surprisingly, even counterintuitively, people do not lose hope in the face of death. It has been widely
observed that people who are facing death very soon do not give up hope
or, rather, do not give up hope easily. Without doubt some individuals do
give up hope—are demoralized by the prospect of death and become deeply
depressed for a while. Some individuals even commit suicide rather than
simply wait for the end. But by far the majority of people in these mortal circumstances do not give up hope—they hope to live longer than anyone ever
expected, including themselves. In fact no one can say when you will die. People have gone into remission from serious illnesses even on their hospice beds.
On the other hand, they are more likely to adopt new targets of hope or to hold
these targets along with their desire for long life. They will move subtly from,
or alongside, the widely accepted and taken-for-granted hope of longevity to a
deeper, more substantial hope embedded in their intimate relationships. And
a key reason for this surprising turn of events is that people who know they will
die soon seldom simply lie down and give up. It's simply rarely the case.

As Gillian Rose, the British philosopher who died of ovarian cancer, wrote
in her autobiographical account of her illness: "What people now seem to
find most daunting with me, I discover, is not my illness or possible death,

but my accentuated being; not my morbidity, but my renewed vitality."[1] And vitality, as the philosopher Henry van Dyke wrote in 1904, "is a spiritual force conditioned, but not created, by material embodiment. A vitameter will never be invented, because there is no instrument delicate enough to take the temperature of the inner life. Even in dealing with bodily disease, the wise physician, while he may make his diagnosis absolute, always recognizes an element of uncertainty in his prognosis. 'While there is life there is hope,' he says. He might as well add, 'While there is hope there is life.' Hope has healed more diseases than medicine."[2]

The Fate and Direction of Hope

The fate of hope when dying is, on close scrutiny, not that different from the fate of hope when any major obstacle disrupts one's life and its goals and dreams. When things are bad at work, or you lose your job, your long-time partner and lover, or when you receive bad news from your doctor, hope can sometimes be difficult to find. Many people in these circumstances will and do commonly ask: What am I hoping for in this new loss—a new job that doesn't seem likely? A sudden world cure for cancer or a bad heart condition? But as any skeptic will tell you about human clairvoyance, no one can predict the future. Every person is biologically, socially, and psychologically unique. No one has your exact configuration of genes. When a forest fire or tornado rips through a human settlement, some houses are destroyed and flattened while others, even just next door, stand unharmed. People do die of life-limiting and life-threatening illnesses every day. And many others with the same disease do not or don't die for a very long time. That this is so is the basis for much enthusiastic research on the physiological and genetic basis of disease remission and the phenomenon of individual outliers in life expectancy, that is, of how some people seem to take so much longer to die than most other people suffering from the same disease.[3]

Even today few physicians would challenge William James's view of the fate and uses of hope:

Believe that life is worth living, and your belief will help create the fact. The "scientific proof" that you are right may not be clear before the day of judgment (or some stage of being which that expression may serve to symbolize) is reached. But the faithful fighters of this hour, or the beings that then and there will represent them, may then turn to the faint-hearted, who here decline to go on, with words like those which Henry IV greeted the tardy Crillon after a great victory had been gained: "Hang yourself, brave Crillon! We fought at Arques, and you were not there!"[4]

Hope is regularly identified as both essential to assisting with a personal sense of coping and as feeling widely prevalent in seriously ill, advanced cancer patients. Despite in-depth discussions of depression, anger, bargaining, or denial in Kübler-Ross's early work on terminally ill cancer patients, the feeling of hopefulness is what she identified as the most important and most prevalent experience of dying people. The research on defining hope, and identifying its role in coping, continues in psychology, psychiatry, and nursing in particular. However, almost everyone agrees that hope is a positive quality of mind and feeling that attempts to overcome barriers to achieving one's life goals by identifying, rerouting, or reworking pathways to attain old goals or identify new ones.[5] When some personal goals—such as staying alive—seem almost impossible, identifying and taking smaller steps toward old goals gives further hope of achieving them or other successes that make such achievements less important. The pursuit of quality of life over mere length is one major example of this process.

The academic literature offers literally dozens and dozens of definitions of hope. I am not sure that their different nuances are helpful or useful to an overall understanding of this important approach to life. Furthermore, academics offer dozens of suggestions for the targets of hope. For example, one recent review of the term suggested that we can understand hope as a style of living, in fact, that hope and life are synonymous—that a desire for a future with positive outcomes in life was absolutely essential to a sense of worth and integration in life itself. Without hope, people fail to cling to life, to want life, and therefore such hopelessness can lead to a desire for suicide or euthanasia. Hope may also mean having a positive goal for the future, literally something worth living and striving for.

The list of goals that might qualify as worth living for is endless and highly personal. They include but not exhaustively: hoping for a healing, a cure, a remission; living as normal a life for as long as possible; finding meaning or personal worth in the life one has lived so far; living the final months or days well; modeling these days for others; making dying a special and close time with others; having good symptom control or management; living longer than anyone expected; having a quick death, a peaceful death, having life after death; or having and creating a new awareness about life itself.[6]

Many have argued that, in both spiritual and taxonomical senses, there is no such thing as false hope because such a judgment is a matter of perspective and/or a conclusion that can be confidently made only in retrospect. Again, only someone who claims to be clairvoyant, or those who read odds and probabilities as certainties, can pronounce a hope false before the outcome. As Diane, a dying cancer blogger, observes, "We believe there is no such thing as false hope, all we have is hope."[7] In this context, then, according to the physician Mark Sullivan, the experience of hopelessness is sometimes less about the loss of hope per se than the attachment to a form of hope that is lost.[8] There are many types and targets of hope. The attachment to a hope for a long life may be shaken by bad medical news, but this is rarely the end of the story of hope itself.

In a life-limiting context, attachment to the idea that one will die in one's sleep at the grand old age may be the kind of hope that is difficult to give up and so can cause many people to be hopeless and despondent. But no one really wants to die, and even when an explicitly diagnosed terminal illness is made for people who are older, hope seems to prevail. In a Canadian study of hope in older palliative patients living at home, the experience of hope — the feelings and desire that things will get better — was paradoxically linked with an acceptance of the way things are. This acceptance of the situation, where death is imminent, makes the targets for hope turn, and transform into a desire for good symptom control, a peaceful death, or life after death. The methods or strategies for maintaining such hopes appear to be setting short-term goals; personal faith or spirituality; consciously, carefully, and deliberately holding a positive outlook; and striving for connectedness. This last point is a recurring theme in all explorations of the anatomy of hope.

Putting aside our modern and recent obsession with longevity, the difficulty in letting go of an attachment to a particular form of hope (living to a grand old age) doesn't necessarily mean that all hope is lost or abandoned. In the end, when all reviews of the term and the experience are sorted and digested, it seems that hope is more often about the ability to see positiveness and possibility in the relationships around you, despite physical and social circumstances that tend to dampen or distract you from that life-affirming tendency to be optimistic about your future.[9] In this context optimism is intrinsically linked to the quality and support of one's family, lovers, and friends—in other words, connectedness.

The positiveness and possibility of relationships is the crux of human hope. As the psychoanalyst Victor Frankl observes in his own life and in the lives of others he witnessed during his internment in a Nazi concentration camp, "A man who becomes conscious of the responsibility he bears toward a human being who affectionately waits for him, or to an unfinished work, will never be able to throw away his life. He knows the 'why' for his existence, and will be able to bear almost any 'how.'"[10]

Gillian Rose echoes this emphasis on the hope intrinsic to relationships, a hope that, however imperfect, fragile, and contingent, is always center stage in our lives and hence logically in our dying. We hope, in the shadow of death itself, to continue to mine the infinite possibilities of intimacy and transformation that only love can give, even in our final days and hours—in fact, even more urgently in our final days and hours. Rose writes that "a crisis of illness, bereavement, separation, natural disaster, could be the opportunity to make contact with deeper levels of the terrors of the soul, to loose and to bind, to bind and to loose. A soul which is not bound is as mad as one with cemented boundaries. To grow in love-ability is to accept the boundaries of oneself and others, while remaining vulnerable, around the bounds. Acknowledgment of conditionality is the only conditionality of human love."[11]

Rose goes on to explain—against the proliferations of New Age admonitions and clichés about boundless love, of recommendations to move toward some all-forgiving ideal of love and life—a moving instead toward an understanding of each other that can transcend the limits and boundaries of our imperfect selves, even if only for a short time. She asks us to consider that

> we are at the mercy of others and that we have others in our mercy. Existence is robbed of its weight, its gravity, when it is deprived of its agon. Instead of insinuating that illness may better prepare you for the earthly possibilities, these enchiridions on Faith, Hope and Love would condemn you to seek blissful, deathless, cosmic emptiness—the repose without the revel.

I reach for my favourite whiskey bottle and instruct my valetudinarian well-wishers to imbibe the shark's oil and aloe vera themselves. If I am to stay alive, I am bound to continue to get love wrong, all the time, but not to cease wooing, for that is my life affair, *love's work*.[12]

Most of the important targets of human hope, then, are focused upon a quality of life that is able to, and can ably draw upon, the potential satisfactions, transformations, and reveries of human intimacy — of closeness, kindness, and a shared life characterized by mutual care and responsibility. It is the potential intrinsic to our relationships that draws us compulsively to each other. Yes, most people hope to live long and prosper but usually and fundamentally as a means of enhancing their life and other people's lives. One hopes for length of life — especially in an age where education and social maturity can absorb the first couple of decades or more — because in a postmodern world a career, an intimate relationship, or a life's social and moral contribution can often take a long time. But in the absence of time, and underlying the need for time, is the always the desire, a sometimes unconscious desire, a sometimes conscious and passionate desire, for a love that nurtures and that is nurturing toward others.

We live to overcome our sense of separateness and to make some contribution to the world for the better. Most people want to point to the ways things have improved because they have lived. They point to children, grandchildren, a better social policy, a better workplace, a piece of important art or musical work, a set of accomplishments in parenting, mentoring, or friendships. Some of these goals take time and can be interrupted or simply and tragically blocked. But most of the others remain attainable for most people, as long as they have some warning about their impending death. In this context, then, it should be no surprise that these — one's closest relationships — is where the lion's share of human hope resides when dying. The heart of hope, in dying as in living, appears to be about human intimacy and connection.

The Underrecognition of Love in the Shadow of Death

Thirty years ago, when I conducted my first study of dying behavior, I interviewed one hundred cancer patients with less than a year to live.[13] The interviews covered the main areas of people's concerns at this point in their lives — work life; religious views; sex and marriage lives; social, psychological, and physical adjustments and problems; changes in their friendships, recreational life, and household roles. At that time, the early 1980s, the common view was that people living with a serious cancer were the subject of considerable stigma, social rejection, and negative attitudes — even from spouses. People with life-limiting illness were, according to conventional wisdom, commonly on the receiving end of significant interpersonal fear and misunderstanding about serious disease and death. One of the most memorable findings of my study was what would later be confirmed by dozens of subsequent studies — that most people do not experience this kind of social negativity and rejection. In fact, more than half my sample of interviewees reported no changes or positive changes to their friendships and intimate relationships, especially marriages. Yes, some reported stigma and loss of friendships, but just as many people reported making new friends or being overwhelmed by friends who redoubled their loving efforts on their behalf.

On the whole, however, negative reactions from their social circle represented less than 10 percent of the reactions to the one hundred people I interviewed. The vast majority reported the same or increased levels of affection and care from their spouses, children, parents, coworkers, or friends. So often one finds that bad news travels faster and gains more popular press than the common, more widespread but less sensational news: that people give and receive more love at the end of life than they ever had previously. In the academic and clinical literature this is somewhat of a silent wonder, an underrecognized but widespread element of the inner and public life of the dying person.

The palliative care physician Derek Doyle confirmed these earlier findings when, reflecting on his many years of caring for dying people, he observed that, counter to popular belief or expectation, dying is often a most positive and loving experience. Doyle muses: "Friendships have become richer and love even deeper; differences have been resolved, old feuds forgotten, and enemies forgiven; faith has grown and meaning been found for many of life's mysteries. For some, life only seemed to take on meaning and have a purpose as it came to its end; others felt loved and needed for the first time. What a paradox! Life reaching its climax, not in social or intellectual achievement and success, but in death!"[14]

The psychoanalyst and social theorist Erich Fromm theorized about the human origins of love as being rooted in the solitariness of human existence. Although human beings are group animals because of our primate ancestry, the deeply reflective capacity characteristic of human beings gives each member of our species a sense of separateness. This separateness is a feeling that no one can ever know and feel what the other truly experiences—a sense of being trapped and cut off from others cloaks our sense of self. Only in rare moments of union within experiences of love—between lovers, in some communities, in one's relationship with God, or occasionally in some social movement—do the boundaries between this estranged sense of self and the social world become temporarily blurred and merged. Most of the time, when we are not distracted by work, worries, or our numerous recreational diversions, people feel alone. In fact, most people are drawn to love and the many diversions of the everyday world to relieve that sense of aloneness, that separateness to which the human capacity to think and reflect, combined with our short mortal experience, condemns us. Fromm writes: "The experience of separateness arouses anxiety; it is, indeed, the source of all anxiety. Being separate means being cut off, without any capacity to use my human powers. Hence to be separate means to be helpless, unable to grasp the world—things and people—actively; it means that the world can invade me without my ability to react. Thus, separateness is the source of intense anxiety."[15]

The First Epistle to the Corinthians describes the human experience of love in daunting terms, perhaps in terms of aspiration and ideals. Nevertheless, it captures the spirit of a human emotion and relationship that is notoriously difficult to define in abstract academic terms. Corinthians observes:

Love suffers long
Is kind
Envies no one
And does not vaunt or boast itself.
Love does not behave unseemly
Seeks not itself for self's sake
Is not easily provoked
Nor thinks evil of another.
Love does not rejoice in iniquity

But instead celebrates truth.
Love bears all things
Believes all things
Hopes all things
Endures all things.
Love never fails
Even if prophecies fail
And speaking shall cease
And all knowledge shall fade away
Love shall prevail.[16]

But love does fail, because, as Gillian Rose reminds us, we have a tendency to get love wrong a lot of the time. This limitation of ability for many of us, this lack of concordance and opportunity for some of us, this daily or periodic misfortune for yet others does not make love less attractive. These imperfections of ability, consistency, or opportunity make most of us redouble our efforts with each other—we do not "cease wooing," as Rose observes, because as she rightly argues, this is love's work.

For Fromm love is not infatuation, a falling in love, nor is love a submerging in the other, though it may often have all these elements from time to time. Rather, love is an ongoing form of a relationship characterized by giving. This is giving of one's self based actively on care, responsibility, focus, dedication, and patience toward another; listening with humility, to have faith in the relationship, and to overcome a culturally reinforced tendency toward individual narcissism. These qualities of mind, heart, and spirit, according to Fromm, do require constant practice, like all artistic endeavor, and hence the title of his work on this subject, *The Art of Loving*. The main purpose of such a complex and difficult task is to successfully overcome the anxiety of separateness, to move toward union or, rather, reunion of a self that always feels incomplete without a complementary other. Though this has a biological corollary and origin, its evolution in human life has taken on additional existential qualities that relate it directly to the problem of human existential loneliness and meaning making.

In the face of death, both the feeling of impending aloneness and the need to readdress the anxiety that flows from this new challenge mean that more people facing death will experience greater, not less, need to give and to receive love. In other words, we are not to be surprised that most dying people and those who care for them experience greater love for one another. The very nature of the circumstances of dying—the intrinsic fact that all those who love will face enormous loss—actually encourages them to love more. In other words, people at the end of life will experience the need to care more, to give more, and to do so in a more self-conscious and urgent way. In fact, it would be a surprise if this were not the case when dying. At a basic sociological level, the dying experience the need to give and care more, and this in turn reinforces the need of those who care for them to do the very same. As the British journalist John Diamond wrote about his own renewed love for his family during his terminal cancer journey:

> "It's such a strange time, isn't it?" I said.
> "How so strange?"
> "Oh you know. Strange in that I've never felt more love for you than I have in the past year, that I've never appreciated you as much, nor the children. In a way I feel guilty that it should have taken this to do it, I suppose. But it is strange, isn't it?"
> For the first time, I found myself talking like this without resenting that it had taken the cancer to teach me the basics, without resenting that there was part of me capable of talking like a '50s women's magazine article without blushing.[17]

The care offered to the person living with a life-limiting illness will, of course, be necessary because of the vagaries of the illness, and this will be a subject of concern for the dying person, if only because the increasing burden of care from a spouse or family member will highlight the gifts of love from their carer. This will, in turn, often elicit a similar caring and giving attitude from the dying person. The reciprocity inherent in these circumstances commonly and logically promotes increasing love—not always, not in every case, but surely, repeatedly, and clearly in most cases. The circumstances of dying frequently introduce a fresh perspective and a new energy into each other's love for one another. This is a commonplace experience of the dying person.

An early study of the impact of a diagnosis of advanced cancer suggests that for most marriages the impact is a positive one—there is more love and more expression of love in these difficult circumstances. On the other hand, if the marriage has problems in the first place, a diagnosis of cancer will reduce rather than enhance commitment.[18] A 2005 Dutch study echoed the positive dimension in other family relationships. Physician observations of dying patients in their care showed a strong correlation between dying peace-fully—despite increasing physical discomfort—and the increase in attention from informal caregivers, especially the dying person's children and other family relatives.[19] A study of communication patterns between family caregiv-ers and their terminally ill loved ones revealed that all participants affirmed and expressed their love during the final weeks and days of care, and many also experienced important opportunities for reconciliation within these experiences. For example, one interviewee with a history of rather fraught relations with her mother, who was now dying and being cared for by the respondent, observed:

> I would have to say it took me days to, uh, get myself ready to tell her that I love her . . . it seemed like this huge thing . . . it just had so much emotional baggage with it . . . because she had never told me. . . . [One night] she was ranting about how nobody loves her . . . and it just laid itself out there . . . and I just said, "Mom, I love you dearly. And I appreciate everything you've done for me all of my life." . . . There was all this conflict between she and I . . . and so I cleaned that up. Later the respondent went on to tell the inter-viewer that her mother finally did tell her that she loved her.[20]

Carolyn Ellis wrote an account of her love for her partner during his slow and tortuous decline from emphysema. In the last year or so of this journey, she constantly documented snippets of conversation and love making that illustrated clearly and sharply how her partner's decline actually enhanced their love during this period:

> "Life is absurd, isn't it? It's not going to get us down," we agreed. Yet the real-ization that eventually the disease would defeat us helped Gene and me to be more caring and loving and to face and resolve disagreements more easily. "What can you do?" we asked each other, acknowledging our helplessness, resigned to our fate. Seize the moment and live each second to its fullest.

. . .

That night I get into bed with Gene, and he has enough energy to hold me for the first time since entering the hospital. "This is the most loving we've ever been," he says. I feel it too. "You thought you were losing me, didn't you?" When I nod yes, I feel tears flow down my cheeks.

. . .

We join together in total, committed love in a way that we haven't for a while. Aloneness is not here. We are inside each other. There are no bodies. No boundaries. Our orgasm occurs in our heads, our hearts, our spirits. We cry during and after, happy to be alive. All the pain that I have held back is, for now, dissipated. Our love in all its aspects has escaped from its rational contained cage and remains as strong as ever. Outside of this moment, we recognize our relationship cannot be perfect. The disease is still eating away at his body, and we cannot continue being all things to each other. Day-to-day concerns will make us forget our love. Momentarily. But we will try to remember that our love can be called on when we need it.[21]

Michelle Lynn Mayer, a thirty-nine-year-old mother of two and a former professor of public health at the University of North Carolina, Chapel Hill, was dying from scleroderma and wrote about her experience in a series of Internet blogs entitled, *Diary of a Dying Mom*. In a video recorded about four months before her death and posted on her blog, she recounts her relationship with her husband during the final years and months of her illness:

And everything we've been through, especially over the last year, um, he's just never ever complained about what it's done to his life. And it's made us a more loving couple. I love him more than I ever have, and, I think, that was another gift that the disease brought. I really learned what love is, earlier than I think I might have. I think another, you know, I think it's, I don't think it was so much the disease I just think it was how my husband and I are hardwired as we're both really, really, into laughing. And I always said that I married him because he made me laugh. And he still makes me laugh. And we still laugh; we've laughed in emergency rooms; we've laughed in doctor's offices; we've laughed under the most miserable of circumstances. And that's what keeps us going. It's just somehow in the midst of all this, still being able to find the humor in it all.[22]

The love experienced from and offered to others is not confined to spouses. Friendships are also commonly strengthened. Friends and distant relatives often go the extra mile for the dying person. The sense of temporariness that accompanies the acknowledged prospect of death underscores for everyone how precious friendship is. Dying people feel the need for closeness and support, which they receive because the knowledge that their dying friends are in serious trouble — inside chronic illness, despondency, and/or fear — tends to mobilize people's loyalties and energies. The threat of death focuses not only the dying person but also their friends on a more restricted set of priorities. Natalie Robins, who was living with her own life-threatening cancer, records an instance of her friends' kindness that stems directly from this awareness of the finiteness of friendship in the shadow of death:

Friends are people who listen to your agonies and dreams. After I was diagnosed with cancer, I blurted out to Dalma and Marilyn something basically inconsequential: a wish for something that has been beyond my reach all of my life, yet has remained an ardent fantasy. I said, "One thing I'm going to do now is get myself that black Armani jacket." Of course, such a purchase was still out of the question, what with my steadily increasing medical expenses, not to speak of my son's upcoming college tuition. Yet dreams give one courage, it is said, especially in the face of danger. So I kept on dreaming.

A few weeks later, my husband and I had dinner at Shun Lee West in New York City with Dalma and Richard and Marilyn and Hugh. During drinks, Dalma suddenly turned to me and said, "We have a little something for you." She took a small, oyster-colored shopping bag from her purse. I saw the words Georgio Armani written across the front of it, and my breath stopped. "Is this a trick?" I asked. "No, it's not," Dalma said, smiling. Marilyn and Hugh were smiling too. I reached into the bag and pulled out an elegant card, opened it, and among the many words on it I saw only these: "a jacket." My hands were trembling. I looked around the crowded restaurant. I looked down. I looked at my husband. I burst into tears. My friends had bought me an Armani jacket.

"Oh my God," I finally said. I kept staring at the gift certificate. No one had ever done anything like this for me. I was the one who gave gifts. How in the world could I accept this? It was far, far too extravagant. "We knew you'd feel that way," Dalma said tenderly. "But it's all paid for so there's nothing you can do about it except pick out exactly the jacket you want."

"Now she'll have nothing to live for," my husband quipped, as we all hugged and kissed and cried. My family of friends.[23]

The palliative care physician Susan Block quotes a patient in a similar vein: "I have wonderful friends who are really loving and caring and look after me and it's genuine. And I have my beloved son and my daughter-in-law and my former wife. I'm surrounded by people who enjoy me and care about me, that I've been important to and who are important to me. What this last year has provided me with is the occasion to be deliberately open to receiving other people's love and care . . . and I'm delighted when it happens."[24]

However, it is also important to note that dying people also often feel the need to offer more love *to* others. In other words, it is frequently important for dying people to feel they are continuing to care and contribute to others they care about. Much academic and clinical literature focuses on care of the dying but regularly overlooks that dying people are carers, too. Many dying people feel the hope and the need to play a significant role in their loved ones' lives right up to their own end, if possible. Often they might seek to share their wisdom, life's lessons, or "model a meaningful path through their dying process," or they seek to be listened to and appreciated for what they can offer.[25] For example, the author Egilde Seravalli quotes a patient's poignant expression of love for his physicians:

Once again I return to the hospital to see whether the physicians will succeed with a new treatment. On my part I have no hope, and, besides, nobody has promised me anything beyond an attempt. Yet, I came here just the same and I know why: There was a man who dispelled the passivity in which I was. Not that that person has changed the conclusion to which my thoughts have brought me; what that person did, rather, was make me suspend them, even though deep down I remain with no hope. He did this, I felt, by manifesting concern, even trust. Therefore the willingness to fight the absurdity came back to me. . . . I felt like Don Quixote indeed, but without even the windmills. . . . Is there really a part of me that is so moved when another human being turns to me, that it makes me feel the need to offer something of myself in return? Here is love for those men who ask your heart to give a bit to theirs. Perhaps these are not windmills: to fight not to save myself but to see still in some human eyes the request for help even from me. And so, I am here ready to be punctured and to suffer. And I am not at all courageous since it requires all my will power to overcome fear with pride.[26]

However, many well-intentioned friends and family are prone to doing everything they can for the dying person, which often means that even dying people who feel capable find their roles as carers, lovers, friends, parents, or mentors are taken from them. Although dying people cannot always or regularly perform their valued roles for others, this does not mean that they cannot ever perform them or that they will not still have the occasional desire to perform them. A blanket helping response toward the dying can at times leave them feeling disempowered and useless. When dying, as with all living, people need to feel that they too can express love and care within the cycles of wellness and illness common to the dying experience and that their carers will recognize and support this expression.[27]

Although accounts of generosity and love, of mutual support and exchange at the end of life, are legion, negative and unloving experiences do occur. These may involve a minority of dying people's experiences, but they occur to significant numbers of people and tragically sometimes replace the positive experiences. Marriage failures, relationship disappointments, and emotional estrangement are not unknown even to those at death's door — if only because dying, as it is often said, is not death but a part of normal living. Derek Doyle's book, *Caring for a Dying Relative*, includes chapters entitled "Unmentionable Feelings" and "Secret Dreams for the Future." In these chapters he describes a wife and husband who had an appointment to meet at their lawyer's office to commence divorce proceedings when the husband received a terminal prognosis of lung cancer earlier in the day. The wife remained with him, caring for him to the end, but confessed to not forgetting the past wrongs and transgressions and to looking forward to life beyond her period of care. Doyle describes other experiences confided to him by members of other families:

Some secretly hope to find a new partner, others to start a new life with a lover, or resume a long lost sex-life, while others again look forward to returning to a career or undertaking new training. There are other implications for these jumbled emotions. Some find they cannot cry yet society expects them to. Others find hospital visiting a hypocritical duty. Others cannot speak and behave in the sad, heartbroken way people seem to expect. Their only help lies in sharing these secret thoughts with the family doctor or hospice staff who, not surprisingly, have heard it all before on many occasions.[28]

Even in my early study of people living with terminal cancer, the support of friends was not always an entirely unadulterated pleasure. One man reported that so many of his friends were so supportive and visited so much and phoned so often that he had to spend a set time everyday away from the house just to "get some peace." The support of friends can sometimes be overwhelming. For those who tire easily from their illness or its treatments, friendly attention can sometimes be too much of good thing.

Nevertheless, as Gillian Rose observes in her own journey of living and dying—for better or worse—the crisis of a mortal illness can be an "opportunity to make contact with the deeper levels of the terrors of the soul, to loose and to bind, to bind and to loose."[29] Any crisis provides opportunities to learn what and who are of genuine importance to your life. So often the hope and love many dying people experience is the transformative kind of greater insight and wonderment. Robins puts it well when she observes: "This, too, is what cancer does for you: it gives you communities you didn't have before, or ever thought you'd wanted to be part of, privileges you never thought you'd use, and friendships that are worth going into the lightning for. It can make wives love husbands more, husbands love wives more, children love their parents more, and parents love their children more. It intensifies, energizes, and electrifies all of life, all around us, all the time."[30]

Surprised by Joy

In 1955 C. S. Lewis wrote *Surprised by Joy*, a book about his conversion to theism and then Christianity. This is a quasi-autobiographical work, and an important backstory of the book is the identification, scrutiny, and meaning of the experience of joy. According to Lewis, *joy* is not a synonym for *happiness* or *pleasure*, although the desire to have joy again, and as often as one can, is one quality that joy shares with both happiness and pleasure. On the other hand, and most crucial for its taxonomic understanding, is that joy is an experience that points to something beyond itself. Joy is an emotional and spiritual experience of the inner life of a person. It does not come along everyday, maybe not even every year, in a person's life. Instead, joy is just a rare hint, a suggestion of ecstasy in human life. Lewis provides three examples from his own life: the brief and fleeting memory of his older brother's bringing his toy garden into the nursery for him to play with; the sudden and suddenly gripping impression of autumn gained from reading Beatrix Potter's *Squirrel Nutkin*; and a passage in a Longfellow poem, "Saga of King Olaf," about the death of Balder. Lewis records his feelings about this last experience: "I knew nothing about Balder; but instantly I was uplifted into huge regions of northern sky, I desired with almost sickening intensity something never to be described (except that it is cold, spacious, severe, pale, and remote) and then, as in the other examples, found myself at the very same moment already falling out of desire and wishing I was back in it." For Lewis, joy became "an unsatisfied desire which is itself more desirable than any other satisfaction. . . . It might almost equally well be called a particular kind of unhappiness or grief. But then it is a kind we want. I doubt whether anyone who has tasted it would ever, if both were in his power, exchange it for all the pleasures in the world."[31]

This almost ineffable combination of experience that is at once a hint of wonderment and grief, simultaneously of love and loss, and in the presence of a painful desire for an elusive something or someone, reasons Lewis, points to something beyond itself. For a moment, even a long surprising moment, joy takes us outside our lonely self-absorption and provides a momentary sense of aching awe and intense desire for union with something (or someone) beyond ourselves. For Lewis this imprint in the sands of our mind, this hint of something greater behind our everyday experience yet embedded within it, was a pointer to the divine.

I do not think it is important to follow Lewis to that conclusion, though I think many readers would find his logic persuasive, especially those who have found these moments regularly in their prayer, meditation, solitary reflection, or, more startling, in the unguarded emotional experiences of communing with the aesthetic—in art, poetry, or music, for example. What is fundamentally true of Lewis's account nevertheless is also true of the surprise that dying people experience when they realize just how much they love and care and, correspondingly, just how much they in turn are loved by their friends and family. This is frequently an achingly wonderful surprise, a joyous, fresh, and riveting insight for them.

Dying people are, in the very terms that Lewis describes, literally surprised by joy—a feeling of "wonderment and grief, mixed with love and loss, and of the presence of a painful desire and appreciation" for these others in their lives. This leads one to self-consciously trace, and to see as never before, every kind act and word as a healing, supportive balm for one's fears and pains, and its mirror image—every feeling and act of care that energetically emanates from dying people to those they love.

As Mahmoud Darwish observes, "love, like meaning, is out on the open road, but like poetry, it is difficult," to be sure. The negative social situations and cases described in this chapter are a sure reminder of that. But any review of the experiences of intimacy, care, and hope among dying people would add that, in the vast majority of cases, the difficulties are ultimately worth it. Because, as Rose argues, however imperfect our love will be, or, as Darwish argues, however difficult love can be, and, as Lewis argues, however ineffable joy can be, love points to our desire at the end of life to redouble our efforts to give as much as we can to one another because time has colored our relationships with the hues and streaks of impending loss.

The practical and overwhelming realization of the brevity and fragility of life—not as mere academic or cerebral ways of thinking about mortality in general but rather in real time—sharpens love and friendship in the way that a dark night sky sharpens the outline of a bright yellow moon. Urgency, clarity of purpose, and renewed commitment are the gifts and graces of human relationships, often taken for granted but seen afresh and revealed and renewed by the now-sensitive inner eyes of dying people—and by those they love.

8

Waiting—In-between-ness

I grew up with six brothers. That's how I learned to dance—waiting for the bathroom.

—Bob Hope

Waiting for death has long been acknowledged as part of both dying and death. A significant academic literature addresses these vigils for the dying, describing how friends and family wait beside the bedside of a dying loved one in intensive care wards, hospices, or even at home.[1] After death the traditional waiting originated as a watching over the corpse, to see if the dying person really was dead (to prevent premature burial) and to guard against evil spirits and influences. This is also time to celebrate the life of the dead person. This last period of waiting is usually called the wake.[2] In most countries from Ireland to the Caribbean and, despite myths to the contrary, even in the United States and Europe, both the vigil and the wake have been documented as a public period of waiting for carers and mourners.[3]

What is usually not acknowledged is that dying people also wait for their own dying if they are conscious during this period. Tolstoy's *The Death of Ivan Ilyich* is a popular and oft-quoted fictional account of just this kind of waiting. In Tolstoy's famous novel Ivan Ilyich undergoes a series of emotional and social transformations while waiting to die in the family home. His attitude toward his wife and children runs the gamut from antipathy and loathing to love and forgiveness as he wrestles with the frustration, anguish, and sense of desperateness that accompany him during his mortal journey. The attention to this form of waiting by dying people is often submerged and overtaken today as academics or clinicians talk instead about how dying people see their future or "sense of finitude." But talk of the future is not what I am referring to in this chapter. In fact, many dying people do see a future for themselves, as prosaically or literally as the next hour or tomorrow or more grandly in the hereafter. In this chapter, however, I am referring to the presence and experience of "in-between-ness" — of being neither here (well and healthy like you) or there (dead as the proverbial door nail). In this psychological and social dimension, the dying person experiences a kind of limbo, a place of waiting, of being in a holding space, watched over by others perhaps but alone and without relief until reaching the final destination, whenever that might be. As Harold Brodkey, the novelist and essayist, wryly observed about his own dying from AIDS, "Much of the time I do nothing. I lie in bed or on the porch. I stare at death, and death stares at me."[4] Or as Thomas DeBaggio observed in the last lines of his own memoir about living with Alzheimer's disease: "I must now wait for the silence to engulf me and take me to the place where there is no memory left and there remains no reflexive will to live. It is lonely here waiting for memory to stop and I am afraid and tired."[5]

Sociologists and anthropologists frequently refer to this waiting experience as a "period of liminality," a social space or transitional identity — adolescence, courtship, apprenticeship — that is between one former recognized status (for example, childhood, being single) and a new status or identity (adulthood, marriage, or professional status).

People who go about their lives with few thoughts of death, serious illness, or a death sentence qualify as full and active members of society. When a serious diagnosis, prognosis, or death sentence is pronounced by the relevant civic authorities, one becomes dying, that is to say, begins a trajectory toward another final status — that of being dead. Dying in this anthropological sense of "status passage" or "rite of passage" is yet another transitional state, a state of in-between-ness that provides few rules or even few clues to when the state will end.[6] Being in-between is therefore always a time and existence characterized by understandable levels of apprehension, anxiety, and to some extent mystery — and misery. The state of in-between-ness is rarely an unadulterated pleasure for those inside it. At best it can sometimes be a mixture of pleasant as well as unpleasant experiences, but just as often it can be simply downright horrible and difficult. The important influence in shaping the emotional experience of waiting is the destination. If the destination is pleasant (e.g., promotion and wider access to economic, sexual, or political advantage), then the limbo state can be acceptable and eagerly anticipated. If the destination is unpleasant and feared (e.g., execution), then the liminal state can be quite unpleasant. The problem with modern death is that most people, as I showed in chapter 3, which addresses fear, have ambiguous and conflicting ideas about what they are waiting for, and this makes for mixed emotional and social consequences during the wait to die. Waiting for death today is ambivalent at best, anguishing at worst.

Waiting to die also has a long history. Human beings have existed for 1.5 to 2 million years. Until the last ice age, about 10,000 to 12,000 years ago, most human beings were hunters, collectors, scavengers, or more rarely, herders. After the last ice age, farming and gardening began to proliferate, and the great peasant societies and cities were born.[7] Among hunters and gatherers life expectancy was often short, with death coming suddenly through trauma—animal predation, childbirth, accident, poisoning. Dying from old age, and recognition that dying was immanent in that old age, was uncommon. Nevertheless, hunter-gatherer peoples were familiar with older people, and every generation witnessed their passing. In his classic work reviewing the role of the aged in these kinds of society, Leo Simmons found that abandoning the dying and elderly was cross-culturally common.[8] Simmons examined seventy-one tribes from around the world from existing ethnographies and found information about end-of-life care existed in thirty-nine. Of those, about half demonstrated practices of abandonment and neglect of the dying and elderly.

Commonly, hunter-gatherer communities could not support an unproductive member economically (as a nonproducer but consumer of food) or physically (to carry the dependent on long seasonal journeys and in difficult climate and territorial conditions). This often led to customs of abandoning the dying and elderly. Occasionally, tribes might build a small hut or dwelling and leave some food and water for the older dying person. At other times the elderly were simply left at the last campsite with a handful of provisions. This is the recorded case for Bushmen in Africa, the Euahlayi in Australia, the Ainu in Japan, the Hopi in North America, and the Lapp in northern Europe. Such practices must have led to a period of waiting for the dying, which began with the ritual abandonment and ended when death came, from starvation or dehydration, after their meager provisions had long ran out. This was nearly always a recognized time for the dying and old, a time of sadness but not resentment, for as young people those dying people themselves had probably participated in these rituals for their own parents or other relatives. Simmons quotes the dying African Bushmen found by white missionaries who tried to save them. Some of the dying declined, saying: "My children have left me here to die. I am old you see, and am no longer able to serve them. . . . It is our custom. I am nearly dead: I do not want to die again."[9]

Rituals of abandonment aside, the sentiments and attitudes of accepting the prospect of death and of waiting for it mirror contemporary experiences of dying in affluent industrial contexts. Kristin Wright provides three examples of dying people who discuss their experience of waiting to die:

BRAD: It was certainly intense, to a place that I hadn't ever been before— just attending death. Waiting. Death is the next portal, and you don't know where or when it's gonna be.

FAITH: I'm expecting death now. . . . There was a time when I was looking for it, in the sense that . . . remember way back, a year and a half, maybe even as much as two years ago, when I was still sick [from] the chemo, I was looking for death in the sense of uh, wanting it to happen. I wanted death. . . . As I think about it, the difference [between then and now] is, uhm . . . then, I was looking for death as a sort of relief, something that I wanted . . . to do instead of . . . the chemo. Where now, I'm looking for it in the sense of . . . it's happening, "Is, is it going to be around this next corner?" I'm looking for it in the sense of expecting it . . . waiting for it.

PATTY: I wish it would come and get it over cause I can't do anything the way it is now. When I think about dying, really honestly dying, I don't like it. But, if it's going to be, what are we waiting for? What can I possibly do? What am I possibly doing in my own little niche, let alone for the world, in the, in the situation where I am now. There isn't anything that I am doing that can be construed as helpful. It's as though I'm living my own little purgatory or portion of hell just waiting. I hate to wait for people who are late, you know. . . . I'm always on time, therefore they should be. And death, if it's coming, for goodness sakes, get here. . . . It's past time. And I, I really am very impatient.[10]

Psychological Effects of In-between-ness

Much of the literature describing the experience of waiting tends to emphasize the feeling of stress and strain. The theme is that waiting is a negative time, a down time, a time of apprehension. For example, a lot of the literature about waiting, as modest as it is, describes the waiting experience of organ transplant patients. But that experience of waiting departs in important ways from the waiting for death that is this chapter's primary concern. For one thing, transplant patients strongly desire to overcome their illness and look forward to a time and a life after the transplant. However, there is no time after dying, except for those with religious or spiritual expectations, and certainly little or no perceived time of continuity with the life they have previously known. Notwithstanding this important difference, a health-care study investigating the experiences of waiting for a liver transplant did identify a common element in all experiences of waiting when death was a significant possibility. The investigators argued that "waiting is a time apart. Loss of roles and loss of vitality diminish participation in the objective reality of life outside and beyond the list. Time on waiting lists is a time apart from the narrative of their lives. Those waiting feel held up or on hold in a purgatory with its own clock, yet there is a time to transcend this experience and grow in the midst of the mundane immanence of pain, the clinical routines, and the intrusions of pagers and false alarms. It is a time of utter subjectivity."[11]

On the other hand, when nurses in Uganda were asked what the experience of caring for dying Ebola patients was like, they emphasized the experience of living with the possibility of dying as an experience they shared with their patients. Ebola virus is so deadly and infectious that, as had happened in the past, the health-care workers were heavily at risk of contracting this hemorrhagic fever. They characterized their experience as "a waiting" (for the disease to develop in them), even after the official incubation period of the disease (two to twenty-one days). Because of the type of patient they cared for, they were isolated from family and friends during the worst of the pandemic. This meant that their experience of waiting included isolation, anxiety, a focus on care for others—patients and their coworkers—a preference and need to live life primarily in terms of the present. Waiting to see if they too would become a patient, to see if they too would die like those in their care, meant living an isolated life of selfless care, oblivious to any time other than the present.[12]

Waiting is also an endemic part of living and dying in nursing homes. A study of the waiting experiences of people in long-term care found that wait-ing was a common part of life in such settings—aged care, rehabilitation, and veterans' long-term care. Researchers found that although most people in these settings were angered and irritated by their experiences of waiting, they often used diversionary strategies to distract themselves—knitting, crossword puzzles, listening to music, and so on. These activities assisted in distracting and diverting their anger, which in turn led them to a calmer attitude. These three stages of reaction to waiting—anger, diversion, becoming calm—were essential to coping with the interminable interruptions from medication and treatment regimes that are characteristic of large and complex health-care institutions.[13]

The anthropologist Sharon Kaufman identifies two perspectives on what waiting does. For health-care institutions, waiting enables things to move along. Although sometimes individuals who wait feel that things are in stasis, in limbo, in between, other events and processes—tests, test results, referrals, treatments, consultations, and the like—are under way and drawing people closer to some kind of conclusion. On the other hand, for families or the dying, waiting is characterized by a sense of anticipation, sometimes of hope, and just as often dread.[14] The university professor Lois Jaffe describes in her own paradoxical experience of waiting to die from acute leukemia: "This 'limbo position' poses a paradox. On the one hand, the lives of the fatally ill are often richer and more meaningful because we *are* confronting time lim-its. On the other hand, it imposes a tremendous strain. I cannot plan for the future. I must constantly restructure priorities in the immediacy of knowing that my life is time-limited."[15]

In summary, then, waiting to die is often experienced as full of dread, isolating, strained, like living not merely in limbo but rather purgatory. How-ever, note too that these accounts also balance their remarks by incorporating the paradoxical observations—often overlooked—that waiting can also be a personal experience of growth and self-realization, of hope and anticipation, and reorientation toward others, and a time of calmness and peace. I want to look more closely at the both sides of waiting to die, beginning with the distressing aspects.

Sources of Trauma and Distress

Waiting, whatever its cause, has core elements of being stationary or stalled toward a goal, yet ironically, as I noted earlier, waiting can also be dynamic and active, finding people planning, preparing, distracting, expecting while actively managing an assortment of emotional reactions during their parallel attitude of vigilance. These preoccupations, combined with the feeling of uncertainty, distort clock time as well as the self-told story of one's day, week, year, or life.[16] Psychiatrists who have studied posttraumatic stress disorder have found that simply telling some people that they will develop a fatal disease that will kill them—AIDS, cancer, or premature heart disease—will stimulate long-term traumatic anxiety in many of them. Although in reasonable health, or chronically but not life-threateningly ill, as many as half these people will simply find the waiting for bad news about the development of a disease that will kill them traumatic enough to be disabling in mental health terms. The waiting and anticipation itself rather than the actual news creates the trauma.[17]

The occupational therapist Noralyn Davel Jacques describes a hospice patient's remarks about her own dying from ALS in the following terms: "I sat alone with her for about 20 minutes. She mostly slept. Her breathing was more relaxed, her apnea not as problematic. Annie's friends came back to the room and held her hands. I was at one side of the bed when Annie struggled to say, 'It takes so long to die.' I repeated what she said, as I did with all of my 'guesses' at her words, to be sure I got it right. Annie's friend Mandy could barely control her tears, it seemed like she could burst."[18]

Ann, another patient living her final days in a hospice, observes: "I don't like the idea of lingering. If it's going to happen let it happen; not all this hanging on dying inch by inch, fighting every scrap of the way."[19] Josephine, a nursing home resident, laments her own dying in that place and describes her anguish: "I'm so on edge. I can't hardly talk. I'm so ripped up inside that I don't know what to do or say. I've just quit doin' things. I'm gone. I can't pray like I used to. I don't know anything about it, but I've got to go through it. I'm on the way. I don't know what to do. If I could lay down in the pasture. But I can't. It comes to you so hard, waiting here."[20]

Perhaps the most exaggerated form of trauma appears in the experience of death row prisoners. Here, the experience of waiting to die is compounded by poor environmental conditions, a lack of any individual power or control over the immediate environment, and the uncertainty about how they will eventually die—all common features of many dying experiences inside residential care facilities for the elderly but not completely unknown for some dying people in hospitals.

Caycie Bradford, a lawyer, argues that death row prisoners should be viewed as a type of dying person who is "not quite dead, but surely not alive."[21] The environmental sources of this particularly agonizing and anxious state of dying can be summarized as (1) a lack of notice as to the date and time of execution; (2) the prevalence of public executions; and (3) the well-known proliferation of mistakes in carrying out the execution. These circumstances and conditions of death row prisoners worldwide—the experience of indeterminacy, the prospect of humiliation, and the possibility of an agonizing physical end in full consciousness—makes waiting for death a kind of torture. Such living and dying conditions apply to more than 17,000 prisoners on death row worldwide. Long delays in execution times lead to prisoners' forgoing appeals, volunteering for earlier execution, or living in intense mental anxiety.

The physical conditions of the wait also contribute to the agony of the wait—denied hobbies or distraction and subjected to inadequate sanitation and nutrition, lights left on around the clock, solitary confinement (commonly for all but one hour a day), and temperature extremes. Delirium, hallucinations, and stupor are well-known consequences of such periods of isolation. In medical terms, then, the experience of dying for death row prisoners is a long, painful, stressful period ending in a medically uncontrolled procedure that is itself an additional source of anguish. In the United States wait times for execution are now similar to the life expectancies of many people dying from long-term conditions such as HIV, cancer, or organ failure. In 2006 the average U.S. wait time was twelve years. In California the wait time is approximately twenty years. Unlike people living with cancer or HIV, death row prisoners are not offered services to manage their distress. And although some critics will observe that these prisoners have usually committed heinous crimes, Bradford makes the sober and correct observation that "the psychological effects a death row inmate experiences is not the punishment that these individuals were sentenced to; their sentence was execution."[22]

The Other Side of Waiting: Choosing and Yielding to the Positive

Bob Hope's joke about waiting for his six brothers to use the bathroom highlights the mixed experience of waiting, that is, unexpected learning and humor commonly occur amid distress and tedium. Although not new, this insight is nevertheless commonly overlooked by clinicians, academics, and dying people alike. The surprise, and often the big surprise in waiting, including the wait to die, is the positive social and psychological features that come along and develop in people while they wait.

Several psychological studies of waiting to die have noted that in the depths of their anguish, most dying people rise above the misery. It is not clear from the different studies what proportion of dying people decide that enough misery is enough and another way is possible. However, all agree that many of dying people in many different settings make this choice.

The psychoanalyst Leon Altman observes that, contrary to the popular view of waiting as dead time, waiting is in fact "an activity with a purpose, an intensely busy process rather than a blank state or an absence of functioning."[23] On the one hand, waiting is overtly active, as when one is on watchful alert, on guard for something to happen, expecting the arrival of something good or bad. In traditional vigils for dying or wakes for the dead, this active sense of waiting refers to watchfulness against disturbance of the dying or dead. Waiting in these contexts implies readiness to advocate, protect, comfort, even celebrate. On the other hand, waiting can assume a more passive meaning as when one defers or postpones an action. One waits for the right moment; one waits for a better opportunity or better conditions before acting.

In either meaning, waiting assumes a position in relation or reaction to time—one waits because time decrees it (as a child waits for adulthood) or one waits strategically (as military generals wait for better field conditions for their troops). Waiting in both senses implies active psychological involvement. Indeed, a wait demands an active readiness. The only real question that remains, according to Altman, is the question that waiting itself asks of all of us: Readiness for what? What shall we do in this time of in-betweenness? In this generic way, the question is no different when it applies to waiting for death.

The psychiatrist Merrill Berman put it another way. In the mid-1960s Berman's study of nursing home residents led him to coin a phrase, "the Todeserwartung syndrome," that is, the "waiting to die" syndrome. This syndrome, he argued, is also seen in prisoners on death row, concentration camp residents, and prisoners of war awaiting execution. He drew his conclusions from fifty in-depth interviews with the elderly in a residential care facility. Berman argues:

> This existence of merely waiting to die is not an inference drawn only from working with geriatric residents in a psychiatric clinic. It was overtly and cogently communicated by 90 to 95% of the people interviewed in an old age home once they were allowed to verbalize their true feelings and ideas, not only somatic ailments. When each patient announced that he was useless and hopeless and was only waiting to die, the only appropriate response was, "What are you going to do in the meantime?" This question applies not only to residents of an old age home but to everyone who finds himself in this situation. However, in an old age home, awareness of the effectiveness of the environment and its purposeful manipulation can allow each resident to find his own answer to this all-important question and substitute meaningful social interaction for merely waiting to die.[24]

Observers of death row prisoners make similar observations. The question of what to do quickly becomes, What can help me and make this time meaningful to me? Phyllis Coontz, studied women on death row and made an interesting observation about their waiting experiences. Apparently many of the rules that regulate interactions with other prisoners do not apply to prisoners on death row—because death row prisoners are rarely allowed to interact with other prisoners. Death row women, for example, spend an average of twenty-two hours alone in their cells. The cycles of meals, chaplain visits, family or lawyer visits, clothing and linen changes, mail arrival, and the offer of reading materials both structure the waiting experience and give it meaning. In these mundane ways, according to Coontz, "meaninglessness acquires meaning."[25]

An observer of men on death row goes further. Robert Johnson argues that to psychologically survive the distress of waiting, death row prisoners must or, rather, are compelled to exert efforts toward self-help:

The refusal to die in an environment where death may be the easy way out contributes to the notion that hope can spring eternal, or at least remain alive in the most unlikely contexts. The hope for life among death row prisoners rests on a belief in themselves and in their ability to relate to one another as human beings, even when the obstacles to empathy and support are at their strongest. The prisoners repeatedly spoke of fighting to retain the capacity to care for others, to recognize and respond to the needs of others for attention, concern or help. . . . The men of death row know that psychological survival requires a collective effort at self-help.[26]

In ordinary social circumstances we can think of waiting as part of a power game related to status and prestige in society. Important and powerful people do not wait or do not wait long. Kings and queens are rarely kept waiting, but in a doctor's office most people are kept waiting. Waiting is being asked to give of your time—voluntarily or involuntarily—and since time is money this donation is usually no small matter. Sometimes to offer to wait is to bestow privilege or honor on friends, colleagues, or even strangers. Waiting for death, however, is an entirely different matter. Although, as the saying goes, death waits for no one, death does, on the other hand, make many wait.

We can and actually often do experience this waiting—as many dying people do—in frustrated, restless, anguishing, resentful, or irritated ways. We can cope with these emotions by killing time, by distracting ourselves while we wait, watching the clock the whole while. Or we can reject clock watching for the most part and explore, notice, and use time for ourselves—refusing to see death as an appointment made for us by others or by fate and instead carrying on with might be achieved despite our looming conclusion.[27] A surprising number of dying people accept this challenge and find a positive way to transcend the anguish of waiting, transforming this time into a productive space, or, in the words of Bob Hope, "learning to dance."

Kristin Wright gives three examples of people who are, existentially speaking, able to learn to dance while waiting to use Bob Hope's bathroom. These people show that waiting is not always or only about anguish and personal purgatory. Some who wait are able to both transcend (to go beyond) and exploit (use) their wait to draw out new insights, enjoyment, and meaning from this time.

DAWN: I learned all about my disease. . . . I felt very comfortable going to the Health Sciences Center Library . . . and I'd check out those big texts and take home 13–15 at a time. . . . I'd go in, and I would read and read. . . . I want to know as much as I can about it, and I don't think hiding . . . behind the door, jumping under the covers could help me at all. And, I realized for the first time in my life—really, really realized that I was strong, and I could handle anything. If I sit down and read about myself, it's like, "My God, that's me," you know? Whoa. . . .

CISSY: One thing I did that was my favorite thing . . . like after you die, your clothes and everything get distributed to people. I decided I wanted to do it while I was still here. So, my mother-in-law . . . my sisters . . . my stepdaughters and some friends . . . we went through my jewelry that's been in my family a long time, and . . . I think everybody got what they really loved. . . . It was just so cool to do that, you know. I got pleasure from seeing their pleasure. The parting is . . . well . . . that made it just so much easier. It was so much fun because I got to see the joy and happiness on their faces. I don't know why everybody doesn't do it that way. . . . And you know, I've already planned my complete memorial service with the priest.

. . .

PATTY: I had heard on Johnny Carson's program once. He had a guest, a fellow who had been a prisoner-of-war in Vietnam, and they learned how to keep themselves, their wits about them as prisoner by uh, each playing a different character in a Star Trek program. And they'd say, "Well, I want to be Sulu tonight. I want to be the captain," and so forth. . . . And I thought, "What'll I do, what'll I do when they told me I had cancer, and again years later when I found out I was terminal, so I thought, ""Well, I can do that." I'm an avid, rabid fan of Star Trek, a trekkie like there never has been. . . . And I have watched it, and I tape all the episodes, and I watch it to the point that I've memorized it, and I used to go over that in my mind while I cleaned the floor and as I did other things. In fact, Star Trek got me through a root canal. I was thinking about . . . the pilot of the newest series . . . and the dentist kept talking to me, and I thought, "I wish he'd quit so I could think about Star Trek." . . . In doing that, I'm not thinking about cancer or dying. . . . I think that's how I get through it—in a make-believe world.[28]

David, who lived with a worsening dementia, spoke about his changing attitude toward the illness and his own death:

> In the first year or two I was more concerned about thoughts about death. I'm going to miss my daughter's marriage, one way or the other I'm not going to be around for life events. It's a source of grief and loss. There's lots of fear around the unknown. The "I know how to do this" days are going to go. What's been surprising is getting back to my optimistic side. If you told me two years ago what would happen, stop speaking, stop driving, stop reading . . . what kind of fucking life is that? You've taken all my joys! But you know, out of the unknown, the unexpected good things come up. It's easy to focus on the things that have gone but there's no way of knowing what the new things are that are coming. If I can let go, let it flow and not get too attached and tied up, the more I am open to what is happening.[29]

The writer Harold Brodkey describes about his own dying from AIDS as a roller coaster of personal suffering that is simultaneously and paradoxically both unremarkable and remarkable. He writes about his "final dying," informed by other close brushes with death that he had experienced as a child and young man. Dying, for Brodkey, has a suspended and almost illegitimate kind of life to it. He speaks about his life while dying as a thief speaks about his ill-gotten gain: "In a sense, I steal each day, but I steal it by making no effort. It is just there, sunlight or rain, nightfall or morning. I am still living at least a kind of life, and I don't want to be reduced to an image now, or, in my own mind, feel I am spending all my time on my dying instead of on living, to some satisfying extent, the time I have left."[30]

Nevertheless, despite this confession of passivity in the face of death, Brodkey hints that something more, and more precious, is happening to him during this time of waiting. In the beginning of this dawning awareness, he acknowledges that something important to him is happening, and he is actively interested and invested in this. "Dying, too, has a certain rhythm to it. It slows and quickens. Very little matters, but that little is of commanding importance to me."[31]

Brodkey rejects the idea that this time of waiting to die is, or can be, filled with "potent meaning" or transcendence. Dying is not a sacred or special time. He endows it with no special pleasures or gifts. His mind and words convey an almost harsh, rough handling of the topic of his own dying and death. At the very least his writing is as unsentimental as it is unsparingly sober, yet other, often parallel, reflections betray the very elements he dismisses. The language of his judgments tells two stories, not one: "Death is a bore. But life isn't very interesting either. I must say I expected death to glimmer with meaning, but it doesn't. It's just there. I don't feel particularly alone or condemned or unfairly treated, but I do think about suicide a lot because it is so boring to be ill, rather like being trapped in an Updike novel. I must say I despise living if it can't be done on my terms."[32]

In these passages Brodkey seems unaware of his own irony—that he is living his dying on his own terms. He continues to write as ever, to make notes, to reflect as a writer and observer of human nature, and even travel until he is too ill to do so. His relationship with his beloved, Ellen, continues and deepens, as does his friendship with his physician. In the second to last page of his memoir, Brodkey observes, with not a little incredulity, that his dying is somewhat more or less than his other, earlier judgments about the boredom of dying and death: "The world still seems far away. And I hear each moment whisper as it slides along. And yet I am happy—even overexcited, quite foolish. But *happy*. It seems very strange to think one could enjoy one's death. Ellen has begun to laugh at this phenomenon. We know we are absurd, but what can we do? We are happy."[33]

Brodkey has learned to dance while waiting for the bathroom. He has learned what many dying people—certainly not all, but many people nevertheless—observe: that dying often confers strange and unexpected gifts, even to the cynical, the fearful, the skeptical, the unhopeful. There is surprise in dying, and it often silently emerges inside the forced experience of waiting: "I don't want to praise death, but in immediacy, death confers a certain beauty on one's hours—a beauty that may not resemble any other sort but that is overwhelming."[34]

This beauty reveals itself in watching physical scenes of nature but also in the relationships around Brodkey. Although he sometimes came to view and speak of death as a bore, he would later often speak of it as a beautiful and happy bore to be with. Brodkey was surprised by dying. He was surprised by what it gave him and what he learned in its presence. And he learned something new, something he found hard to describe but that was nevertheless real, unexpected, and wondrous. Toward the very end of his life and memoir he muses about a metaphor that might also easily serve as a reflection on his final days: "I remember Chartres in 1949 before the stained glass was restored. No one I had spoken to and nothing I had read had prepared me for the delicacy of the colors, the pale blue, a sky blue really, and the yellow. The transcendent theatre of the nave while the light outside changed from moment to moment—clouds blowing over—and the colors brightening and darkening in revolving whorls inside the long, slanted beams of lady-light. I had never been *inside* a work of genius before."[35]

Inside the World of the Feeling, Changing Self

The experience of waiting to die can be surprising, running strongly counter to the television stereotype of the condemned man tearing his hair out. Reviews of studies of waiting to die, and of individual accounts of that experience, do reveal plenty of stories of people living and stewing in their own anguish, killing time (literally), pursuing trivial distraction while painfully watching the time and their bodies pass. Many of these people are not on death row but inside nursing homes or indeed their own homes. Many of these individuals go to their emotional or spiritual deaths in a kind of self-described limbo or purgatory that will seem more like hell to many readers. Yet many others do not choose to experience their waiting in this way.

Large numbers of other dying people, whatever the actual proportions might be, experience waiting to die in another, more positive, more satisfying way. Waiting to die, for this group of people, poses a question about what to do, and they answer it, at first slowly and reluctantly and then later with more effort and some consolation. I have detailed some of the experiences of those who have yielded to the positive side of waiting, and these reveal a set of seriously important personal, social, and spiritual benefits to waiting to die. Waiting to die, as a circumstance, prompts dying people to ask themselves some serious questions about what to do with their remaining time. This time and these questions are themselves a benefit and often yield responses that surprise people.

An important way many dying people have coped with waiting is to take a renewed, and sometimes new, interest in the welfare and care of others around them. Some dying people realize that dying is not all about them but rather about others. The centrality of others and their welfare becomes an important insight in transcending the suffering of waiting. It transforms the experience by linking passive acknowledgment of one's own short life to an active concern for the longer life and love of others. This rejoining and recommitment to others is life affirming and transcending, and its renewal is a surprising source of consolation and strength to the self.

For other people waiting to die, the time of waiting stops clock time, a suspension that permits and encourages them to notice their own character. Such stillness and cessation can be both terrifying and satisfying. It allows people to feel the outlines of their taken-for-granted or long-ignored reserves of strength, love, and commitment. They can also identify their own weaknesses and commit to finishing their life by addressing these in the time they have left—for their own reasons, if for no other. Insight into your own character can come as a surprise to many people, and it is common and satisfying for many of those who wait to die.

As Brodkey showed about living with AIDS, and David about living with dementia, learning to let go and accept are both hard lessons and hard-won lessons. Such changes in personal attitude allowed, indeed encouraged, both men to develop a curiosity for the new and the new positives in their lives. This was a surprising development and a source of wonder, even incredulity, to them. Yet learning to let go and accept helped them to lay difficult but important emotional foundations. These insights helped transform their view of their life at the end of that life. David eventually received a satisfying answer to his earlier question: What kind of fucking life is that? It seems it was a surprisingly good one. And Brodkey found that, while waiting to die was a bore, it was an unexpectedly charming and happy bore.

And Patty the Trekkie demonstrated that people waiting to die can creatively make new emotional and spiritual spaces inside themselves. The construction of these new spaces and places requires no small psychological effort, but they are rewarded by the realization that their own autonomy and strength have not deserted them, even in what must often feel like desperate times. Furthermore, the exploration of these new worlds of fantasy, memory, and aspiration may promise or challenge them to think, or dare to think, that their dying may offer more power and possibility than the fading social and physical world of biological dying.

The simple but powerfully renewed pleasures of noticing, really noticing, the relationships around you—in the people around you, in the natural world around you, and within the feeling world of the self—suddenly become a diverting, even exciting, source of focus, satisfaction, and hope. In this context it is easy to see why Brodkey and many others confess rather shyly, even feeling foolish while saying so, that they are happy. However strange and difficult as it is to imagine, believable or not, but happiness while waiting to die apparently exists as commonly as the usual tales of anguish and strain. Who knew you could learn to dance while waiting for the bathroom? And who could possibly believe—without listening to a full range of dying voices and texts—that happiness is truly, genuinely, and practically possible to experience again, in the often overlooked darkened corner of waiting to die?

9

Review and Reminiscence—Remembering

In that part of the book of my memory before which little can be read, there is a heading, which says: "*Incipit vita nova:* Here begins the new life." Under that heading I find written the words that it is my intention to copy into this little book: and if not all, at least their essence.

—Dante Alighieri, *La Vita Nuova*

Because we are animals, many of our reactions to death are or come from instinctual reactions to threat and from the deep organic drive to overcome and survive it. However, it is also important to emphasize that, unlike most of our ancestors and relatives in the animal kingdom, we are storytelling animals. Our cerebral functions have evolved not only to analyze a situation, like most complex animals, but also to build upon and go beyond that store of experience. Unlike most animals, we try to find patterns that might reveal to us a greater meaning behind the good and bad, threat and safety, absent or present, many or few. We always seek a pattern behind things.

Furthermore, our evaluations of the world are not simply practical but deeply moral. Things are bad not only because they hurt or harm us but also because they make no sense, or their apparent sense threatens a set of values or a way of life that we have built and hold dear. In every individual life a complex and intricate pattern of interrelated stories about the self and others supports, revises, or dismisses these values. We are organic machines held together by flesh, blood, and our stories. As human beings we ask why things happen. Is there more meaning beyond the parade of minute-to-minute events that daily traipse past our eyes? We theorize, and we share those different theories. We try to make sense of what has and is happening to us so that, among other things, we can anticipate, be better prepared for, the next challenge. We strive to overcome not only our present trials but, as all experience tells us, the ones that will inevitably come to us in the future. This is a human habit borne of our experience from birth and is not blunted or stopped by the historically recent view, however tightly held by some people, that death ends all.

As storytelling animals we are hardwired to continue to try to make sense of things in order to be better prepared for the future. That future-oriented characteristic of human storytelling has been one of our important evolutionary advantages, and it seldom stops because we are facing death. As the British psychologist Peter Coleman reminds us, *story* and *history* share the same root word, *estoire*.[1] In fact, etymologically *story* - has been used only recently (circa 1500 A.D.) to mean a tale told for the purposes of entertaining.[2] The link between identity and one's own story, one's history, is widely recognized by communities of all sorts as well as individuals. No one can know someone without knowing something of their history.

Health-care professionals are so conscious of the link between the act of review and reminiscence and identification of the self that this is often incorporated into the practice of taking the history of patients. We have no chance of knowing or getting to know people without knowing something of their history. For example, the book *Crossing Over: Narratives of Palliative Care* examines twenty cases and introduces all the patients with a brief review of the individual's personal, family, and work history. This gives the reader, as it always does, a sense of the person whom we will read about and try to understand.[3]

According to Robert Butler's classic essay about life review among the elderly, the life review is not exclusive to the elderly but is used by all those who look back on their life while confronting death.[4] In this way Butler includes younger people dying of life-limiting illnesses and those facing death in prisons and extermination camps. The act of looking back over your life has many literary (Orpheus in Greek mythology) and even biblical counterparts, such as Lot's wife in the Bible. Sometimes the act of reminiscence occurs as memories involuntarily injecting themselves into someone's daily thoughts for immediate consideration. At other times a person's recall is more voluntary, occurring more freely without the distraction and defense of a work life. People analyze, reanalyze, revise, reorganize, and then integrate their past, leading to a substantial reorganization of the personality for most people.

Butler argues that remembering the past has a number of important psychological functions for those who engage in it. Looking back is not without its hazards, but it is valuable in times of change and is critical to people's ability to adapt to and resolve new conflicts or obstacles in their life. According to Butler, "Memory . . . serves the sense of self and its continuity; it entertains us; it shames us; it pains us. Memory can tell us our origins; it can be explanatory and it can deceive. Presumably it can lend itself towards cure. The recovery of memories, the making the unconscious conscious, is generally regarded as one of the basic ingredients of the curative process. It is a step in the occurrence of change."[5]

Although how widespread review and reminiscence is for most populations is a matter of some debate and controversy, we do know that it is common practice for most people facing death. People often think that reviewing and remembering one's life is a key activity of the elderly, and no doubt it is for many. Butler cites a typical example of a seventy-six-year-old man he spoke to about this: "[He] said: My life is in the background of my mind much of the time; it cannot be any other way. Thoughts of the past play upon me; sometimes I play with them, encourage and savor them; at other times I dismiss them."[6]

But remembering in this way cannot usually be separated from the context of a person's life. We all reminisce or review our lives from time to time, but an imminent confrontation with death is one among many events that strongly prompt such conduct—whatever one's age.

Mortal Contexts of Review and Reminiscence

The psychologist Mark Freeman argues that the art of looking back and drawing out a story that make sense to us is crucial to self-understanding. Furthermore, hindsight plays an important role in deepening our moral life, not only clarifying for us when or where we have behaved badly or well but also when we have modified how we live and conduct ourselves in the world more generally.[7] Looking back has its obvious perils concerning accuracy and honesty, but notwithstanding these internal tests, remembering remains the main basis for our ability to build and evaluate ourselves. Review and reminiscence in these ways are the building blocks of self-understanding and self-evaluation. Even more, these products — self-understanding and self-evaluation — are fundamentally about self-discovery and identity maintenance.

This is simply another way of saying that when we look for what we are or who we are, for clues we turn to memories of what we have done and what we have experienced. We are our experiences. Facing death, the prospect of losing their self prompts many people in these circumstances to examine their lives once more to see who they have become and to ask whether their life was worth it and to whom. Derek Miller, a Canadian who died of metastatic complications from colon cancer, illustrates much of this self-discovery through personal history. In a final blog published after his death he introduces both the topic of his death and an aspect of his identity that remains alive: "Here it is. I'm dead, and this is my final post to my blog. In advance, I asked that once my body has finally shut down from the punishments of my cancer, then my family and friends publish this prepared message I wrote — the first part of the process of turning this from an active website to an archive."[8]

He goes on to acknowledge that most people close to him would have already heard the news of his death from his family and friends. But instead of simply mentioning that his wife would have also been one of these sources of news about his death, he identifies her in a brief review of his past life:

Of course it includes my wife Airdrie (nee Hislop). Both born in Metro Vancouver, we graduated from different high schools in 1986 and studied biology at UBC, where we met in '88. At a summer job working as park naturalists that year, I flipped the canoe Air and I were paddling and we had to push it to shore.

We shared some classes, then lost touch. But a few years later, in 1994, I was still working on campus. Airdrie spotted my name and wrote me a letter — yes! paper! — and eventually (I was trying to be a full-time musician, so chaos was about) I wrote her back. From such seeds a garden blooms: It was March '94, and by August '95 we were married. I have never had second thoughts, because we have always been good together, through worse and bad, and good and great.

However, I didn't think our time together would be so short: 23 years from our first meeting (at Kanaka Creek Regional Park, I'm pretty sure) until I died? Not enough. Not nearly enough.[9]

Those facing death are not the only ones who look back. Knowing that you have more of your life behind you than in front of you has a way of making most people look again at that past. Although many people think of living and dying with dementia as a problem with losing memory, Thomas DeBaggio reminds us that, for people living this kind of dying, memories become even more cherished and important. Reviewing and remembering that life is a critical part of holding on to a slipping sense of self. DeBaggio models this attachment in his own memoir of living with dementia, which he describes as "an unfinished story of a man dying in slow motion. It is filled with graffiti, sorrow, frustration, and short bursts of anger. While the narrator suffers his internal spears, he tries to surround himself with memories in a wan attempt to make sense of his life and give meaning to its shallow substance before he expires." Elsewhere he explains: "To retreat from my lonely internal immersion with myself and the disease, I started a diary that has become this book, as unique perhaps as the disease itself—*sweet memory, the unreliable handmaiden of the past.*"

In the very next line he launches his story with his childhood: "I was born in a wicked midwinter Iowa snowstorm and my father, proud and happy after the delivery, took the news to his parents in their little restaurant a few steps from the hospital in Eldora, Iowa. I was taken to a small white house where many of my parent's friends arrived with good wishes and grand hopes for the future." Remembering and reviewing the past provides DeBaggio with a storytelling device that is as identity affirming as it is comforting—needs made greater by a disease biologically designed to aggressively erode both. He reports, "Even in this time of failing memory, I am happy to stay closeted in my mind and bring up broken memories to paw over."[10]

For people like DeBaggio the problem of the reliability of memory and the propensity to deceive oneself is beside the point. Ultimately, remembering is a diminishing precious resource; aside from any other existential or spiritual function, it is a receding opportunity to see himself again. And since no one knows when total memory death (and hence the death of self) might come in living with dementia, authenticity is less important than the reassurance that you are still here, living, breathing, and loving—tasks that are much more valuable because of their diminishing opportunities. DeBaggio writes: "Clouded memories flit through my brain, wandering moments in a jumble of events only half-remembered. Faces smiling and sullen rise through a mist of years. Is any of this true? Can memory lie? It is too late for me to judge. Days are numb with forgetfulness and verbal stumbling."[11]

Life review is also a key element in trauma and dying. Reviewing their life has been widely reported by people who were convinced they would die but survived. Among the many examples are those who survived serious mountaineering falls, car accidents, or heart attacks. These accounts of reviewing life are core parts of academic and clinical accounts of near-death experiences.[12] They even predate modern accounts. In religious studies, for example, the idea of a book of deeds or a time of judgment and review of life is a common theme in Christian, Jewish, and Muslim eschatological traditions. Though most of these accounts involve departed souls, nevertheless countless Christian and Semitic legends of death and survival report similar experiences.[13]

The pervasiveness of life review in accounts of near-death experiences has even produced philosophical speculation about their ultimate moral and spiritual meaning.[14] People who have fallen off a mountain or suffered cardiac arrest later report reviewing their lives instantaneously, experiencing a different kind of time, or gaining the ability to see their lives as a whole in a self-admittedly short space of real time. The cardiologist Michael Sabom quotes one Vietnam veteran who described his experience of life review while he lay wounded on a battlefield: "When I came down and hit the ground (after being blown up by the explosion), I remember sitting up and I saw my right arm gone and my right leg gone and my left leg was laying off to the left side. I fell back . . . and my whole life was just going in front of me like a very fast computer and I kept thinking about all the different things I had done or perhaps I hadn't done.[15]

Zaleski quotes at length one woman's account of her near-death experience and life review in which she refers to herself in both the first and third person:

And into this great peace that I had become there came the life of Phyllis [the author of this account] parading past my view. Not as in a movie theatre, but rather as a reliving. . . . The reliving included not only the deeds committed by Phyllis since her birth in Twin Falls, Idaho, but also a reliving of every thought ever thought and every word ever spoken PLUS the effects of every thought, word, and deed upon everyone and anyone who had ever come within her sphere of influence whether she actually knew them or not PLUS the effect of her every thought, word, and deed upon the weather, the air, the soil, plants and animals, the water, everything else within the creation we call Earth and the space Phyllis once occupied. . . . I had no idea a past life review could be like this . . . it was me judging me.[16]

Between the modest autobiographical remembering styles of people living with advanced cancer or dementia and the more grandiose and mystical life review commonly encountered by people who have near-death experiences serious accidents or heart attacks comes yet another style of life review. A remembering and looking back that showcases the flooding and no less irresistible creep of small past memories into daily life. This is the kind of review and reminiscence more common among those who are in prison. Victor Frankl recalls this kind of review in his own remembering of his time in a German concentration camp:

This intensification of the inner life helped the prisoner find a refuge from the emptiness, desolation and spiritual poverty of his existence, by letting him escape into the past. When given free rein, his imagination played with past events, often not important ones, but minor happenings and trifling things. His nostalgic memory glorified them and they assumed a strange character. Their world and their existence seemed very distant and the spirit reached out for them longingly: In my mind I took bus rides, unlocked the front door of my apartment, answered my telephone, switched on the electric lights. Our thoughts often centered on such details, and these memories could move one to tears.[17]

These three examples of review and reminiscence reveal three very different styles of remembering. People who review their lives while living with a serious life-threatening or life-limiting illness experience their remembering as a controlled and selective review that focuses on relationships or events important to them. Some of these relationships or events may seem small or minor to readers or listeners, but the important characteristic of these recalled memories is that they seem important and major to the one who recalls them. For people dying from a serious illness, review and reminiscence appear to hold the promise of self-understanding and identity maintenance. A clear purpose is to establish, if it wasn't already, who and what they are as people and in relation to other people in their lives. To some extent too, a selective recall of the past, a turning over, or a pawing through, important events and relationships is also about identifying, holding, and then letting go of our most important losses. This is the work of an anticipatory style of grieving. This is a hanging on to memories as preparation for letting go.

On the other hand, the life review in traumatic events seems invariably to be of the overview and scanning type. Reviews are nonselective, uncontrolled—the memories flood the consciousness, and the person experiences this as a roller-coaster style remembering that is both overwhelming and riveting in both good and bad senses. To those who have experienced such remembering, its main purpose is one of moral evaluation and judgment about one's own life. Death is imminent, and the dying people are in a hurry, so the scan of their lives is both panoramic and almost instantaneous. Typically, people who report these kinds of life review are in dire straits for only a few minutes. This is a review designed for a personal letting go in quick time.

Finally, the remembering of those incarcerated in prisons or death camps seems mundane in comparison to the remembering that occurs in illness or trauma. The memories are often partial and not always social, such as opening their office door or catching a bus. In this kind of remembering, the incarcerated person relives these memories for compensatory reasons, drawing a certain and sometimes substantial comfort from what these small memories supply—the recall of better times or better life. The memories are most often used to deny or obliterate, however temporarily, the terrible sufferings of the present. In significant measure, the review of these kinds of memories helps the person to live in the past since the future appears unlikely and the present appears impossible. This is a review that holds on to memories for their own sake—to hold on to a past life in order to obliterate a present one.

I list the different purposes of review and reminiscence to introduce a deeper discussion of their role near death, but I do not want any readers to think that such purposes or styles of remembering are exclusive to one context and not another. Clearly, using remembering to compensate for present losses and suffering may be found in people dying of illness, just as it might be present among patients in residential nursing care. The pursuit of self-understanding goes on in death camps just as it does in those who seek to make a judgment about their quickly ending lives during experiences of sudden trauma. My point is only to emphasize what appear to be the primary—but not sole—purposes of these different styles of remembering and to suggest the main roles that the different social contexts clearly play in prioritizing these purposes for those in each circumstance.

Nevertheless, whether in trauma, illness, or confinement, what and why we each seek to remember in the face of death is clearly an essential part of making meaning out of this last time for us. When we speak about meaning making at the end of life, we are referring to these themes. We seek self-understanding or self-knowledge; we seek to manage our grief and loss; we seek judgment and evaluation of our lives; and we seek to distract ourselves from our present suffering and indignities, whatever method we use. What is the purpose of these goals when someone is dying?

The Meaning of Review in Lives Facing Death

According to the famous Swiss psychoanalyst Carl Jung, human beings are an enigma to themselves.[18] They lack similar beings to which they might compare themselves. Clearly we are animals, but just as clearly something is different about us. The elephants have not put one of their number on the moon. Chimpanzees have yet to produce a Mozart. Even if we underestimate the intelligence and spirituality of animals—and I'm sure we do, as volumes of new philosophical work on their nature have begun to argue and describe—yet they are not like us in major ways—at least in aesthetic, moral, and aspirational ways. Jung continues his argument by adding that without a clear someone to compare ourselves with—an angel, a god, or an interstellar humanoid of alien origin, for example—self-knowledge is difficult. Instead, from Jung's point of view, we have only two alternative sources of self-knowledge: other people, that is, other members of our species, and the memories of our evolved and evolving self through autobiographical recollection. Both options, argues Jung, seem deeply unsatisfactory.

Comparing ourselves to others is often doomed to be an unsatisfying pastime, not least because we are constantly reminded how individual we all are. But if there is no one similar enough to allow comparison, how are we then to objectively observe and assess what we are? Enter here the possibility of comparing our past selves with the self that is evolving now. It is in this territory, the territory of memory, that Jung seems to have underestimated the fertile possibilities for learning. Here in memory we do see a being much like our self: not an angel, God, or alien, not even ourselves as we experience ourselves in the present but a self in recollection. Our present self and our self in the past have physical, social, psychological, and moral similarities. The image of our self yesterday looks much more like the one we are today than our memory of who we were twenty years ago—but they are all technically not us today. Because we experience our self only momentarily, that is, moment to moment, we gain a deeper understanding of our self when we step out of that daily stream of consciousness and rely on review and reminiscence—our ability to tell a coherent story about how these other past selves connect and make sense to all who know us, including our current self.

What does "making sense" mean? For dying people it means weaving coherence—a story must have a beginning, a middle, and an end. The adventures and trials between the beginning and the end must all be related somehow, perhaps joined by a purpose—always maintained, or viewed and understood in retrospect. In this way, when we tell the big overarching autobiographical narrative to ourselves in the final days of our lives, we look not just for coherence but for the basic message or messages underlying these past selves. This message might be elicited by our own questions asked in trepidation: Was it worth it? What was I? What was my purpose? Will I continue, and in what ways, for what reasons? These are philosophical questions, to be sure, but they are also spiritual questions in the sense of establishing a broad transcendent meaning for one's own life, that is, a meaning that goes beyond and behind the apparent parade of patterned events and relationships. It is the meaning behind the apparent order (or disorder) in one's life. As the psychologist Coleman observes: "Central to the task of creating a life story is achieving reconciliation between conflicting elements. This means facing up to discrepancies between reality and ideals, hope and experience, and building bridges between them so that they are united once again. Providing coherence, assimilating what is difficult to understand, recognizing original purposes and their endings, and being true to oneself and others are all aspects of reconciliation."[19]

Any major life crisis can bring you to a point where you will interrogate the "past selves" in search of a discovery or rediscovery of the meaning of self, but dying will often do this too for many people because dying is the final roundup of all meaning about their life. People review their lives for another reason, too. Sometimes, it is a simple reacquaintance with the contents of memory.

Dying people may review their lives in anticipation of their demise. In other words, dying people may experience what psychologists commonly call anticipatory grief.[20] In this form of grief the dying person (and their carers) will begin to grieve for their future loss. Much has been written about this from a carer's perspective, but here we are concerned with the dying person's point of view. Review and reminiscence may play the role of reacquainting one's self with important events, cherished relationships both past and present, and valued and sometimes secret personal experiences. Looking back at these memories is an act of visitation — to people, places, and experiences for the purposes of saying good-bye.[21]

The grief psychologist Bill Worden argues that using memory in the service of anticipatory grief helps dying people adjust and accept their own impending demise. Such processing may arouse significant anxiety and depression and can lead to premature withdrawal of the dying person well before, for example, the actual terminal stage of an illness. But it can also help settle dying people emotionally for the next emotional tasks of grieving, such as accommodating themselves to a world from which the dying are missing.[22] Reviewing memories can also prompt the dying person to make psychological and social preparations for a future world where they are missing. These private reviews prompt social conversations with family and friends about how the dying person would like these people to live without them. Dying spouses may encourage remarriage or at least give their surviving spouse permission or reassurance that such future arrangements meet with their understanding and approval. Dying parents may make recordings, write letters, or leave gifts or financial arrangements based on their desire to be present and active in their children's future.

By making preparations for survivors, ensuring a presence of the self in the future world without them, dying people accommodate themselves to that future world. Review and reminiscence thus bring memories to the fore—to reacquaint, to remember the priorities in the dying person's life, to say good-bye, and to provide stimulus for planning and preparing for survivors' future.

The third meaning of review in dying people's lives is self-assessment or, to put it another way, judgment and evaluation of their life. This is common in near-death experiences but is certainly an element in all reviews and reminiscence to some extent. The psychologists Jeffrey Webster and Barbara Haight have identified several distinct purposes of personal reminiscence, many of which are covered by my earlier discussion of grief and self-understanding. But one of the key other factors they identified was a tendency to obsess about unresolved past events (bitterness revival). A subsequent study by other psychologists found that, apart from some people with a low tendency to reminisce, older people in particular either fall into negative reminiscing or use reminiscing to find story and meaning in their lives.[23] In these circumstances judgment and self-assessment prevail. This can lead to contentment, but it can also lead to bitterness as people remember the failures, disappointments, and wrong-doing by themselves and or others. Here the story of past selves linked to the current self is disappointing. The life story makes the person angry, unhappy, grief stricken, regretful, and depressed.

In circumstances of sudden trauma such as falls or accidents, for example, the prospect of a long, drawn-out assessment of one's life is impossible, but the need to make some assessment of one's life apparently is not. In these kinds of dying, the dying person cuts to the heart of the matter and asks: What kind of life did I lead? However, in the case of near-death experiences, the overwhelming majority of life review experiences seem to be positive or at least performed self-consciously with a certain detachment and self-acceptance. Why should this be so, in direct contrast to the observations reported by Webster and Haight of similar self-assessment by the elderly?

Webster and Haight's report provides no prevalence data on the proportion of elderly people who experience so-called bitterness revival—it may be quite small in comparison to those who assess their lives more positively. Nevertheless, other psychological characteristics of remembering provide some clues to the differences in these two groups. In the elderly, and especially in the elderly experiencing a slow and uncertain process of dying, memory will be selective, as it is for most people dying of an illness. This allows them to carefully and slowly choose what concerns them most—both positive and negative—and therefore what they will dwell on. On the other hand, near-death experiences elicit life reviews that are characteristically panoramic and oriented to the entire context of the person's life. People who experience this kind of life review consistently mention that they have no control over or choice about what they see parade before them. They tend to see large numbers of both positive and negative events, experiences, and relationships. It is a context-style review par excellence. The option of singling out a particular incident, relationship, or part of one's life simply isn't made available by whatever drives this type of remembering.

Notwithstanding the different outcomes of judgment—selective or not, bitter or not—the purpose of such reviews seems to be to abandon the niceties of meaning making or storytelling about one's life and to prioritize the task of self-assessment. It is difficult to say why judgment becomes so prominent in life review in the face of death, at least psychiatrically, but the social reasons may have to do with the long-standing and cross-cultural association of death and religion. In most of the world's religions, and hence in most of the major cultures of the human race, the spiritual meaning of death openly suggests a final moral assessment of character and lifestyle. Whether a dying person is religious or not, few people on Earth can escape the unconscious association of death and moral evaluation of a life, even if that judgment comes from the self rather than any divine source. Even modern newspaper obituaries for famous people, or death notices written by funeral homes for a deceased person without any public profile, commonly provide a review and (usually) sympathetic assessment of a deceased person's life. So do survivors who give eulogies at funerals or memorial services. Death, even in today's secular society, suggests a time of judgment about a life, and this seems to be a secular continuity of an old, more religious, tradition. If survivors cannot avoid these habits in eulogies, what chance is there that dying people would avoid judging themselves while approaching death? Self-assessment of a life is a deeply cultural activity in the social psychology of life review.

Finally, people review their lives to distract themselves, sometimes from boredom and sometimes to avoid or deny great suffering.[24] Reminiscence can be a helpful way to avoid living in a world one hates—a nursing home, a death camp, a hospice. Just as fantasy and daydreaming can be pleasurable ways to avoid painful or boring experiences, so too can review and reminiscence. As Frankl observed in his own experiences of the death camp:

> A man who let himself decline because he could not see any future goal found himself occupied with retrospective thoughts. In a different connection, we have already spoken of the tendency there was to look into the past, to help make the present, with all its horrors, less real. But in robbing the present of its reality there lay a certain danger. It became easy to overlook the opportunities to make something positive of camp life, opportunities which really did exist. Regarding our "provisional existence" as unreal was in itself an important factor in causing the prisoners to lose their hold on life; everything in a way became pointless. Such people forgot that often it is just such an exceptionally difficult external situation which gives man the opportunity to grow spiritually beyond himself. Instead of taking the camp's difficulties as a test of their inner strength, they did not take their life seriously and despised it as something of no consequence. They preferred to close their eyes and to live in the past. Life for such people became meaningless.[25]

All these key meanings of life review in the face of death — self-understanding, grieving, self-assessment, and distraction — to some extent show the different spiritual levels dying people inhabit. Some dying people wish to live and die with a life examined. This helps them prepare for death socially, psychologically and spiritually. It also helps them grieve and opens them to the ambiguities of anxiety and transcendence. But it also leaves them vulnerable to other feelings behind other memories — hate, resentment, fear, bitterness, regret, and disappointment. And at the end of life it is difficult to know what emotional weaponry to use to fend off such surprises and sirens. At the very basic level, review and reminiscence may hold no gifts or virtue. Remembering may instead provide simple reverie, a spiritual boat ride away from the unpleasant and painful indignities of a dying life without any control other than what dying people can exert within themselves. This is remembering as comfort and anesthesia. Frankl may regard such acts disapprovingly, although even he claims a limit to understanding, cautioning that it is ultimately impossible to know the moral and emotional complexities that dog human beings facing their own death. The dying may close their eyes and live in the past, but that does not necessarily mean that life has become meaningless. It may be that they are in hot pursuit of meaning in a place where Frankl cannot follow. As Mahmoud Darwish reminds us, a fundamental purpose of reminiscence is remembering who you are, especially in adversity:

> Remember yourself
> before all turns to dust
> so that you may grow up
> Remember, remember
> your ten toes and forget the shoe
> Remember the features of your face
> Forget the winter fog
> Remember your mother and your name
> and forget the letters of the alphabet
> Remember your country and forget the sky
> Remember, remember![26]

Problems and Tensions in Remembering

Some have suggested that the life review is not universal — that these personal processes are most likely linked to cultures that value individualistic forms of identity or that these processes are more likely to be prompted by a variety of age-related stimuli — for example, bereavements, retirements, or questioning from others, especially new acquaintances or grandchildren. Indeed, the sociologist J. B. Wallace argues that life review is less about age or the prospect of death per se than about forms of social activity required by certain situations that may or may not be age or mortality related.[27] Some times and some circumstances are more likely than others to demand a review to answer questions or to establish identity, access, or rapport with others. Reminiscence is a common interpersonal tool in many forms of social interaction.

Nonetheless, whatever else might also prompt life review, the prospect of death remains one important stimulus. While academics make good points about the variety of events that can trigger life review, few studies include the terminally ill, and facing your own death will always be a primary impetus for such a personal review. In any case, most studies show that the majority of the elderly actually do perform life review — prompted by a variety of sources. Many dying people may not do this, but this does not mean they didn't do it at an earlier point in their lives. Sometimes a decision not to review may itself be a sign of some deep grief about an important part of their life.[28] Finally, life reviews do seem to be peculiar to cultures that value individual autonomy, and so are mainly prevalent in Western or highly industrialized societies. But for many of those people in these places, the life review is an important and vital element in their social and psychological response to death. Looking over one's shoulder as one disappears over the horizon of life itself is an understandable final act.

Other psychologists warn us of the unreliability of perception and memory, as if this somehow makes a difference to life review in mortal circumstances. Perception, as psychologists are always reminding us, is often both selective and notoriously unreliable, and memories too are both selective and unreliable. To put it another way, one's idea of one's self is drawn from two notoriously difficult, complex, and ambiguous sources of information — perceptions of the present and memories of the past. This leads to the contemporary academic models of the psychology of self that suggest everyone tends to have multiple selves, which we use in different social contexts or different relationships. Each version of the self tells slightly different versions of the same story about daily incidents, past memories, or future aspirations, shaped to the needs of different audiences and selectively prompted and encouraged by the different listeners. Because no one remembers everything — we simply forget large tracts of information or cannot access them because some memories are less important than others — all remembering is to some extent a rationalization, simply for the purposes of ordering and consistency, if nothing else. This can and does lead to significant faulty and outright false memories as well as the development of different versions of events recalled from the distance of many years.

Overall, then, the research on remembering highlights the fine line between the simple memory of a basic few facts (a house move, a marriage breakup, or the earning of a university degree) and the development of a narrative or story about how and why these events occurred. In other words, remembering is a small matter of facts and largely a matter of making sense.

This latter function of making meaning is where remembrance and the personal construction of the self—who we think we were, who we think we have become, or are becoming—do battle. And in the end, the literal end, the meaning, sense, and discerned purpose (or not) is what counts for people near death. Facts and accuracy are necessary but not sufficient conditions for satisfactory self-storytelling. Having an accurate memory doesn't help with discerning a meaning in one's life anymore than having a poor memory does. One can misinterpret or miss the whole point with or without the facts. This has been true for the writing of history and autobiography. In reviewing our lives we are not keeping records—we are making them, we are creating—demolishing with one hand and shaping with the other. After all, as the Canadian pop philosopher of media Marshall McLuhan once observed in the 1960s, the medium is the massage, that is, the medium is what makes the biggest difference to people, not the message.[29]

Finally, in a major British ethnographic study of hospice patients' experience of the process of dying, the sociologist Julia Lawton noted a paradox between day-care patients at the hospice and residents, who sometimes described their time as a "waiting game."[30] Patients with a degree of independence and health, although avowedly keen to live in the present, nevertheless incorporated the past by sharing photos or reminiscing about the past with other patients of a similar age.

On the other hand, the more incapacitated and high-dependency residents were less willing, or perhaps less able, to reminisce in the more public way as the day-care patients. For the residents the time for review may already have passed, and the time had come for focusing on other matters, perhaps inward concerns for the present or perhaps other contemplation of what is to come.[31] Lawton believes that the cessation of a concern for the past or the future that she sees in "high-dependency" patients may be part of what she calls "loss of self," or moving toward a "state of unbeing." However, that is a serious example of unverifiable speculation. As some philosophers warn about the limits to academic observation, the absence of evidence does not necessarily provide evidence of absence.[32] Because I do not answer the door when you knock is not hard evidence that I am not home. I may simply refuse to answer the door for my own reasons, and your guesses about my lack of appearance run wild without my participation.

Is Remembering Useful?

Review and reminiscence have social and public value. Remembering is not a self-indulgence for the maudlin and self-absorbed. Sharing a review and reminiscence has great value, and no one can know what value listeners and readers will make of such acts. As Gillian Rose, the philosopher who wrote her own remembrance of her life and dying, observed:

> Who is entitled to write his reminiscences?
> Everyone.
> Because no one is obliged to read them.[33]

Writing one's reminiscences does not require being a great person, a notorious criminal, a celebrated artist, or a diplomat — it is quite enough to simply be a human being, to have something to tell, and not merely the desire to say it but at least have some little ability to do so. As Rose said, "Every life is interesting; if not the personality, then the environment, the country are interesting, the life itself is interesting. Man likes to enter into another existence, he likes to touch the subtlest fibres of another's heart, and to listen to its beating . . . he compares, he checks it by his own, he seeks for himself confirmation, sympathy, justification."[34]

The act of review and reminiscence is not only a personal and private task. It can be, and has been, a public task shared with audiences both intimately small and infinitely great. Its value is fundamentally about reminding those around the dying person that, ultimately and literally, we are all making the same journey and must face the same psychological and spiritual challenges sometime. Sharing one's remembering can model that task for each of us.

And finally there is the matter of memories as a source of learning for the future. As someone once said, "We remember not for the past but for the future."[35] But do the dying have a future? I think we can definitely conclude that, despite popular myth to the contrary, the dying do have a future. Their future is projected into the lives of all their surviving friends and family, the many individuals and attachments that populate the dying person's mind during a review and who prompt that person to secure a place in their lives. Furthermore, the dying are not dead, and certainly until they are, a future however short exists for them to act in. In that future, such as it is, reminiscence may allow a more peaceful and accepting passage. In mining the past the dying may identify a psychological and spiritual way forward for themselves in their final minutes of life here on Earth. Beyond that, the future of human survival beyond death is not established. The easy answers to the question of human survival of death belong to the smug in religion and in science. The greatest openness to this question of death is often to be found in those who stand at its doorway. Only the dying person knows if she or he has a future of this kind, and the acts of review and reminiscence help the dying determine what to take into that bold and mysterious future.

10

Aloneness—Disconnection

This young woman knew that she would die in the next few days. But . . . she was cheerful in spite of this knowledge. "I am grateful that fate has hit me so hard," she told me. "In my former life I was spoiled and did not take spiritual accomplishments seriously." Pointing through the window . . . she said, "This tree here is the only friend I have in my loneliness." . . ."I often talk to this tree," she said to me. . . . Was she delirious? Did she have occasional hallucinations? . . . I asked her if the tree replied. . . . She answered, "It said to me, 'I am here—I am here—I am life, eternal life.'"

—Victor Frankl, *Man's Search for Meaning*

Dying as an experience of aloneness—felt as a lonely experience—is invariably viewed as a negative experience and existentially as a deepening of a modern malaise that generally leaves people feeling lonely and cut off from each other despite the presence of others. It is not that people simply don't have company but that this company frequently fails to provide individuals with a sense of connection with one another. People die alone not only at the hour of their death but well before, sometimes months or years before. Dying—as an extended period of living before imminent death—attracts experiences of social disconnection from others because the destination is often too difficult for other people to accept or confront.

The philosopher John McGraw reminds us that this experience of being alone was one of the first things in the world that the biblical God named "not good" and that it was the primary divine motivation for creating woman.[1] He even reminds his readers that Mother Teresa claimed that loneliness was *the* problem of modern times. Nevertheless, although the problem of existential loneliness is clearly related to the loneliness of dying, it is only the cultural background to the more specific, more intense, and unavoidable loneliness of confronting our own death. All experiences of being alone, and of loneliness, are obviously symbolic of dying to some extent, presaging the more acute experience, but whereas "existential loneliness" may be defended against—by working on love, intellectualizing its immediate effects away, keeping busy, or expressing the feelings and spiritual problems creatively, even artistically, the loneliness of facing imminent death is less amenable to rationalization and sociological massage.[2]

The aloneness of dying places the individual not on the proverbial mountaintop for reflection but in a corner. Time is not abundant but short. The problem is not merely troublesome but urgent, acute, devouring, affecting. The difference here is between contemplating one's mortality while in health and addressing the same topic while facing death. The experiences have some resemblance, but the quality is entirely and fundamentally different.

Philosophers have stressed the importance of the basic conceptual distinctions in isolation (being physically separated from others), solitude (being alone and liking it), and loneliness (being alone and not liking it).[3] Philosophers have tended to argue that isolation is an existential quality of being human, that is, to some extent we all feel separate from one another and that's why we pursue social activities to transcend or overcome those feelings of aloneness. In this view, the prospect of death has no particular special ontological status except in so far as death itself represents the ultimate threats to being. In other words, the major threat that death offers to most people confronting it is the loss of who they are, have been, or ever will be. In short, it is the threat of separation from self and others that fuels the anxiety behind the experience of being alone.

While some experiences—such as marriage or an initiation rite into adulthood—will yield a grief reaction to the loss of one part of the self (usually a former role such as bachelorhood or childhood), death can mean a confrontation with a total loss of self. Dying in this way places a person in a slow, incremental, and inevitable process of socially disappearing. Or, to put it another way, the social death precedes the physical one—parts of the self become less sharable and visible the deeper the physical, emotional, and spiritual processes of dying become. That kind of loneliness is commonly described as a total lack of relatedness—like screaming and waving at others from a soundproof room high up and away from street level. You're there—but not there. You still exist, at least to you—but you don't, at least to other people. Dying, in this isolating sense, is the gradual moving toward such invisibility and isolation.

Aloneness in Early Experiences of Dying

The psychiatrist Robert Butler notes the relationship between social disconnection and the experience of dying in a long tradition of writing. He says: "The writings of Cannon, Richter, Adland, Will, and others suggest a relationship between isolation, or loneliness, and death. 'The feeling of unrelatedness is incompatible with life in the human being.'" This observation is supported by his citations to anthropological studies of voodoo death, the study of sudden death in animals and humans, and several essays on the loneliness of aging, written by, among others, Frieda Fromm-Riechmann and later Norbert Elias.[4]

Perhaps the most important social science book to directly address the problem of aloneness in dying is Norbert Elias's *The Loneliness of the Dying*, published in 1985. This book is more a long essay that focuses on the situation of dying people in the industrial West. It is a book of theoretical reflections from a man who is more widely known for studying and explicating the development of the civilizing process in Western societies from the Middle Ages to the present. Some of Elias's observations about death are period specific because hospice and palliative care now address some of his early concerns about pain management—but most of what he has to say about the modern circumstances of dying remains relevant today. Although the hospice and palliative care movements in the United States, United Kingdom, Canada, and Australia provide both physical and social support to dying people, few people die under their care. The vast majority of dying people still die in hospitals, nursing homes, or at home. In the United Kingdom, for example, less than 5 percent of dying people receive palliative care.[5] But whether they die under this form of care, or in hospitals or nursing homes, Elias's general observation of the modern circumstances of dying remains true: "Never before have people died as noiselessly and hygienically as today in these societies, and never in social conditions so much fostering solitude."[6]

Elias argues that modern dying has three main sources of aloneness. First, sharing the actual physical and emotional experience of dying with anyone who is not dying is almost impossible. Second, also impossible to share is the loss of our own uniqueness—memories, emotions, knowledge, and dreams. Finally, loneliness can be the more social feeling that most, and sometimes all, the people to whom we feel attached leave us alone to die.[7]

The earlier meanings of aloneness arise from the relatively recent emphasis on what Elias calls individualization, a process that accelerated during the Renaissance. This is the cultural change that socializes people to think of themselves as enterprising, problem-solving, and careerist individuals in social orientation, not bound to a group mentality tied to family, village, or tribe. This encourages a kind of atomized form of individualism that makes each of us think we are alone and must make our way in the world through individual effort and achievement. Such thinking inevitably leads people to view themselves, upon their deathbed as in life, as lone helmsmen. Undoubtedly such a cultural orientation does lead to a baseline experience of aloneness and disconnection while dying, at least emotionally.

However, Elias is describing more than this. Compounding this social psychology of the modern individual are other social and political facts about the dying experience itself. Dying people often find themselves in institutional and physical circumstances that leave them victims of disenfranchising social processes. Those who are aging and dying, for example, are subjected to insidious social processes as they get older that prepare the way for more openly aversive reactions at the deathbed. Elias gives a couple of insightful personal examples of how this begins:

Now that I myself am old I know, as it were, from the other side how difficult it is for people, young or middle aged, to understand the situation and the experience of older people. Many of my acquaintances say to me words of kindness such as: "Astonishing! How do you manage to keep so healthy? At your age!" or: "You *still* go swimming? How marvelous!" One feels like a rope-dancer, who is quite familiar with the risks of his way of life and fairly certain that he will reach the ladder at the end of the rope and come down to earth quietly in his own good time. But the people who are watching him from below know that he might fall from his height at any moment and look at him thrilled and slightly scared.[8]

These examples refer to the emotional isolation and loneliness specific to the aging experience, which seems only to deepen as fragility increases with age, or as serious disease enters these circumstances, or as an old person leaves home to enter an institution such as a hospital, hospice, or nursing home. Such disenfranchising experiences have also been commonly reported by people with terminal illnesses. Trillin recalls her own cancer experience as including such times of social alienation:

> I have no horror stories of the kind I read a few years ago in the *New York Times*; people didn't move their desks away from me at the office or refuse to let their children play with my children at school because they thought that cancer was catching. My friends are all too sophisticated and too sensitive for that kind of behavior. Their distance from me was marked most of all by their inability to understand the ordinariness, the banality of what was happening to me. They marveled at how well I was "coping with cancer." I had become special, no longer like them. Their genuine concern for what had happened to me, and their complete separateness from it, expressed exactly what I had felt all my life about anyone I had ever known who had experienced tragedy.[9]

Grace Chow, a thirty-two-year-old dying from a rare cancer, had similar experiences with well-intentioned friends. She wrote on her blog:

> What do you say to friends who say *"I'm sure you will get well soon"*? What is the basis of their faith that I'm actually not dying, but merely undergoing a phase that will be temporary before life starts kicking in again? Do they know something that I don't? Do they realize the seriousness and extent of my disease? That tumors tend to grow rather than shrink spontaneously? That death is statistically, historically, even philosophically more certain than life?
>
> The enthusiasm to believe that I will get better is based on the reluctance to think about the concept of death, to try to understand what death means. Of course death is frightening. That's a natural biological reaction.

Every living thing strives to stay alive. And death is all the more frighten-ing when you have to watch it unfold before yourself. But you achieve absolutely nothing by refusing to acknowledge it. You do not comfort me with your assurance that I won't die, because escaping death is not what I'm longing for. What I'm longing for is for *you* to understand what death is. Look it in the eye and see it for what it is. And then you'll see that under-standing death is the only one and true liberation.[10]

Furthermore, these incremental reactions of lack of empathy or under-standing become open aversion when the dying person's body begins to fail and break the usual social and cultural boundaries. The presence of odor is one of these cultural taboos and social alarms. Aversion and increasing isola-tion are the result. Elias recalls the predicaments of both Freud and Sartre as they were dying:

Freud's protracted death from cancer of the larynx is one of the most tell-ing. The growth became more and more ill-smelling. Even Freud's trusted dog refused to go near him. Only Anna Freud, strong and unwavering in her love for the dying father, helped him in these last weeks and saved him from feeling deserted. Simone de Beauvoir described with frighten-ing exactness the last months of her friend Sartre, who was no longer able to control his urinary flow and was forced to go about with plastic bags tied to him, which overflowed. The decay of the human organism, the process that we call dying, is often anything but odorless.[11]

Finally, Elias writes about the loneliness of people who may not neces-sarily be dying from illnesses but who are surrounded by others — in nursing homes, hospitals, or death camps — who ignore them. This is a loneliness that comes from being surrounded by people for whom "it is a matter of indifference whether or not this person exists." The dying person is no one of any significance, and the last "bridge of feeling" has been broken. Such circumstances apply to many of the homeless or vagrants but also those in torture chambers, death camps, or those on death row. Such dying people die alone, physically and emotionally.[12]

The palliative care researchers Lisa Sand and Peter Strang conducted an in-depth study of twenty palliative care patients about their existential loneliness.[13] They found a variety of different sources for dying people's sense of loneliness or feelings of isolation. A few of their respondents mirrored Trillin's and Chow's experience—that the joking behavior, unrealistic comments about health and appearance, or other comments that minimized the gravity and difficulty of the patient's situation made dying people feel invisible.[14] Few people acknowledge the place of death inside the patient's everyday experience, inside their daily thoughts and feelings. This disenfranchised them from their usual social circle, made them feel isolated. These feelings of separation would also arise or were compounded by other social experiences of interaction, such as when one patient managed to go out with old friends but wore diapers. The experience of wearing diapers and of having physical suffering and psychological anguish are difficult to share with those who have no previous basis for empathizing with these experiences.

Furthermore, dying people often felt that introducing such topics of discussion was inappropriate or depressing in social situations, forcing dying people to conceal, or surrender to, feelings of aloneness within their new world of living with dying. There were yet other sources of aloneness, too. The "most severely ill" dying people in Sand and Strang's study shared their concerns about the loneliness of actually dying:

> I wonder, what is happening when you die? Is it one moment like this and suddenly you are gone? I think that if I can sit here and fall asleep, what would the difference be between that and if I were to go into a coma? . . . Just sit here and suddenly stop existing . . .
> [Interviewer] Are you afraid of that?
> Yes, I am afraid of that situation . . . (*long pause*) . . . And being alone here at home. I don't want to just sit here and deteriorate and struggle and experience a hard time all alone.[15]

Aloneness in Late Experiences of Dying

When being alone becomes completely unavoidable because an illness or a set of mortal circumstances nearly or completely severs the social contact a person can have, a different kind of loneliness can ensue. In these cases of severe estrangement, withdrawal, or separation from the world, what does a dying person do? Grace Chow gives us a clue. Chow expressed her view of dying, literally only days from her actual death, when she observed: "Soon, I will be dead. I have a recalcitrant tumor in my neck, and it's a real pain. It's given me plenty of time to prepare for my death, and now it's finally going for the kill. I am completely powerless in the face of it. My only option is to flee to my mind, where I have so, so much to say and tell. . . . But I have no one to tell it to. This is the loneliness of death."[16]

This disengagement from the outside world and simultaneous retreat to the mind is the most common response to severe isolation and recalls a wealth of psychological and anthropological literature and research on how, when the stimuli from the external world recede, the stimuli from the internal, psychological world begin to move to the foreground of our experiences. Psychoanalytical theorists in particular have made much of this psychological shift.

The psychoanalyst Frieda Fromm-Reichmann stresses the importance of at least two factors in preventing loneliness from turning into madness, in a psychiatric sense.[17] According to Fromm-Reichmann, loneliness can fuel or even create a psychotic state in people who experience extreme loneliness. The protective factors seem to be voluntarily opting to be alone and lonely or devotion to a cause or belief system. These two factors seem most important to the mental and spiritual health and well-being of isolated people, and they are commonly found, for example, in hermits, explorers, or those in isolating occupations such as lighthouse and polar expeditionary work. Mental disturbance during forced isolation such as solitary confinement or sailing solo is common except where such people hold strongly to some transcendent belief or cause. Often such people strive for order and distraction in their isolation, allowing them to have some control over the rising dominance of their inner life. Thus choice and faith, to use the more common terms, seem psychologically protective in the often-slippery transitions from aloneness to loneliness to further progressions into regions of intolerable and painful loneliness, at least so say the psychoanalysts.

Against this rather armchair view of loneliness come ethnographic and historical objections from two sources—the lives of castaways, and the lives of hermits and recluses. In the first case, being marooned on a rock, coral reef, small island, or ice shelf is not voluntary, and, in the second, the life of the traditional hermit and recluse is a chosen one. Belief in survival has a limited role to play in both cases, for toward the end of their lives, in both cases, we have ample evidence of death and dying as recorded in diaries and other observer accounts. The freelance researcher and writer Edward Leslie compiled a list of castaway accounts from several hundred years ago to the present in a book whose title could describe many people's personal experience of dying—*Desperate Journeys, Abandoned Souls*.

In many of these accounts the castaway journeys are lone journeys characterized by severe trials, physical pain, psychological anguish, a spiritual turn toward religion or spiritual matters, and—rather interestingly—visions and hallucinations. In one account of a nameless man left stranded alone on Ascension Island in the eighteenth century, the castaway desperately battled a lack of water on the island. In the end, unable to find a reliable source of water to sustain him, he began to locate and kill large turtles, cutting off their heads and drinking their blood. Eventually this practice only made him vomit continually, undoing the hydration it was supposed to supply. To solve this problem he began to mix and drink both the turtle's blood and urine so as to thin the more ghastly taste of the blood alone. Under these conditions of privation the castaway records his constant hallucinations or delusions of seeing sails or boats on the distant horizon. He also experienced visitations by spirits, demons, or monsters. These would taunt him, swear profanities at him and remind him of his failures: "In the solemn gloom and dead of night I was surprised by an uncommon noise that surrounded me, of bitter cursing and swearing mixed with the most blasphemous and libidinous expressions I ever heard. My hair stood on end with horror and cold sweat trickled down my pallid cheeks."

Later he was visited in broad daylight by a former lover who he "perfectly knew," and they conversed extensively. Another time he was visited by a skeleton that pointed to its own throat. This last apparition he took to be a prophesy of his own fate.[18] Such accounts are not unusual in the annals and diaries that describe being castaway with little or no resources and facing certain death without rescue. Indeed, these accounts seem most common in those whose belief in rescue has failed them. In the end the castaway described here dies on the island, his diary found much later. The last entry in his diary declares: "I am becoming a moving skeleton, my strength is entirely decayed. I cannot write much longer. I sincerely repent of the sins I committed and pray, henceforth, no man may ever merit the misery which I have undergone. For the sake of which, leaving this narrative behind me to deter mankind from following such diabolical inventions. I now resign my soul to Him that give it, hoping for mercy in."[19] Here the diary ends.

When the famous French aviator Antoine de Saint-Exupéry was interviewed about his many near-fatal crashes and marooning at sea and in the desert, he too pointed to that mixture of inexplicable vision and sensation of the eternal that long periods of isolation seemed to bestow on him and those in similar situations. As Leslie records it:

> The repeated brushes with death, far from frightening him, actually seemed to give him a sense of ease and a reaffirmation of his existence. He had long since given up conventional religion, but in these moments he sensed, as he said of yet another near-fatal accident, "a new undefinable intelligence"; he glimpsed a "world from which one does not often return to describe." Recalling the serenity with which his beloved fifteen-year old brother accepted terminal illness, he wrote, "One does not die. . . . There is no more death when one meets it. When the body breaks apart, the essential is revealed. Man is a knot of relationships."[20]

On the other hand, hermits and recluses — as volunteers for aloneness and disconnection — do not have a peaceful, serene life quite different from those involuntarily thrown into isolation. In fact, a review of the lives of hermits and recluses in England by the medieval historian Tom Licence reveals that their lives were devoted to eschewing life's many pleasures, and their key goal was preparing their souls for the afterlife with God. They did this preparation through constant prayer and isolation, torturing themselves with self-inflicted pain and discomfort, and by fasts and severely restricted diets. Furthermore, many kept the prospect of imminent death before them deliberately and sometimes dramatically by kneeling in open graves for long periods, or even living in small cells with open graves dug and constantly present before them.[21]

Such experiences of aloneness, pain, and suffering, and the chosen lifestyle of leaving themselves alone with their own thoughts for long interminable periods also prompted hallucinations and visions — both welcome and unwelcome. Licence devoted a whole chapter to these mystical experiences: "Wicked spirits arrived . . . to beat the hermit, smash his possessions, and toss him from his bed. [The spirits would] . . . attack him while he prayed. . . . pelting him with projectiles. . . . Others took the form of wolves, bears, bulls, lions, 'poisonous' toads, and ravens. [They would] . . . approach him with hammers, clubs, pincers, burning splinters, and bloodthirsty hissing. In the dark they would rise from the floor or burst through cobbles.[22]

But there were better, more pleasant visionary experiences, experiences of bliss or of rescue from demons by other saints or divine figures such as Mary, the mother of Jesus. Visions that terrify commonly occur alongside earlier or later visions that are uplifting, even plunging the hermit into experiences of ecstasy. These have been long recorded in medieval Christian history as well as contemporary near-death experiences.[23] In fact, the matter of supernatural visions is a vexed one—not simply for their medical or psychiatric explanations or even because the debate about their causes continues to rage today—but primarily because even those who are dying agree on little about the prevalence and meaning of these visions. A raft of different people from different times and in circumstances of dire need and privation—from shamans, trapped coal miners, and castaways to hermits and recluses, and those dying from illness—have reported having visions of deceased human beings, supernatural figures, and divine vistas, both good and evil.[24] The psychologist Peter Suedfeld notes this about this diversity and its psychological consequences:

> It is also quite frequent among tribal cultures to incorporate a period of solitude in the life history of every individual, or at least every male. . . . Adolescents passing into adulthood would, after appropriate purifications and ceremonies, leave the community to wander alone in the desert, mountains, forest, or prairie. The particular kind of puberty rite has been reported in scores of cultures in North and South America, Africa, Asia, and Australia. The specific details (and goals) differ. In some groups, physical deprivation, pain, or fasting accompany the isolation procedure. The duration of aloneness may be only overnight or as long as several months. . . . But in all cases, the individual was expected to . . . and generally did . . . grow beyond his usual self to achieve some higher level of consciousness.
>
> Frequently the actual phenomena that were experienced bore close similarities to those reported by the castaways and prisoners discussed previously. A modern Western psychologist would have seen hallucinations,

illusions, delusions, inappropriate affects, disorganized cognitions, and bizarre behavior. But the tribe saw only the manifestations of the supernatural, or perhaps the more deeply natural. And since the events were not categorized as symptoms, no one realized that there was anything to worry about. As a consequence, no one worried, and no one was damaged.[25]

The conventional academic and clinical wisdom suggests that the attitude of the person in privation is important to the positive or negative quality of these experiences, but whatever their quality, such experiences do come nevertheless. They perhaps come to a minority of all those in these circumstances, but they come so regularly to those dying, and those in severe privation, that the importance of their appearance cannot fairly be ignored.

Although being and feeling depersonalized can be deliberately produced, or be an unintended consequence of forced social withdrawal and aloneness, we must also acknowledge that when such aloneness becomes severe, for example, late in the course of the dying journey, it can and does produce an involuntary psychological orientation toward the spiritual and supernatural. Or to use the alternative, more felicitous, phrase offered by Suedfeld — perhaps a more "deeply natural" chain of experiences. At this point the psychoanalytic commentators and the religious philosophers appear to momentarily converge. The psychoanalyst Melanie Klein claims that everyone's loneliness more or less springs from the infant's yearning for an "unattainable perfect internal state" that remains in our unconscious life throughout our adult years.[26] That pursuit of the perfect internal state may be what some Christian thinkers view as communing with the eternal or the divine. Thomas Merton argues in this way that "it is in silence, and not in commotion, in solitude and not in crowds, that God best likes to reveal Himself most intimately to men.[27]

And Paul Tillich observes: "It is the presence of the eternal upon the crowded roads of the temporal. It is the experience of being alone but not lonely, in view of the eternal presence which shines through the face of the Christ and which includes everybody and everything from which we are separated. In the poverty of solitude all riches are present. Let us dare to have solitude: to face the eternal, to find others, to see ourselves."[28]

Suedfeld argues that modern urbanites have been socialized to think of isolation or aloneness as a bad thing and so they react accordingly. He reflects the widely held view that if the environment is approached more positively the experiences encountered while alone will be neutral or even positive.[29] But this sociological assertion about the causal parameters of positive or negative experiences while alone seem rather tenuous and fragile when reviewed in the comparative light of involuntary castaways and voluntary hermits. After all, even though members of the first group commonly battle uncertainty and their own fears of death and abandonment, and the second group instead embraces isolation and seeks the face of God in constant prayer, both are pelted by a diversity of visionary experiences, both good and evil. The social, psychological, and spiritual consequences of aloneness while dying do not appear to have a ready set of easy explanations for the often perplexing, frightening, or ecstatic emotional experiences that dying people commonly experience. What is certain is that, to create a version of Merton's important words, "it is in silence, and not in commotion, in solitude and not in crowds," that something religious, spiritual, or eternal commonly occurs, and that is also true for the aloneness of dying. I will return to this theme at the end of the chapter, but in the meantime, it is also worth noting that other stories of dying alone present a less passive image. Some dying people have a more active, self-directed response to the prospect of their final social disconnection.

Other Responses to Dying Alone

As I showed in the first part of this chapter, dying people have difficulty receiving honest communication, empathy, and or understanding that truly reflects their situation early in their dying. For most of the twentieth century that would have been a common experience because for most of that century death was a taboo subject for public conversation (as were sex and madness during the same period). Furthermore, even late in the course of dying from an illness, for example, the dying were often isolated in hospitals or at home, away from other dying people. The only people they could discuss their dying with were people who did not have a vested emotional connection with the dying person—cleaners, medical students, or visitors who were strangers to the patient.[30] Today, however, it is possible for dying people to link up with each other over the Internet in an attempt to bypass the more disenfranchised connections with people they know. No longer content to speak to a good listener who isn't dying, dying people now use the Internet to connect with other dying people. A growing, if small, community of dying people are using personal web pages, blog pages, or social networking sites to compare notes and support each other. In these ways some modern dying people resist the aloneness and loneliness of dying, at least in the earlier stages of fatal illness.

Here Bill Howdle—a man dying from a brain tumor—creates a blog to discuss the experience and meets up with people who are dying from other conditions. Sometimes they are able to share their experiences of loneliness while dying and to gain both empathy and companionship for this special and elusive experience.

> I heard something one time that went something like this: "sometimes one of the loneliest places in the world can be when you are in a room full of people." If we think about that I think we can all understand that at least to some extent. Imagine you are invited to attend a huge party or celebration of some sort, hundreds of people will be there and if for some reason you have to go alone. Suppose you know no one at the party, how are you likely to feel? At times sheer numbers can be over whelming. Others may go out of their way to try to welcome you. You may realize all the others there are close friends with whom you have nothing in common. It can be a lonely place to be you can feel the odd man out. Having something in common is at least a good starting point in being able to strike up a conversation. Having something in common will allow that conversation with someone that has some knowledge or understanding of the subject you are discussing.
>
> What if you are dying? Who can you talk to then? Now, I do not mean in any way for this to slight or insult all the wonderful loving care-givers out there. What you are doing is fantastic, please keep it up. Your help and support means more than you will ever know.
>
> It is just if you are dying, that thought can play a prominent role in your mind. Some times you just need to talk about it. All those around you may be the most wonderful, loving caring people you can imagine. All trying to be as loving and as supportive as possible and yes I am sure you can talk to them. It is just no matter how hard they try they can't truly empathize which [sic] what you are going through. When it comes right down to it, what you are going through is a private, individual journey of life. But, if

you can talk to another person in your situation, they will at least have a better understanding and be able to relate to some of those thoughts and feelings that can haunt us.

I know that feeling of loneliness very well. I am so very blessed to have the blog here. I can express my thoughts and feelings and have received the loving support of so many. I will be eternally grateful.

I have recently put up a couple of posts about a lady I have been conversing with. Yes again, this is the lady with the hot air balloon ride and the cooking lessons. Her name is Meg and after some coaxing and encouraging she had [sic] joined us here on the blog.

She speaks so well of the loneliness of dying in a comment yesterday. Now I do know for a fact many don't always read the comments left and that is such a shame. In those comments is so much more than I can ever offer. Because of this I am posting Meg's comment as part of todays post.

Hi

I am the woman who has been in contact with Bill for the last eight months. I have been humbled by his generosity of spirit and time since I first came across his blog and I see that same generosity reflected in the comments left by those who visit his blog.

I wonder how many people who still inhabit the world of the living, rather than the living-dying, can truly appreciate what Bill and his blog has given to those of us in the last stages of our life. I doubt it—try mentioning death in casual conversation and then sit back and watch the ensuing fidgeting and discomfort and unease. I think the dying process is one of the best-kept secrets we have in our world. It saddens me for at a time when connections and relationships are so important it sometimes feels we suffer a "social" death long before our biological bodies draw their last breath.

I have spent my professional career working with people who are dying and my own biggest fear was never death itself but dying alone, not just physically alone but emotionally alone if people in my life were unable to accompany me into the void if their own fear of death overwhelmed them. I have no family and when my husband died I threw myself into my work as it was the only part of me I felt safe in. Now I find myself facing my own certain death and although I am physically alone, Bill and his blog had brought me a comfort that mere words on a page could never convey.

Sharing my dying process and engaging with Bill in his dying process has given me a sense that I matter and I will be missed, personally.

I am so grateful for the kindness and warmth that saturates the comments left in response to Bill posting my e-mail and will treasure each as a precious memory that will give me a longed for buffer during the journey that lays ahead. Who knows, perhaps I can develop some friendships here amongst like-minded people who "get" this whole dying thing from the inside.

With love to all who share Bill's blog and bask in his kindness, openness and warmth — truly one of the world's "good eggs."

Meg [31]

So although some dying people do find their experience of aloneness a desperate journey and feel like abandoned souls, an increasing number do not, choosing instead to reach out to people in similar circumstances. Furthermore, just as some people choose the secluded life of a hermit or recluse, so too some dying people choose to be alone.

Not all dying people find the situation or the feeling of aloneness difficult — or, if they do, they prefer it nevertheless. A small but significant group of older people, often with multiple life-threatening conditions, prefers to live with the risk of dying alone at home than be subject to greater professional surveillance and care. Many of these people are found dead at home some days, weeks, or even months after their death.[32] Often the media, local governments, or local communities see such deaths as failures of the health or social care system, but investigation usually later reveals people with a strong will for independence and autonomy. They resisted efforts by others to get the dying people care for their conditions under terms set by the health authorities, especially if those terms meant being away from their own homes.

A British report cites the case of a ninety-three-year-old woman who had a heart attack but lived alone at home.[33] She insisted on discharging herself from the hospital amid doctors' warnings that they could not properly care for her unless she stayed as an in-patient. She left anyway — and promptly died at home some days later. For some dying people, especially for some aging and dying people, dying alone does not necessarily equal dying lonely. In fact the prospect of dying alone is less of a problem for them than dying away from home or losing their independence to others.[34] Many members of voluntary euthanasia movements around the world identify with such sentiments.[35] Dying alone holds no fear, certainly less fear for them than the loss of independence, dignity, and personal control.

Aloneness and the Eternal

In the opening example of aloneness in this chapter, Victor Frankl recalls the dying of a young woman in a German World War II death camp. Despite being surrounded by others, and even others facing certain death, she reveals her personal experience of loneliness in the line, "This tree here is the only friend I have in my loneliness." But the tree is no ordinary tree from her point of view. This is a 'speaking tree,' a tree with a spiritual meaning others cannot see or hear, a tree that *means* something to her in her dying state. The tree conveys an important and enigmatic message. It says: "I am here—I am here—I am life, eternal life." This vignette of dying is emblematic of many people's experience of dying—the sense of isolation even among others; the turn toward self-examination and reflection so common during extended periods of aloneness (voluntary or not); and the re-orientation toward the spiritual, eternal, even supernatural.

Being alone, to use Aldous Huxley's phrase, often forcibly opens the "doors of perception."[36] This prompts many dying people to find personal or social insight (insight into interpersonal, institutional, or cultural relationships), encourages a kind of spiritual awakening, and often opens the way for supernatural visions and experiences. For example, in recent studies in Europe and Asia about 30 percent of dying people in different samples reported deathbed visions of deceased relatives or friends.[37] This conservative figure (because not all dying people share these occurrences with their carers, and these studies survey carers' perceptions of the dying) means that approximately one in three dying people are having unusual mystical, paranormal, or "deeply natural" experiences near death that may be attributed to their isolated social or psychological state. As the examples of dying explorers, castaways, death camp inmates, hermits and recluses, as well as those dying from cancer, show, the experience of aloneness may prompt forms of transformation in dying people, whether they like it or not, whether they expect it or not, whether they seek this or not.

In the end, as the horizons of the outer world begin to recede, at first socially, then in totality, the lifelong taken-for-granted presence of the inner self and its companions begins to sound louder. From within the self of the dying person can emerge legions of which the self has no knowledge. This is what the mystics and the hermits have consciously sought for millennia, but it is also often true, sometimes surprisingly true, that when those forced into aloneness disconnect, they do so only to learn of a new connection. The inner life no longer simply provides a running commentary and reflection on the outer world but soon becomes the world itself, slowly or suddenly becoming its own all-consuming reality. The rhythm of the heartbeat is soon submerged by the rhythm of the increasingly louder music of the spirit. In the poetic words of Victor Hernandez Cruz:

it's been so long
speaking to people
who think it all
too complex
stupidity in their eyes
&
it's been so long
so far from the truth
so far from the roof
to talk to
or a hand to touch
or anything to really
love
it's been so long
talking to myself
alone
in the night
listening to a music
that is me.[38]

11

Transformation—Change, Change, Change

"Who are you?" said the Caterpillar.

This was not an encouraging opening for a conversation. Alice replied, rather shyly, "I—I hardly know, Sir, just at present—at least I know who I was when I got up this morning, but I think I must have changed several times since then."

"What do you mean by that?" said the Caterpillar, sternly. "Explain yourself!"

"I can't explain *myself*, I'm afraid, Sir," said Alice, "because I'm not myself, you see."

"I don't see," said the Caterpillar.

—Lewis Carroll, *Alice's Adventures in Wonderland*

Most people think of dying as a descent, even a descent into hell. If you have read this far, you will have realized this is far from what happens. From an anthropological perspective, it is important to stress that what carers often see of the outward expressions of dying—as family, health professionals, or coworkers and friends—does not commonly reflect the inner life of the dying person. More often than not, the two realities are substantially different from one another and reflect different perceptions, experiences, and internal realities. As I have shown, dying people some years, months, or days from their death have a rich and diverse set of experiences that are both positive and negative, ever changing, and characterized by frequent moments of despair, even terror, but also elation and love.

The insider view of suffering is frequently and surprisingly different from what others observe. It is intricately complex. This often difficult-to-discern aspect of the inner life of the dying person continues to the last point in life, to death itself. Here too, in the last minutes and seconds of life, dying people can experience substantial change, even transformation of their lives, that can take them to places of peace and rejuvenation, alongside or even beyond their commonly observed difficult and frightening experiences.

Although it is always true that responses to life and death vary widely from person to person, the sociological truth is that—more often than not—definite positive patterns tend to emerge and compete alongside the obvious negative experiences. Palliative and hospice care narratives commonly record both peaceful and difficult deaths. As the widow of one palliative care patient reported about the death of her husband: "He was conscious of everything up to a few minutes before he died. He was happy in his room and in his bed. He knew that we were there and were helping him. I was happy for him because he had his daughter and son with him. He died peacefully. He didn't appear to be suffering. I'm at peace with the fact that he stayed at home. And I think, for him, absolutely, it was wonderful. He didn't have much pain. He died in his room, with all his pictures."[1]

On the other hand, the same book from which the last account is taken reports:

> The following morning a hospice nurse found Ms Cook "wildly anxious." Ms Cook was refusing to be discharged from the hospital, crying out that she was afraid to die. When Keisha arrived to pick her up, she found her sister rolling feverishly in her bed. She had lost control over her urine, and defecated involuntarily. Frightened and agitated, Ms Cook asked Keisha to hold her hand. She looked like she was struggling to breathe. "Can't you make this stop?" she asked Keisha in a panic. Keisha took hold of her sister's hand and tried to calm her. Gently, she encouraged her to close her eyes and rest. As Keisha started to rub her leg, Shamira stopped moving. A few minutes later, Keisha realized that she was dead.[2]

Such contrasting experiences occur in the final moments of other forms of dying, too. For example, the academic Robert Johnson reports: "Beyond the expected physical indignities and pain, the death sentence calls for a trial by ordeal, in which the inmate ideally completes his last walk under his own power and faces his sentence with some poise and composure. Most prisoners, in fact, walk to the electric chair with surprising calm. Some fall apart during their last walk, and must be dragged kicking and screaming to their deaths. But 'the rule,' as attested to by many observers, 'is for the condemned to walk toward death passively, in a sort of dreary despondency,' as though resigned to their fate."[3]

In 2004 Bechor Aminoff and Abraham Adunsky conducted a medical study of seventy-one inpatients in the geriatric department of a large American hospital.[4] They found that 70 percent of these patients did not die calm and 15 percent were screaming from the severity of their suffering. Every experienced hospice physician and nurse is also familiar with at least one case of a dying person whose last physical act was to vomit bile or blood while passing out for the final time — an extremely distressing last memory for family and other carers. Without doubt, then, the care (or uncaring) environment, the final attitude of the individual in the last days and hours of dying, and the sometimes uncontrollable intrusiveness of certain physical symptoms during dying and death play a pivotal role in the direction of any psychological and spiritual transformation, both experienced and observed. However, several crucial and overriding factors also play a role in the widespread experience of transformation while dying.

Above all, we must remember that positive transformations that see dying people rejuvenate their perceptions of the world and others often occur well before the final weeks and days of life. We often think of *dying* as a word that refers to the final days and therefore overlook transformations that have occurred earlier in dying people. Sometimes the dying do not share these positive experiences and perceptions with carers or onlookers for a variety of reasons: that their views will be received as silly or overly sentimental or maudlin; some may fear that some of their new perceptions and experiences might not be believed; some dying people might view these changes as a gift and keep them private.

Second, in the thirty years I have worked with dying people and alongside those who care for them in palliative care, my impression (and the impression of most of these professional carers) is that most people die without terrible drama and distress. Dying from serious illness means it is not always possible to die a perfectly peaceful death without some discomfort. However, the discomfort that many dying people experience in serious illness tends not to overtake or overshadow positive, intimate last moments and exchanges for those who remain conscious to very near their end. Here, at this late stage, many dying are seen to experience positive alterations to their inner life and outer demeanor. Other dying people are simply not conscious at the end and so do not have dramatic psychological or spiritual changes that are observable to others.

Third, many people who do suffer terribly often do not suffer so terribly in the last hours or minutes before they die. A frequent observation of physicians such as Kübler-Ross or Hinton is that people do not commonly experience a "crisis of distress" in their final moments. Furthermore, two studies reported have unusually high prevalence figures, of comforting deathbed visions (18 percent) and of near-death experiences(33 percent).[5] These prevalence figures must be conservative because they do not and cannot report those people who have these experiences but die before they can share them with anyone. Clearly, dying people are pushed and pulled toward their physical and psychological limits — by their own acute or prolonged suffering, by their own bouts of despair and loss, by the love of those who care for them, by the vast isolation and loneliness of simply dying, so much so that their inner life is frequently able, under these extraordinary circumstances, to touch something that the rest of us believe is untouchable. In this way, at least psychologically, symbolically, and spiritually, if you push and swing us hard enough, our sense of self may often reach new and previously unimagined heights and turns. From those unexpected swells, tides, and eddies in our last experiences may come other, equally unexpected, experience. Such graces, new vistas, or personal insights are rarely observable to onlookers, who can only hear the last clatters and turns of the dying body before them. For in the matter of watching others die, it is wise to remember that, as commonly happens in the rest of life, appearances often deceive.

Before going further I will briefly clarify what I mean by the term *transformation*. Transformation is the process of becoming something else while fundamentally remaining the same. In mathematics, for example, transformation describes changing the form without changing the underlying value — the substitution of one geometric figure for another of equal magnitude.[6] The term is widely used to refer to a change in character, form, and even function, but throughout the change the basic nature remains. Oxygen may be a gas but can become liquid. Voltage may change but remain electricity. Children grow up, change, and become adults but remain fundamentally as we knew them. Transformation that is radical and total is usually obliterating or annihilating. This is not mere shape or character changing but outright destruction and rebirth.

In this chapter I am not referring to such a radical change to the inner life of dying people but rather to the shift and alteration of perception and experience that, whatever the changes experienced, maintain the usual presence and integrity of the person at the center of the new experience. John Smith as the person we know remains, but he is now different. He sees things differently; he has become something more than he was. He has something new inside him and with the new eyes sees more in the world than he once did. John Smith is now a transformed man. As the Portuguese poet Fernando Pessoa so beautifully expressed this:

> The startling reality of things
> Is my discovery every single day.
> Every thing is what it is,
> And it's hard to explain to anyone how much this delights me
> And suffices me.
> To be whole, it is enough simply to exist.[7]

Transformations in Early Dying

Transformations can occur early in the dying experience. Weeks and months before death occurs, some dying people already are noticing the world is different for them. They see the world afresh; their perceptions are rejuvenated; they start to notice things they did not see before in their environment. These dying people's altered perceptions provide them a new appreciation of life and what it is offering them day to day. Helen and Faith, cancer patients with advanced disease, spoke of their transformations in the following ways:

HELEN: I might not be here next month or in 2 months time or on my next birthday. You then become much more aware of people, your beloved people around you. You know, my little, my little granddaughter . . . I keep on hugging and kissing her because I don't know how long I will be able to do that. And your senses are sharpened. Suddenly pink roses are much pinker than they used to be, and the blue sky is bluer than it used to be. And you just observe things in a different way. Most of us take things for granted — that's human nature, you know?

. . .

FAITH: Everything is in focus. Uh, I call it crystal. What this crystal means, it's like after snow, on a real cold night when there's fog in the air and every tree branch is covered with ice the next morning, and the sun shines, and it's just a different world — beautiful. That is as close as I could come to describing crystal. My world is in focus. It's . . . crystal-ized. It is that this moment with Kristin [the researcher conducting the interview] is of an extreme value to me, and it is a high point in my life, and it is just enjoy the moment. Don't worry about the next one. . . . It is an enjoyment. Every moment has meaning to me.[8]

The Reverend Dr. Giles Fraser, a priest of the Church of England, remembers his grandmother in a BBC broadcast and reflects on the transformation he saw in her after her diagnosis of dementia:

Much of her life she had suffered from a crushing sense of social inferiority. With Alzheimer's disease came an unforeseen release. . . . During this time her characteristic frown slipped into a grin. And so it seems to me that right at the end of her difficult life, as she potted about helping fellow residents and experimenting with her wardrobe, she gave some indication of the person she might have been had she found earlier release from her demons. . . . Perhaps that's what a rightful mind looks like. When all our plans and plotting, all our resentments and knotted histories have become foggy and indistinct, perhaps then we are released to become something like the sort of person that God has always wanted us to be.[9]

An eighty-two-year-old former senior academic reflects about his dying from a spreading prostate cancer:

I'm learning, and it's just nourishing. For me, to learn is almost an appetite, and that appetite is being met. It's wonderful. I'm learning to die. It seems that, under certain circumstances, there's room for growth, which

I never expected. You know, I used to think dying was like going downhill and into the bottom of a cone. It's not that at all. I feel a new dimension in me, which I will tell you, serves me. I'm very curious to know for myself how I'll respond to a worsening condition. If tomorrow the metastases do something, I really think I would take it with equanimity.

This voyage is just expanding onto horizons that I've not quite made out. It's all very affirmative, very freeing. I'm almost enjoying studying it. Who would think that a dying person is capable of making it worthwhile for others to nurture him? What is a dying person capable of? There is something worthwhile in this. It means that not so much will have been lost. It will have made life a success. Not only my life, but it confirms that human life can be very good, even in very dire circumstances.

The interviewer-author goes on to observe that this man "entered a hospice unit where he experienced a slow decline in his health, but he remained conscious until the end — writing, reading, and talking about dying."[10]

These horizons that Robert has "not quite made out" suggest more to life than his dying would have originally have suggested to him. When he speaks about dying as "going downhill" and "going down into the bottom of a cone," he speaks not only for his own former view but for that of many readers of this book, I suspect. Rather unbelievably, Robert is expecting more, not less, from his future, from his dying life. He is curious to see what lies just over those horizons of his new experience. For some readers his enthusiasm might elicit cynicism or dismay, but (1) he is not alone or atypical of those experiencing dying this way, and (2) these transformative experiences seem to keep occurring later and later in the course of the dying experience. The poet Stephen Crane describes the counterintuitive nature of pursuing a horizon that few except those nearing death can see:

I saw a man pursuing the horizon;
Round and round they sped.
I was disturbed at this;
I accosted the man.
"It is futile," I said,
"You can never" — "You lie," he cried,
And ran on.[11]

The perceptual fact is that many dying people are themselves amazed at how the world around them seems so different and how their inner life seems so in the throes of transformation that ever newer, more novel, ever strange, and foreign experiences seem not only to be possible but even very likely to them. Many dying people at the center of these new perceptions and changes come to expect more alterations to their inner realities and experiences. As the writer Philip Toynbee attempts to explain about his own iterative transformations while dying from cancer: "Looking up at the window through the lower halves of my spectacles I see not much more than a blur of green, with vague recessions here and there. Pushing the spectacles down on my nose a marvelous clarity is provided, and many details of perspective. Imagine another and equivalent clarification, and then another, and another. . . . Working toward the Beatific Vision."[12]

Transformations in Late Dying

John Hinton, the physician and pioneer researcher of the dying, once made the following observation about the final moments of death. Much of what he said in this 1967 statement remains true today, at least in medical terms: "The moment of death is not often a crisis of distress for the dying person. For most, the suffering is over a while before they die. Already some of the living functions have failed and full consciousness usually goes early. Before the last moments of life there comes a quieter phase of surrender, the body appears to abdicate peacefully, no longer attempting to survive. Life then slips away so that few are aware of the final advent of their own death."[13]

This observation also remains true for many terminally ill patients even without major medical support. In the Republic of Moldova, for example, I recently conducted a study of family observations of the dying process in relatives under their care.[14] Despite much physical and emotional suffering wrought by the ravages of advanced disease with little medical support and palliation, most dying was reported to be peaceful in the last hour or minutes of life.

However, Hinton's assertions that "full consciousness usually goes early" may be both an oversimplification and premature in its conclusion. A more modest and precise observation would be to say that communication with others usually goes early. The terminally ill often lose (observable) conscious-ness as a result of the advance of the disease, but this does not necessarily mean that (unobservable) conscious thought and emotional processes have ceased. Evidence of conscious processes and responses have been detected and documented in coma patients who appear to everyone as insensible to external stimuli.[15] Moreover, significant numbers of revived patients—from accidents, surgical unconsciousness, and from comatose or clinical states of death—have subsequently reported their conscious experiences of thought and feeling while in these states.[16] In these contexts it may well be that "few are aware of the final advent of their own death," but just as surely—from the empirical evidence in contemporary studies of those near death—many oth-ers are actually aware of their own death. These studies suggest and describe transformative psychological, social, and spiritual experiences that occur, for some people at least, even into the first few minutes after a medical judgment of death has been pronounced.

Often in late dying, people might report or simply experience that their perceptions of the world have altered in rather radical ways. For one thing, they could now see their dead. These were transformative experiences in two senses. First, even those people who were dying and who reported sights and conversations with their dead would often acknowledge that these were unprecedented experiences and perceptions for them. Their direct personal experience of the world, and their expectations about what to expect from the usual world of experience, had changed dramatically.

Second, the experience of seeing, and often conversing with, dead friends and relatives was itself transforming. The overwhelming majority of people who report such experiences say they are comforting, reassuring, and posi-tive. These experiences provide company and support in circumstances that are increasingly isolating for those who are dying from advanced terminal illnesses. The prevalence of deathbed visions is estimated to occur to about a third of all dying people, especially in developing countries.[17] This preva-lence is much lower in industrialized nations where the use of opiates is higher and seems to suppress these type of visions.[18] Typical family observa-tions of these visions include:

> She had visions very often. She would be sitting at the table and at one
> point she would say, "can you not see that I have guests, lay the table to

welcome the guests . . . here is my mother, right beside me." Then she would talk to someone who was not there. This sort of thing happened very often.

. . .

She had visions too. She would lie in bed, look into a corner of the room where the icon was hung, and talk to those who had died. If I asked her who she was talking to, she would say, "What, can't you see them sitting there, calling me?"

. . .

He had visions. He said there was a man who stayed with him and talked to him all the time.

. . .

I don't know if she had visions but she would often be in a trance when she spoke to my father, who was dead, or with my mother [likewise, she had been dead for many years], and she would also speak to a child.

. . .

Yes, he had visions. He would look out the window and call people who were already dead to come to him inside the house. He would tell me he could see them looking at him. He saw several dead people. He practically listed all our neighbors and relatives who had long died.[19]

These kinds of personal experiences at the deathbed appear to be quite old, are cross-cultural, and are not always associated with the presence of medications such as painkillers or sedatives. Furthermore, unlike hallucinations and delusions, their imagery and emotional content are remarkably consistent. In other words, deathbed visions do not enjoy a wide variety of images and do not usually provoke distress or fear in those who perceive them. Such visions are also not predicted by diagnosis, religion, ethnicity, class, gender, or age. Compare the following two experiences of young children dying in two quite different countries and more than eighty years apart. The first case describes the deathbed vision of Anita, a case I collected with medical colleagues in India.

> The mother of 8 year-old "Anita" recounts the following story. Anita was dying from AIDS but had no medical history of opioid or other pain killer use. In the week leading up to her death, her prescribed pharmacotherapy consisted of some anti-emetics, antibiotics, and antivirals but most of these were refused by the child during this period. On the day that she died, Anita announced to her mother, in a very matter of fact way, that her late grandmother had come to sit with her. (Her grandmother had died four months previously). The grandmother would sit beside her and chat, occasionally calling for her. "Amma" (Mamma), she had said, "don't hug or hold me anymore; don't put me on your lap because it's time for me to go, so don't do any of these things for me. I need to go now." And later that day she died.[20]

The physics professor William Barrett describes a similar incident in a schoolchild of unspecified age more than eighty years earlier in the United States: Barrett retells a childhood recollection by a Dr. E. H. Pratt of Chicago about the day his sister died:

> She knew she was passing away, and was telling our mother how to dispose of her little personal belongings among her close friends and playmates, when she suddenly raised her eyes as though gazing at the ceiling toward the farther side of the room, and after looking steadily and apparently listening for a short time, slightly bowed her head, and said, "Yes, Grandma, I am coming, only wait just a little while, please." Our father asked her, "Hattie, do you see your Grandma?" Seemingly surprised at the question she promptly answered, "Yes, Papa, can't you see her? She is right there waiting for me." At the same time she pointed to the ceiling in the direction in which she had been gazing. Again, addressing the vision she evidently had of her grandmother she scowled a little impatiently and said, "Yes, Grandma, I'm coming, but wait a minute, please." She then turned once more to her mother, and finished telling her what of her personal

treasures to give to different ones of her acquaintances. At last, giving her attention once more to her Grandma, who was apparently urging her to come at once, she bade each of us good-bye. Her voice was very feeble and faint, but the look in her eyes as she glanced briefly at each of us was as lifelike and as intelligent as it could be. She then fixed her eyes steadily on her vision but so faintly that we could just catch her words, said, "Yes, Grandma, I'm coming now." Then without a struggle or evidence of pain of any kind she gazed steadily in the direction she had pointed out to us where she saw her Grandma, until the absence of oxygen in her blood stream, because respiration had ceased, left her hands and face all covered with the pallor of lifeless flesh.[21]

The prevalence of deathbed visions is dramatically lower in societies where heavy drug administration is routine in the care of dying. In developing countries such as India or the Republic of Moldova, where we have recent data on deathbed visions, we tend to see peaceful and transformative deaths, with the dying accompanied by what they believe are their deceased friends and relatives. With more widespread terminal sedation practices and the use of opiates for dying people, some wonder whether these late experiences in dying are being subdued under our greater modern anxiety about the amelioration of any discomfort near death. As early as 1980 Lewis Thomas, then president of the Memorial Sloan-Kettering Cancer Center in New York, had occasion to reflect and wonder about the increasing so-called beneficent role of technological interventions for the dying:

> I do not know what we are doing to the first-hand experience of dying itself with technology, but I suspect we may often be interfering with an important process. The awareness of dying can be an extraordinary sensation, described from time to time as a feeling of exaltation. In the days when tuberculosis was the commonest disease, causing death after a prolonged, exhausting illness, doctors could tell when death was near by a remarkable change in the patient's attitude. It was called "*spes phthisica,*" and it was marked by a sense of tranquility and great peace, and something like pleasure.[22]

Yet transformative spiritual experiences still seem to occur among the dying—in countries without such heavy pharmacotherapy involvement at the end of life, at homes, even in residential care facilities where dying comes under less surveillance and control. Furthermore, studies of near-death experiences also indicate that those dying from trauma have experiences similar to those who die slowly from serious illness under hospice or home care.

Transformations at Death

A long tradition of medical, psychological, religious studies, historical, and parapsychological work has examined an equally long body of empirical cases of people's accounts of revival from states of clinical death.[23] The most impressive thing about such cases is their overall consistency. If these experiences are dreams or hallucinations, a lot of people are having the same dream or hallucination—a feature not usual for either. The cases are usually derived from people who have experienced cardiac arrest as a consequence of other illnesses or major injuries from trauma.

For example, a person with end-stage liver disease spoke about the life-changing effects of nearly dying during an acute episode of her illness: "I had for me what was a deeply religious, religious is the wrong word, deeply spiritual thing happen to me before I ever got to the hospital, in the process of actually dying before anyone got to me. I feel very, very lucky because God gave me a chance to set things right. . . . So anything that happens now . . . if I go tomorrow, it's really okay."[24]

Although the debate rages in many different academic fields about the cause of such experiences under fatal medical circumstances—because, apart from anything else, reason the many, there shouldn't be any experiences under these conditions (i.e., clinical death)—few people now contest that the experiences are real and do exist, as the people who recall them assert. In these experiences dying people who are later resuscitated recall experiences of leaving their body as a "spirit-like" person and being able to look back at their physical body and the resuscitation attempts on it. They will often report being drawn into a dark but peaceful place. They might meet a being of light or appear in a place of great light. Sometimes they will report meeting deceased friends and relatives or even seeing supernatural vistas, such as a countryside of uncanny beauty or a beautiful and luminescent city in the distance.

Most reports describe sensations of great peace and calm following earlier experiences of prolonged pain, tiredness, or other physical suffering. The transition to feelings of peace, calm, and security is dramatic. Their new state of consciousness is described as nothing short of transforming. Raymond Moody, a former academic philosopher who became a doctor, described some early examples of these phenomena, which have subsequently been reported over the years with little change or variation.

> I had heart failure and clinically died. . . . All this time I was perfectly conscious of everything that was going on. I heard the heart monitor go off. I saw the nurse come into the room and dial the telephone, and the doctors, nurses, and attendants come in.
>
> . . . . And I rose up and I was a few feet up looking down at my body. There I was, with people working on me. I had no fear. No pain. Just peace. After just probably a second or two, I seemed to turn over and go up. It was dark — you could call it a hole or tunnel — and there was this bright light. It got brighter and brighter. And I seemed to go through it.
>
> All of a sudden I was just somewhere else. There was a gold-looking light, everywhere . . . beautiful. . . . There was music. And I seemed to be in a countryside with streams, grass, and trees, mountains. But when I looked around — if you want to put it that way — they were not trees and things like we know them to be. The strangest thing to me about it was there were people there. Not in any kind of form or body as we know it; they were just there.
>
> There was a sense of perfect peace and contentment; love. It was like I was part of it. That experience could have lasted the whole night or just a second . . . I don't know.[25]

Paul Swain, an Australian film and television camera operator and producer, recalls how in the 1970s he was accidently electrocuted while disassembling some lighting in a studio. After grabbing a live light with both hands, he received a boosted 320-volt shock of alternating current that, because of his electrocuted contracting muscles, he was not able to let go of. During those few minutes of constant electrocution he fell back and lay on the studio floor with the current continuing to surge throughout his body. He said he initially remained able to think and feel as he usually did.

Then, within that few seconds, this peace, this incredible calm came over me. . . . I then found that I was no longer inside myself under the light but I was, in fact, quite high in the room looking down at myself and I could see my whole body laid out. I could see the light across my chest and I could see my own end. I could see it all happening. . . . Then I saw this . . . the only way I can describe it is that I saw a doorway. It was like a doorway and the door was slightly ajar. There was this brilliant light, this very intense light, coming through the doorway and I drifted towards it. When I looked at that light my mind, whatever my conscious mind was, was saying to me that to go through the doorway would be beautiful, absolutely beautiful. At the same time I had this awareness that to go through the door would mean death, that I would die and I would have no return. . . .

I moved toward the door and I came into the light and it hit me all over. I stood in the light, but I didn't go through the door. While I stood in the light, for that split second or few seconds or few minutes, whatever it was in time, I had this feeling of just total understanding. It was just being part of that universal spirit, part of what you can only describe as being all. Everything. You know — positive and negative — and it was the most inspiring and, I guess, the greatest single experience I've ever had in my life. It was just incredible.[26]

A Reality Check: What Should I Believe?

The philosophical, parapsychological, and medical literature engages in a long and complex debate about the nature of deathbed visions and near-death experiences. Furthermore, so-called skeptic organizations actively contribute to these debates — organizations of rational humanists who have a vested interest in believing and advocating to the rest of the world that what is not observable or measurable doesn't exist. Finally, members of New Age and spiritualist movements — both formal and informal — believe that these experiences are evidence for an afterlife, a personal life beyond death. Clearly, many of you will be asking yourselves what to believe about the accounts I have detailed in this chapter, most especially in those sections dealing with mystical transformative experiences such as deathbed visions and near-death experiences. Just so that we are all on the same page, that both writer and reader understand each other clearly, let me point out some basic information about these experiences and my avowed purpose in presenting them here.

First, despite popular and academic beliefs to the contrary, the matter of the ultimate meaning of these experiences is not settled. Neither in philosophical circles, parapsychological circles, nor medical commentary is this matter safely concluded. Not even close. Some readers may be familiar with the view that such near-death and deathbed experiences might result from the side effects of oxygen deprivation in the dying brain. Often this explanation is given with such technical flourish and confidence that readers can be forgiven if they are quickly convinced and taken in by such reductionism.[27]

However, we have an abundance of cases in which all the important features of these visions and experiences have happened to people who are perfectly conscious and not near death—reports of castaways, trapped miners, bereaved people, or those undergoing shamanic initiations. Also, even if the oxygen deprivation explanation were true, it would not solve the greater philosophical and religious question about the relationship of mind to brain. If you believe that mind is the brain, then oxygen deprivation causes hallucinations, and that is that—because nothing except the physical, biological realities exists. If, however, you believe that the mind expresses itself through a brain, and that damage to the brain may trigger the release or altered perception of the mind, then oxygen deprivation is merely a trigger for mystical experiences that go beyond the mere biological. This is an old philosophical chestnut—does the radio play the music, or is the radio a mere conveyor of it? This question has no empirical resolution, simply because these different viewpoints reflect assumptions or principles first and to them are added fortifying evidence and arguments. No matter what you believe, the old saying, that things may not be what they seem, holds true.

Also the sheer insistence and conviction that skeptics, humanists, rationalists, or materialists display in regard to the mystical is equaled only by the calm and equally strong conviction of those who report these experiences—many of whom are from the ranks of science and medicine themselves. I readily confess that believing an incredible, even fantastic, story that has little or no precedent in one's everyday experience is difficult. This is an understandable reaction from anyone, let alone from those who have an investment in a worldview limited by the senses and an overconfident attitude toward what science can tell us about life. Caution, if not skepticism, is both an understandable and a safe approach. After all, anyone with Internet access today has a sound and day-to-day understanding of scam, deception, and the vulnerability of the credulous.

Yes, some people peddle snake oil. We are mostly right to be cautious. It is, however, also true that few explanations about the world—historical, sociological, and scientific—are black and white, that is, obvious and plainly correct or incorrect. Most people, and most academics and clinicians, use their own experiences to weigh the evidence before them. The research into deathbed visions and near-death experiences is controversial, peppered with vested interests not always disclosed and dogged by insufficient data and balanced reflection. But the field is new. Each of us will need to decide what we are seeing, feeling, and meeting when faced with the transformations that dying can bring. This is only partly an academic exercise; it will ultimately also be a very personal task. Each of us will need to make our own judgments when we are confronted by these experiences, or when we observe these experiences happening to those we love who are dying. We are not well served by prejudgment without actual experience (commonly called prejudice), and we are not well served by ignoring the nuances of complex experiences, the multiple perspectives that all experiences tend to generate, and the importance of their recognition and careful handling for future scientific work and personal insight. For the purposes of this chapter, it is enough to acknowledge that deeply transformative experiences come to the dying, and our task here is to recognize and appreciate the important features and benefits of these experiences, however they may be explained in the future.

In short, the salient observation one is compelled to make is that all these experiences are transformative for those who undergo them. No one anywhere is really disputing their perceived reality by dying people. It matters not a jot whether deathbed visions are hallucinations or something else. That most dying people believe their visions are real, or reflect another, alternative reality, is the only important point to take away from this chapter and the only point I wish to defend and support. What I am saying here is that deathbed visions and near-death experiences suggest—empirically, reliably, and convincingly—that transformative psychological and spiritual experiences occur widely to people while dying, and they occur quite late in the course of the dying journey.

No matter what we may eventually discover about the ultimate biological causes of such events and experiences, these visions do provide a strong, historically consistent, and culturally widespread source of personally transforming experiences that go to the heart of personal hope, companionship, and transcendence of suffering. These experiences are both personally important and a rather common feature of the dying experience. They should be taken together with the less perceptually dramatic changes, documented earlier, that cause people who know they will soon die to see the world in fresh ways.

Mystical experiences while dying seem to be related to these earlier, more commonplace personal experiences of transformation. All are important to note because all underline something commonly overlooked: transformative experiences often come unbidden to the dying. No matter your usual professional or personal values, no matter how unshakable your usual views about how the world works, and will always work, extraordinary things can and do commonly occur while dying. It can begin with a slight alteration to the way people appreciate small human acts, or the trees outside the bedroom window, but it can escalate and intrude forcibly to include surprising visitors and vistas from an incredible, even unbelievable, place. Belief in these things seems beside the point—for the experiencer or the academic observer. The important point is to acknowledge that they occur and that they seem to inevitably bring to many of the dying benefits that are often positive and transformative. Participating in debates about what is *really* real in life and what is not is beyond the purposes of this book. The transformative dimension, and the usually positive aspect of that dimension, is the most important theme to note in this rather common aspect of the inner life of the dying person. In this way, it is the journey as experienced in the here and now and not what happens later that mostly matters to people who are dying. If any of these transformative experiences do ultimately unfold into a personal afterlife for dying people, those dying people know soon enough. Only those of us who remain behind are left to grope in the dark, left to our theories, guessing and wondering in the absence of experience about the eventual whereabouts of all who have gone before us.

Transformation in Dying—and Its Consequences

Reviewing the different examples of transformation that seem to commonly occur to dying people makes it possible to discern a core pattern to their development. Although these might overlap with transformative religious experiences in general, certain features of the personal experience of transformation for dying people have a unique pattern of psychology. Clearly, not everyone who is dying seeks or receives a fresh view of life and its newly held wonders in the months, weeks, or days leading up to death. But just as clearly many do. More empirical research needs to be done on the potential psychological and social precursors and prevalence of such alterations in perceptions. However, failure to experience alterations in perceptions of life during months or weeks before death does not mean dying people would not have such experiences on or near their final deathbed circumstances. Some people — with or without witnesses, with or without personal disclosures at the time — may experience a major shift in their perceptions that enables them to see, sense, or feel events or experiences without precedent.

Furthermore, we know from countless cases of near-death experiences that such transformative experiences might occur during the death process itself — whatever organic theories a reader might want to entertain about their source. As the little prince reminded the lone aviator Antoine de Saint-Exupéry while he was stranded in the desert after his plane crash: "The thing that is important is the thing that is not seen."[28]

In fact transformative experiences are common to dying, and they may occur in different ways at different points in the dying process. At this stage of the contemporary research into these things, we know little about what influences the why, how, and when. The social process, however, appears to evolve something like this:

1. Foreign circumstances demand one's attention, creating new receptivity. A background of suffering, isolation, personal review, and often-radical changes to one's usual physical or social environment is preparatory to transformation. This leads to parallel changes in identity, leading to the first and most fundamental observation about transformation: one leaves one's former self to become a new self or to integrate a new sense of self. A prolonged ordeal is especially likely to give one a new sense of limits and strengths. These self-realizations, and the new social information about others, form a new identity while a person endures the new reality of dying. The world is inexorably altered. There is no turning back, nor is there any, or rarely any, biographical precedent for what is happening to the self. Without this sense of jarring, crisis, or erosion of the old life and self, a new perspective on what

is happening rarely takes place. In other words, people must experience some sense of disorientation for some reorientation to take place.

2. New experiences and perceptions come unbidden. Most people's lives in most cultures follow a social script provided by the dominant institutions of their culture. However, most of the time, for most people, the script of school, work, family, health, or religion does not come with major surprises, shocks, or trauma. When the unexpected does happen, people learn something and acquire new perceptions. The more severe the change, the more serious the learning and subsequent experience, assuming they survive such change at all. In the case of illness, most people expect to recover or simply to go on with chronic illness. The first surprise is when they understand that they will die from the illness. The second is the realization that they will die soon. The final disorientation often comes when people realize just how difficult and traumatic their inner struggle can be, let alone any of the social and medical difficulties they might experience. The same is true for those who commit crimes that lead them to death row, those who suddenly and unjustly find themselves interred in a death camp, and those who are castaway or marooned, and so on.

3. A shift in self occurs. The shift in psychological perspective is commonly provoked by a parallel shift in the physical and social location of the dying person. The more dramatic or disconcerting the shift or the greater the physical or social distance between the person's current location and the new one, the more likely the person is to experience a shift in perception, thinking, or feeling. Every traveler, explorer, or shaman knows this principle in elementary form. Obviously, an actual physical or social shift will be accompanied by new experiences, for that is what happens in all movement. But the person's perception of events and those experiences also shift, more subtly, perhaps less consciously experienced at first. New experiences have a way of altering how we perceive them as we experience them — stimulating old memories and feelings, not always consciously, but also suggesting and creating new desires or fears at the same time. The transformative dimension of dying experiences is just this kind of process but in more dramatic, sustained, and isolating form.

4. The self experiences the shift — often while alone. Prolonged suffering, prolonged personal review, and a growing sense of isolation tend to give primacy to the inner world of self. This does not necessarily mean that the outer

world of experience becomes less dominant or important but rather that the inner world of memory, reflection, personal soliloquy, and self-observation grows in significance. The inner world of memories, dreams, and reflections takes its place alongside, even rivaling, the world of external experience. But this new relationship between the inner and outer worlds alters both.

People see the world freshly again, often in a surprisingly novel frame. They view anew things they have taken for granted. They notice things they never noticed before. They are receptive to new content in the world and have a new interpretation or appreciation of vistas new and old. These interpretations and new observations can be as surprising to people experiencing them as they nearly always are to people who are told about them. In this way, any new content or the new meanings and interpretations of old content can seem foreign to the person's old audiences and networks. Regular companions are often unable to genuinely share the new experience or the new perceptions. It is not simply the so-called mystical experiences that create barriers to sharing but also equally and problematically the more banal and worldly social, psychological, and physical experiences, whatever their different sources and content.

In other words, dying moves individuals to such a new existential location that the view from there is usually almost impossible to share—unless with someone who is also there. Perhaps this is the fundamental meaning of the term *transcendence*. Dying people's altered inner life often enables them to go beyond the ridges and reaches of everyday experience to see or understand something beyond those appearances—and to receive by virtue of these insights the promise of more. As Antoine de Saint-Exupéry reflected from his downed plane in a Libyan desert, with no hope of rescue for days:

> For the first time I understood the cigarette and glass of rum that are handed to the criminal about to be executed. I used to think that for a man to accept these wretched gifts at the foot of the gallows was beneath human dignity. Now I was learning that he took pleasure from them. People thought him courageous when he smiled as he smoked or drank. I knew now that he smiled because the taste gave him pleasure. *People could not see that his perspective had changed,* and that for him the last hour of his life was a life in itself.[29]

5. The self opens to the promise of yet more such experiences. The gradual new reflections and perceptions of human acts, or of trees, colors, the sky, or a last cigarette, open people up to the possibility, indeed even the expectation, that their views and experiences might continue to change. They might realistically expect to ask: What else might change that I had not expected? What, for example, is next? As one dying man remarked earlier in this chapter, the "voyage is just expanding onto horizons that I've not quite made out." Dying people commonly express a new and provocative openness towards their personal experience and future, and this suggests more, rather than less, experience is likely to occur at the end of life. As Harold Brodkey himself muses in the final entry of his "story of my death": "Peace? There never was any in the world. But in the pliable water, under the sky, unmoored, I am traveling now and hearing myself laugh, at first with nerves and then with genuine amazement. It is all around me."[30]

And David, a man dying from dementia whom I quoted in chapter 8, remarks: "It's easy to focus on the things that have gone but there's no way of knowing what the new things are that are coming. If I can let go, let it flow and not get too attached and tied up, the more I am open to what is happening."[31]

Historically the world over, people on their deathbeds are not surprised to see their dead visiting them. From where does this equanimity derive? Are we to believe that religious belief or the utter fatigue of dying bestows otherwise ordinary people with a sudden and remarkable acceptance of the fantastic? One of the more interesting observations about deathbed vision accounts is the lack of religious interpretation and the dominance of the sheer *social* pleasure of the encounter for dying people. What emerges strongly from these accounts is the expectation that they will experience more of this. This is also true of those who recount their near-death experiences—many of which are told by people with no active religious commitments or background.

Notwithstanding the different and often contradictory academic views of medicine, psychoanalysis, experimental neuropsychology, or world religions, the transformative experiences of dying people suggest—controversially, tantalizingly, provocatively—that dying can bring positive change experiences. These fascinating experiences and perceptions often give dying people an expectation that more lies within the doors of the dying experience than any of us—or them—ever thought possible. Not science, religion, or philosophy had prepared most of them for life's final and bittersweet lessons in humility and reorientation. As the late poet Mahmoud Darwish warns us about all mystical experiences:

> It will come like a sovereign, without permission, as does love. It will come when you are not waiting for it, transparent, so that you know you are asleep, not dead. It might take you by the hand to inspect the ruins of your forgotten self in a distant land. You say: I am he and he is the shadow, and you run through your memory. When the dream sees that you are about to notice the map of memory, it lends you one of its wings and takes off with you to orange groves hanging above the clouds, to unfamiliar birds that speak to you in their own language, which you understand without difficulty. A higher self is borne of you. You embrace the universe and it embraces you, your interior becomes your exterior and your exterior your interior. And you say: I am I![32]

12

Some Final Reflections

And now that his story is told, what does it mean?
How can I tell?
What does life mean?
If the meaning could be put into a sentence
there would be no need of telling the story.
—Henry van Dyke, *The Friendly Year*

My review of the inner life of the dying person is almost complete. What general lessons might we glean from it? The main emotional, social, and spiritual experiences of dying people leave little doubt that the difficult, and frequently terrible, trials that dying people undergo are commonly counterbalanced, often even eclipsed, by an overlooked and underdescribed array of adaptive, positive, and transcending dimensions of personal experience. Suffering, fears, isolation, resistance, or the sadness and anger that dying people experience are not one-dimensional experiences of singular negativity. Within even these difficult experiences are to be found surprising insight, humor, positive changes, new and frequently enhanced relationships, and the birth of other feelings, perceptions, or perspectives. An emotion like anger, like the experience of suffering itself, is a journey and not merely an event.

These journeys, like all journeys, offer the traveler a complex set of vistas and reactions—and reactions within reactions. Journeys take time, and time offers the opportunity for travelers to change their mind about what they see and experience. Their reactions change, evolve with experience, are molded by reflection, comparison, and contrasts within the experience itself. Nothing stands still. This is what happens in the inner life of dying people because this is what happens to the inner life of all people in the journey of life.

What is notable and striking in the experience of dying is how much of this alteration of experience seems to be positive. The stories that people tell about their dying—about their fear or their experience of resistance—are frequently stories about the meaning of other people in their life. The observations made about, or stories people tell about, the courage of dying, or the sadness and hopes that dying people have, are about keeping others safe and supported. The inner life of dying people is replete with stories whose central meaning is about embracing life, particularly in the affirmation and enhancement of personal values and intimacy.

Dying as Life Embracing?

This review of the inner life of the dying person has discussed the multiple ways in which dying is commonly life embracing. Dying people commonly affirm important values and relationships in their life, strengthening them or further supporting them, and experiencing newer and novel experiences that enhance their enjoyment or insights into life. The evidence for these general remarks is everywhere in the accounts of dying people themselves.

Dying is life affirming in that it forces people to examine again how life is or is not working for them. Suffering and the experience of aloneness tend to ask dying people to affirm their beliefs and values, and in this context forces them to make choices about the practical use of these beliefs and values in their suffering and isolation. Courage in dying offers dying people the chance to protect others, their own sense of self, or their own values, and this too affirms the value intrinsic to the life they have lived and for whom they have lived it.

The experience of resistance helps dying people maintain the current quality of their relationships as givers and receivers of care and love but also ultimately helps them negotiate the terms and conditions of their release. Resistance offers both dying people and those around them the opportunity to affirm their relationship and to come together to fight and then to take their leave when the time comes for surrender, reinforcing their long alliance and bonds as parents, children, friends, and lovers. Finally, the experience

of waiting heightens dying people's daily experience of reality and of relationships, affirming both, and reinforcing their importance and value to the
dying person. In all these ways dying is a conscious experience of affirmation
of all the things—especially relationships and values—that were and remain
important to the life of the dying person as a living member of family and
community.

*The multiple core experiences of dying also function as life-building pro-
cesses.* In other words, the behavior and reactions of the dying actually
construct additional forms of emotional, social, and spiritual spaces and
connections because these people now face death and separation. This is
demonstrated in the way dying pushes people into new emotional territory
and coping when they suffer. Courage in dying creates mental and social
spaces for others—buying them time, saving their lives through sacrifice,
or leaving legacies of affection and memory in writing or phone messages.
Courage also has survival value for dying people; sometimes it has extended
their lives, sometimes it has prevented them from dying too soon. The courage to face and resist dying, at least initially, buys time not only for the dying
person but also for others. This gives others time to act, time to reconcile, to
say good-bye.

Even sadness and anger encourage a reassessment and realignment of
existing relationships and, alongside the experiences of hope and love, commonly forge reconciliation and resolve conflicts between the dying person
and friends and family. The experience of waiting for death has also been
fundamentally about promoting personal choice about what to do with one's
remaining time, encouraging new learning, and a new appreciation of the
life one has and has often taken for granted. These new social and aesthetic
lessons rebuild or add to the dying person's inner life. Review and reminiscence build bridges of new understanding through the realization of new
connections and insights; when shared these have offered others opportunities for their own reflection, insight into mortality, or role modeling for end
of life conduct and values.

Furthermore, the experiences of review and reminiscence, as well as the
transformative experiences of the inner life of dying people, tell us that these
too are life-building experiences. Life review gives dying people a new and
perhaps novel view of their own future, commonly the realization that the
future is not merely a personal reality but a shared one. That their own life

is embedded in, and wedded to, others' is not commonly appreciated until extensive review and reminiscence are begun in earnest. Such challenges to a usually individualized view of one's future commonly open up other ideas and possibilities about personal continuity, building within the dying person new understandings about the possible. Fresh ideas about the future become possibilities: how the dying and their influence might reach beyond the present limited view of the future.

The transformational experiences of dying people commonly reorient their attention toward their own inner life. A fresh and growing appreciation of the outer life around them emerges as a result. This reorientation to the inner life is a counterbalance to their usual sense of living with a contracting sense of time and gives them a sense of growing depth. Their understanding of life's usual dimensions begins to become distorted, with what was once an emphasis on length of remaining life giving way to a sense of quality or depth of experience. This leads in turn to a new realization that depth brings with it its own sense of length, a new sense of distance to travel, and with this even a new sensation of time.

This new sense of life inside a moment, inside a brief experience, provides the dying person with an often-startling realization of a new possibility— something the person often has already partially lived and felt—the possibility of timelessness as a real lived experience rather than a mere poetic metaphor. Within this new timelessness is the surprising, if not shocking, possibility of new life. Ulla-Carin Lindquist, the Swedish television producer with ALS, found just such a possibility:

> Gustaf comes and stands behind my desk.
> "Do you write all the time, Mummy?"
> "It takes such a long time," I reply. "I only write with two fingers now."
> "Mummy, I'm a miniature human being."
> "What?"
> "You're big and I'm little."
> "No, Gustaf. You're big. You have your whole life in front of you. The future. Now it's me who's getting smaller."
> "Mummy, every second is a life," he says gently.
> "What did you say?"
> "Every second is a life."

"Where have you heard that?"

"Nowhere. I just made it up."

And he carries on: "You have hundreds and thousands of lives left, Mummy."

"Every second is a life," I echo.[1]

Finally, the key experiences of the inner life of the dying person reviewed in this book have revealed not only that most of these experiences are affirming and building of life—regardless of the definition of *life* you choose to entertain—but that the core experiences of dying are also commonly life enhancing. If the diverse experiences associated with dying do not affirm what the dying person values, or build new emotional and social spaces in that person's existing social relationships and perceptions, these experiences instead often strengthen, fill, or round out a personal sense of life and of living. People facing death commonly report, paradoxically, that they feel better, stronger, happier, more able, and more confident than they had before the confrontation with death and in these ways were surprised by what they had become as dying individuals.

Dying experiences create a new awareness of dimensions within the self that people previously did not notice or appreciate. Dying people are so often forced to confront and live with fears that in better times they had thought they dare not confront or live with. They often are forced to make choices when they seem to have no choices available or none to make. Fear makes both cowards and heroes of people, and at different times, but more often than not mortal fear simply makes them more creative about how to live with limited choices in the midst of great trials.

In these ways, experiences of courage, fear, anger, or sadness force dying people to draw on strengths they didn't realize they had; on personal power, autonomy, or hopes they did not know they had; on personal values that they now can clarify and push into active service. The transformative experiences of dying people force them to attend, notice, and see afresh their existing relationships to family, lovers, friends, and community as well as nature itself. From this new perspective the dying can experience a new appreciation for the social exchanges of giving and receiving; of surprise, humility, and wonder before strange new experiences; and of the value of the small act and the overlooked scene.

Whether religious in outlook or not, whether naturally cynical and world weary or not, whether unsentimental in disposition or not, large numbers of dying people report a spiritual awakening that surprised them. They find themselves opened up to new experiences—many altered by their new outlooks on life, some forced upon them by periods of isolation or altered states of consciousness encountered near death or in unexpected physical and emotional crises. Whatever the route, whatever the past occupation, whatever the usual personal disposition, surprise and wonder seem integral to the dying experience and indeed seem to be necessary by-products of the trials and suffering associated with it.

Like the dying leaf in autumn, and the cocoon casing of the moth, the process of dying includes life-affirming, life-building, and life-enhancing processes for most life forms, maybe all life forms, for all we know. Like the defensive reactions of prey in the plant and animal kingdom, dying is more than the destructive meanings projected by predators and killers, more than the loss and grief of carers and members of the same species. Perhaps because of these dominant (and domineering) death-at-a-distance meanings, we have only just recently noticed that other, more life-affirming, processes are alive and active within ourselves, even as we die. The fascinating and intriguing challenge, both in identifying these adaptive processes and in making any positive generalizations about them, has been the sheer number of individual variations in expressing them.

Furthermore, our observations and judgments about dying have suffered from being event related (deathbed observations) or perspective distorted (privileging observer rather than participant descriptions). In this book we have taken a longer view of dying as an evolving and changing personal journey over several minutes, months, or years and privileging the voices of those who have undergone this journey. This approach gives us a more positive view of the diversity of experiences associated with approaching death, a balance of experiences that resembles that found in the rest of the organic world of animals and plants. Dying is a set of life-affirming experiences for human beings, just as it is for the rest of the natural world. After all is said about the differences between ourselves and the rest of life, then, the elementary observation about our primeval similarity in this one respect should come as little surprise.

Nevertheless, although we might speak about courage in the face of death, or about the loneliness of dying, or the sadness in the gradual realization of what we lose when we die, everyone dies in a different way. People's courage and their sorrow, their particular transformations or their special style of resistance to the many challenges that approaching death sends, are part of their story, one each of us tells our self about our ending. This is a story prompted by a sense of an ending that we realize only inside ourselves. We are compelled to tell a new story about ourselves when dying because, as Henry van Dyke suggests in the opening lines of this chapter, our meanings *are* our stories. Our sense of an ending requires us to rise to the challenge of coherence and finish the tale of what *I* thought it meant to be *me*. For however poorly or partially realized, however imperfect that story may be to us in the end, our final story may yet be our most important companion—the best light we have to guide us into that dimly lit journey ahead.

Life-embracing Dying or Happy Dying?

Most of the dying voices heard in this book appear to discuss lives that are able to affirm, build upon, or enhance their remaining life, prompted and stimulated by the knowledge that they will die soon. These adaptations of the inner life clearly show that positive and constructive forces are at work within the dying experience. We know that such forces are not unprecedented in the organic worlds of all life forms and that these long-standing functions at the end of all life should have told us of their parallel presence in human endings, too.

However, I remind the reader that this positive and constructive dimension of dying does not equate with the experience of being happy. Most dying people would still say that they would be happy not to die at all, not be parted from those they love, not leave until whatever work they value is finished. I must here emphasize to the reader that the positive, life-embracing features of dying do not make dying less sad, less lonely, or even less fearful for many dying people. But life-embracing features of the inner life of dying *do* make the process of dying more bearable—often providing much-needed support, unanticipated purpose, coherence and insight, openness, direction, and strength, even choices in how to live the remaining time. After the initial darkness passes, a darkness that necessarily accompanies a person's initial sense of the end, comes a surprising reawakening toward life—a development experienced rather differently, and at different times, by each dying person.

There is, of course, little positive to say about being the victim of murder or terrorism, suicidal despair, or of a life cut short in childhood from incurable disease. Nevertheless, even in these and other extremely tragic examples, saying that the positive forces of life are sorrowfully absent is simply not true. Our horror, grief, and even anger as onlookers to these kinds of dying and death have traditionally clouded our judgment, compromised our ability to see more clearly the subtle positive dimensions of the dying people who defend against the forces that eventually overcome them. Some of these defenses, even in sudden mortal events, bring a merciful peace, strength, or unexpected psychological experiences or reorientation to the dying person, whereas onlookers see only violence, horror, and grief. Clearly, the longer the time for dying, the greater the possibility of a mobilization of a wider range of defenses to the threat of death that will leave the dying person with some additional parting graces and gifts. The story of this book has been to show how much more common these graces and gifts are than we had previously supposed.

It is also important to say that such life-embracing dimensions of dying are never a rationale for the act of killing others because such acts are decided, and should be decided, on other cultural, political, and psychological grounds and not solely on the psychological or spiritual positives associated with the nature of death. Responsibility toward others, toward oneself as someone inexorably linked to others, and the intrinsic value of the preservation of all life—these are the basis of contemporary bioethical, moral, and political debates about the sanctity of life and not positive dimensions of the dying experience.

However, identifying the positive dimensions within the end of life so that they may take their rightful place alongside our understanding of the negative dimensions of the end of life does provide us with a clearer, more balanced, and more substantial picture of what contemporary debates about quality of life, dignity, hope, and living until we die might mean. So often such phrases and words seem more like empty clichés and catchphrases and not the serious pointers to genuinely real, detailed, and holistic experiences of the inner life of dying people. Worse still, such phrases are commonly overburdened by negative, life-detracting, or grief-stricken images of living with dying. In both of these latter cases, living with dying can sometimes appear to others as pointless, singularly tragic, and a time (and a role) to be avoided at all costs. A review of the life-embracing aspects of living with dying shows that such terrible images and stereotypes of dying are untrustworthy at best, untrue at worst. When we discuss the future of dying and its care, it is essential that we take a more balanced view of this final time of life.

In this way, to identify and describe the life-embracing dimensions of the inner life of dying people is to sketch some detail and add some genuine color to what we mean when we allude to positive and constructive changes while dying. In their turn, these details and colors compete against the better-publicized and more familiar negative aspects of dying that commonly bias public debate and overwhelm policy formulation. We know that many people die unsatisfied with both their life and death. We know that, every day, people are deprived of their lives by random and intended violence, unstoppable disease, accidents, or global apathy. No remarks or descriptions about the positive dimension of dying described here should be taken to slow our opposition to, detract from, or partly rationalize away any of these wider and often preventable life-stripping forces.

However, dealing with threat has some undeniably positive features, and within these are some of the more conscious processes of the dying experience itself. In this book I have reviewed the abundant evidence for these features in the current clinical and academic literature, and it is high time we publicly acknowledge them. This should give a measure of comfort to those who even now confront their own death as well as to those who care for them. This underrecognized insight about life is one we should receive gratefully. For though many of us are no longer sure what lies beyond death, there is consolation in the rich abundance and depth of life that seems to accompany each of us within our journey toward its mysterious embrace. Nakae Chomin, a Japanese journalist born in 1847, gets the last word on this as he reflects upon the news that he will not have long to live:

One day I visited Dr Horiuchi and enquired how many days and months before my death. I asked him to speak truthfully and hide nothing. With much to do and enjoy, I wanted to use completely every last day. To make plans for my remaining days I asked how long I had to live. The rather innocent Dr Horiuchi thought for a few minutes and then replied rather uncomfortably, "One year and a half; perhaps two years if you take good care of yourself." I told Horiuchi that I had expected to live only five or six months and that in one year I could certainly reap a rich harvest from life.

Some of you may say that one year and a half is very short; I say it is an eternity. But if you wish to say it is short, then ten years is also short, and fifty years is short, and so, too, is one hundred years. If this life is limited in time and that after death is unlimited, then the limited compared to the unlimited period is not even short: it's nothing. If you have things to do and enjoy, then isn't it possible to use quite well one year and a half? As fifty and one hundred years disappear, so, too, does the so-called one year and a half. Our life is nothing but a single empty boat on a non-existent sea.[2]

Notes

1. In the Beginning . . .

1. Bracha, "Freeze, Flight, Fight, Fright, Faint."
2. Ratner, "Comparative Aspects of Hypnosis"; Knudsen, "Dying Animal."
3. Knudsen, "Dying Animal," 40.
4. Kellehear, "A Social History of Dying"; Porges, "Orienting in a Defensive World"; P. A. Levine, *In an Unspoken Voice.*
5. Lingle and Pellis, "Fight or Flight?"; Ford and Reeves, "Fight or Flight"; Eilam, "Die Hard."
6. Ford and Reeves, "Fight or Flight."
7. Dhabhar, "A Hassle a Day."
8. Edinger and Thompson, "Death by Design."
9. Greenberg, "Programmed Cell Death"; Jacobson, Weil, and Raff, "Programmed Cell Death in Animal Development."
10. Baehrecke, "How Death Shapes Life."
11. Nuland, *How We Die,* 134.
12. Moody, *Life After Life,* 28–29.
13. Most of the human record of these experiences comes from the field of near-death studies, in other words, from investigations of survivor testimony from motor vehicle and industrial accidents, war injuries, near-fatal drownings, mountaineering falls, and other sudden trauma events/experiences.
14. Bauby, *Diving Bell and the Butterfly,* 138.
15. MacDonald and Rich, *Look Me in the Eye,* 108–109.
16. The distinctions between *imminent* and *immanent* come from the critic and literary theorist Frank Kermode, who discusses their role in fiction in his aptly titled book, *The Sense of an Ending.*
17. This is often why sudden death is so difficult to understand and why most onlookers and loved ones have major difficulties in discerning a meaning, and also why even those who have survived such sudden attacks or accidents commonly report disorientation and shock. In these cases, no one has time to discern meaning or

purpose. Dying in these cases is more a case of suddenly becoming dead rather than a gradual process of leaving life, as we commonly define *dying*.

18. I am not trying to replace Kübler-Ross's five stages in *On Death and Dying* with twice that number of my own. Instead, I am attempting here to outline what I consider to be the core elements of the inner life of dying. Most important, the ones I have chosen to outline are the ones that seem to repeatedly occur and to dominate a wide diversity of autobiographical writing and other self-reports about the experience of dying. These personal elements of experience and response have no necessary or natural sequential value for humans, although it must be said that in animal studies the elements of fear, courage, resistance, and transformative experience, for example, tend to occur to the dying animal in this basic sequence, depending on how quickly a deadly attack takes place. I have used that broad biological template of ordering as both a token acknowledgment of the origins of these experiences and responses and as a convenient basis for organizing the book as a whole. Notwithstanding this liberty of style, it is crucial to note that the elements themselves—and not their sequence—dominate accounts of dying as reported by dying people. Many of the different elements often occur together, simultaneously. When these elements occur separately, they may be experienced cyclically and in highly diverse configuration, driven as they always are by the individual personality and the innumerable cultural influences that petition and shape it. This is the way it is for all our living, and so this is the way it is for the last part of that living—our living while dying.

2. Suffering—Enduring the New Reality

1. Amato, "Politics of Suffering"; Bowker, *Problems of Suffering*.
2. Bowker, *Problems of Suffering*, 2.
3. Levertov, "Age of Terror," 201.
4. Wilkinson, *Suffering*; Kellehear, "On Dying and Human Suffering."
5. Bourdieu, *Weight of the World*.
6. Saunders, "Philosophy of Terminal Care." See also Saunders, *Hospice and Palliative Care*.
7. Cassell, *Nature of Suffering*. See also Kleinman, *Illness Narratives*.
8. Geertz, *Interpretation of Culture*.
9. See Frank, "Can We Research Suffering?"; Kleinman and Kleinman, "Suffering and Its Professional Transformation"; Kleinman, "Pitch, Picture, Power"; Das, "Suffering, Theocidies."
10. Kleinman, "Pitch, Picture, Power."
11. Schwarcz, "Pane of Sorrow."
12. Lubbock, "Tom Lubbock: A Memoir."

13. Rich, *Red Devil*, 67.
14. Gregory and Russell, *Cancer Stories*, 90.
15. Bassett, "Facing Mortality," 225.
16. Rossi, *Waiting to Die*, 33.
17. M. Miller, "You Just Shed Life," 27–28.
18. Lawton, "Dying Process," 89.
19. Perera, "Faith Keeps Me Going," 86.
20. Arriens, *Welcome to Hell*, 252.
21. DeBaggio, *Losing My Mind*, 87.
22. Brodkey, *This Wild Darkness*, 159.
23. Lymphopo, "The Missing Weeks, Part 2," *As the Tumor Turns* (blog), November 7, 2006, http://spinningtumor.blogspot.com/2007_05_01_archive.html, accessed June 15, 2011.
24. J. Diamond, *C: Because Cowards Get Cancer Too*, 171.
25. Rich, *Red Devil*, 81.
26. Arriens, *Welcome to Hell*, 239.
27. Lymphopo, "Little Miss Meltdown," April 30, 2007.
28. Bassett, "Facing Mortality," 226.
29. J. Diamond, *C: Because Cowards Get Cancer Too*, 171.
30. Saba, "Trying to Be Normal," 12.
31. Casson, *Dying*, 23–24.
32. Arriens, *Welcome to Hell*, 177–78.
33. DeBaggio, *Losing My Mind*, 193.
34. Gregory and Russell, *Cancer Stories*, 40.
35. Ibid., 68.
36. For a recent public overview of the social research into this problem, see PBS's coverage (T. Miller, "In Many Countries").
37. Jarman, *Smiling in Slow Motion*, 110–11.
38. Rich, *Red Devil*, 103.
39. Ibid., 57.
40. Ibid., 22–23.
41. Frankl, *Man's Search for Meaning*; see also Frankl, *Doctor and the Soul*.
42. Frankl, *Doctor and the Soul*, 109, 114.
43. Ibid., 116.
44. Ibid., 67.

3. Fear—A Threat Observed

1. Krishnamurti, *On Fear*, 92.
2. Penson et al., "Update: Fear of Death," 162.

3. Craib, "Fear, Death and Sociology," 286.

4. Kierkegaard, *Fear and Trembling*, 151.

5. Boston, "Klara Bergman: Burdens from the Past," in Barnard et al., *Crossing Over*, 77.

6. DeBaggio, *Losing My Mind*, 80.

7. Roth and Massie, "Anxiety and Its Management."

8. Plath, "Elm," 26.

9. Eliot, *Waste Land*, 28.

10. Darwish, *In the Presence of Absence*, 41.

11. Eliot, *Waste Land*, 41.

12. Langner, preface to *Choices for Living*, v.

13. Feifel, Freilich, and Hermann, "Death Fear in Dying Heart and Cancer Patients," 161–66.

14. See Cassidy, "Emotional Distress in Terminal Cancer"; Parkes, "Dying Patient"; and Penson et al., "Update: Fear of Death."

15. Rachman, *Meanings of Fear*, 58–59. See also Thomson, "Concept of Fear," 22.

16. Lubbock, "Tom Lubbock: A Memoir."

17. Lloyd-Williams et al., "End of Life," 62.

18. M. Miller, "You Just Shed Life," 32.

19. Ritchie, "Listening and Understanding," 122.

20. Savary at al., *Listen to Love*, 41.

21. Bourke, *Fear: A Cultural History*.

22. Gill, Hadaway, and Marler, "Is Religious Belief Declining in Britain?"; Bruce, *God Is Dead*.

23. Wink and Scott, "Does Religiousness Buffer."

24. Trillin, "Of Dragons and Garden Peas," 699.

25. Entwhistle, *The Child's Livingstone* (London, 1913), 10–11; Bourke, *Fear: A Cultural History*, 384.

26. Kaufman, *And a Time to Die*.

27. Craib, "Fear, Death and Sociology," 291.

28. Ibid., 292.

29. Henderson and Oakes, *Wisdom of the Serpent*. See also Kellehear, *Eternity and Me*, 51–54.

30. Warner, *Monsters of Our Own Making*.

31. Lymphopo, "Life Beneath the Superdome," *As the Tumor Turns* (blog), November 12, 2006, http://spinningtumor.blogspot.com/2006_11_01_archive.html, accessed June 15, 2011.

4. Courage—Facing the Overwhelming

1. See Putman, "Philosophical Roots of the Concept of Courage."

2. Lopez et al., "Folk Conceptualizations of Courage."

3. Tillich, *Courage to Be.*
4. Walton, *Courage: A Philosophical Investigation*; Scarre, *On Courage.*
5. Scarre, *On Courage*, 32–34.
6. Walton, *Courage: A Philosophical Investigation*, 76–96.
7. Scarre, *On Courage*, 112–24.
8. Walton, *Courage: A Philosophical Investigation*, 91.
9. Leslie, *Desperate Journeys, Abandoned Souls*, 161.
10. Ibid., 91.
11. Faust, *This Republic of Suffering*, 19.
12. Ibid., 16–17.
13. Moran, *Anatomy of Courage.*
14. Remarks by the President George W. Bush at Presentation of Medal of Honor, April 9, 2008, in Rate, "Defining the Features of Courage," 50–51.
15. See Nagatsuka, *I Was a Kamikaze*; Ohnuki-Tierney, *Kamikaze, Cherry Blossoms, and Nationalisms*; Cook and Cook, *Japan at War*, 305–26.
16. Nagatsuka, *I Was a Kamikaze*, 189–90.
17. Reuter, *My Life Is a Weapon.*
18. Ibid., 1.
19. Atkins, *9/11 Encyclopedia*, 1:285.
20. Noonan, "Sounds That Still Echo from 9/11."
21. H. Jackson, "524 Killed in Worst Single Aircraft Disaster," *Guardian*, August 13, 1985, http://www.guardian.co.uk/fromthearchive/story/0,,1017027,00.html, accessed July 12, 2013.
22. Noonan, "Sounds That Still Echo from 9/11."
23. J. Diamond, *C: Because Cowards Get Cancer Too*, 72–73, and 76.
24. Rich, *Red Devil*, 122.
25. Rawnsley, "Recurrence of Cancer," 166.
26. Ibid., 166.
27. Hinton, *Dying*, 92.
28. See Frankl, *Man's Search for Meaning.*
29. Herbert, "Constancie," in Scarre, *On Courage*, 158.
30. Van Dyke, *Friendly Year*, 154.
31. Scarre, *On Courage*, 30.

5. Resistance — Facing the Choices

1. Plath, "Lady Lazareth," 17.
2. Alvarez, *Savage God*, 18.
3. I discuss this in my review of Alvarez's work — see Kellehear, "Classics Revisited."
4. Goodall, "Personal View."
5. McPherson, Wilson, and Murray, "Feeling Like a Burden to Others."

6. Lederer, "Dark Victory." See also Patterson, *Dread Disease.*

7. Also Seale, "Sporting Cancer," and "Cancer Heroics." The work of Juanne Clarke is also instructive and typical of this genre, for example, Clarke, "Cancer Meanings in the Media." In the clinical literature see Byrne et al., "Patients' Experience of Cancer"; Skott, "Expressive Metaphors in Cancer Narratives."

8. Nuland, *How We Die,* 265.

9. See the early work of I. Illich, *Limits to Medicine,* 179–211, and also more recently Sherwin Nuland, *How We Die,* for a wonderfully reflective series of essays about the overzealous culture of medical rescue in the United States. For an anthropological account, see Kaufman, *And a Time to Die.*

10. Hu, "Fighting for a Peaceful Death," 213

11. Marcus, "Loneliness of Fighting a Rare Cancer."

12. Skott, "Expressive Metaphors in Cancer Narratives."

13. Helm, "Fighting Demons, Fighting Cancer."

14. Bytheway, *Unmasking Age,* 94.

15. Conway and Hockey, "Resisting the 'Mask' of Old Age?" 481.

16. Thomas, "Do Not Go Gentle into That Good Night," in H. Gardner, *New Oxford Book of Verse,* 942.

17. Kellehear, *A Social History of Dying,* 228.

18. Tennyson, "Ulysses."

19. Smith, *Passive Fear.*

20. Carson and Fiester, letter to the editor.

21. Byrne et al., "Patients' Experience of Cancer."

22. McPherson, Wilson, and Murray, "Feeling Like a Burden"; Taylor et al., "Biobehavioral Responses to Stress in Females."

23. See "'Fighting Spirit' After Cancer Diagnosis"; Petticrew, Bell, and Hunter, "Influence of Psychological Coping"; Boer et al., "Psychosocial Correlates of Cancer Relapse."

24. Santayana, "A Silent Hope," in Savary et al., *Listen to Love,* 303.

25. Gilbert and Gilbert, "Entrapment and Arrested Fight and Flight."

26. Seligman, "Learned Helplessness."

27. Kübler-Ross, *On Death and Dying,* 100.

28. Ibid.

29. Cowan and McQuellon, "Turning Toward Death Together," 395

30. I. R. Gardner, "Not Dying a Victim," 53.

31. Rose, *Love's Work,* 102.

32. Howse, *Deaths of People Alone,* 22. See also Richards, "Fight-to-Die."

33. Kellehear et al., *Care of the Dying.*

34. Kellehear et al., *Deathbed Visions,* 2011–12.

35. Darwish, *In the Presence of Absence,* 67.

36. Brontë, "Spellbound," in H. Gardner, *New Oxford Book of Verse,* 676.

6. Sadness and Anger—Facing Loss

1. Bassett, "Facing Mortality," 227.

2. Averill and Nunley, "Grief as an Emotion."

3. Ibid., 84. See also Horwitz and Wakefield, *Loss of Sadness*.

4. See Chochinov, "Depression in Cancer Patients," and "Dying, Dignity, and New Horizons."

5. Blazer, "Depression in Late Life."

6. Bowlby, *Loss: Sadness and Depression*, 245.

7. Barnhart, *Chambers Dictionary of Etymology*, 950 and 1036; *Oxford Illustrated Dictionary*; *Roget's Thesaurus*.

8. Worden, *Grief Counseling and Grief Therapy*, 18, 96–97.

9. Pastan, *Five Stages of Grief*, 48.

10. Lindquist, *Rowing Without Oars*, 182.

11. Robins, *Living in the Lightning*, 33, 82.

12. Saba, "Trying to Be Normal," 23.

13. Kübler-Ross, *On Death and Dying*, 77–78. Emphasis added.

14. Pastan, *Five Stages of Grief*, 52.

15. Ibid., 14.

16. Ibid., 313–17.

17. See Houston, "Angry Dying Patient"; Philip et al., "Anger in Palliative Care."

18. Barbato, *Caring for the Dying*, 203.

19. Tavris, *Anger: The Misunderstood Emotion*, 46–47.

20. Gilbert and Gilbert, "Entrapment and Arrested Fight and Flight."

21. Greenwood et al., "Anger and Persistent Pain."

22. DeBaggio, *Losing My Mind*, 170.

23. Frankl, *Man's Search for Meaning*, 24.

24. Donaldson and Donaldson, *How Did They Die?* 384.

25. Barnard et al., *Crossing Over*, 145.

26. Jaffe and Jaffe, "Terminal Candor and the Coda Syndrome," 201.

27. Killick and Cordonnier, *Openings*, n.p.

28. Lindquist, *Rowing Without Oars*, 183–84.

29. Robins, *Living in the Lightning*, 16.

30. Trillin, "Of Dragons and Garden Peas," 700.

31. For a review of the relative importance of all these factors and influences, see Berkowitz and Harmon-Jones, "Toward an Understanding." For guilt, anger, and pain see the early works of Engel, especially "Psychogenic Pain," and Pilowsky and Spence, "Pain, Anger and Illness Behavior."

32. Eliot, *Silas Marner*, in Hackett, *My Commonplace Book*, 159.

33. Barbato, *Caring for the Dying*, 193–94.

34. Tavris, *Anger: The Misunderstood Emotion*, 318–19; emphasis in original.

35. Masson and McCarthy, *When Elephants Weep*, xiii.
36. Ibid., xxi.
37. Sullivan, "Hope and Hopelessness," 393.
38. Lindquist, *Rowing Without Oars*, 1.

7. Hope and Love—Connection

1. Rose, *Love's Work*, 79.
2. Van Dyke, *Friendly Year*, 14.
3. Some of these thoughts have been drawn from Kellehear, "World of Hope," in *Book of Gentle Wisdom*, 4.
4. James, *Will to Believe*, 62.
5. See Kellehear, introduction to Kübler-Ross, *On Death and Dying*; Gum and Snyder, "Coping with Terminal Illness"; Felder, "Hoping and Coping."
6. Kylma et al., "Hope in Palliative Care."
7. Diane Lee DeTar, "A Survivor's Gift," *Diane's Story of Living Life with Breast Cancer and Dying with Dignity* (blog), n.d., http://diane.ponpines.com/dianes_last_thoughts_gift.html, accessed June 15, 2011.
8. Sullivan, "Hope and Hopelessness."
9. Eliott and Olver, "Hope and Hoping."
10. Frankl, Man's *Search for Meaning*, 80.
11. Rose, *Love's Work*, 105.
12. Ibid., 106.
13. Kellehear, *Dying of Cancer*.
14. Doyle, *Caring for a Dying Relative*, 4.
15. Fromm, *Art of Loving*, 15.
16. 1 Cor. 13:4–8.
17. J. Diamond, C: *Because Cowards Get Cancer Too*, 240.
18. Swensen and Fuller, "Expressions of Love."
19. Georgers et al., "Symptoms, Treatment and 'Dying Peacefully.'"
20. Keeley, "Final Conversations," 52.
21. Ellis, *Final Negotiations*, 53, 161, 117.
22. Michelle Lynn Mayer, "Michelle Discusses Her Illness," *Diary of a Dying Mom* (blog), June 2008, http://diaryofadyingmom.blogspot.com/, accessed March 28, 2012.
23. Robins, *Living in the Lightning*, 46–47.
24. Block, "Psychological Considerations," 2902.
25. Ibid.
26. Seravalli, "Dying Patient," 1729.
27. Kellehear, "Social Inequality of Dying."

28. Doyle, *Caring for a Dying Relative*, 61–62.
29. Rose, *Love's Work*, 105.
30. Robins, *Living in the Lightning*, 98.
31. Lewis, *Surprised by Joy*, 20.

8. Waiting — In-between-ness

1. See Donnelly, "Traditions Associated with Dying"; Donnelly, Michael, and Donnelly, "Experience of the Moment of Death at Home"; Donnelly and Donnelly, "Experience of the Moment of Death in a Specialist Palliative Care Unit."
2. See Van Gennep, *Rites of Passage*; Gibson, *Wake Rites*.
3. For U.S. examples see Carr and Fogarty, "Families at the Bedside"; Kaufman, *And a Time to Die*, esp. 145–202. For European examples see Fridh, Forsberg, and Bergbom, "Close Relatives' Experiences"; Woodhouse, "A Personal Reflection"; Abrahams, "Storytelling Events."
4. Brodkey, *This Wild Darkness*, 111.
5. DeBaggio, *Losing My Mind*, 207.
6. See Van Gennep, *Rites of Passage*, and Glaser and Strauss, *Status Passage*.
7. Kellehear, *A Social History of Dying*.
8. Simmons, *Role of the Aged in Primitive Society*.
9. Ibid., 226.
10. Wright, "Relationships with Death."
11. Brown et al., "Waiting for a Liver Transplant," 132.
12. Locsin et al., "Ugandan Nurses' Experience."
13. Mitchell et al., "Exploring the Lived Experience of Waiting."
14. Kaufman, *And a Time to Die*, 148.
15. Jaffe and Jaffe, "Terminal Candor and the Coda Syndrome," 197.
16. Irvin, "Waiting: Concept Analysis."
17. Barak et al., "Stress Associated with Asbestosis."
18. Jacques and Hasselkus, "Nature of Occupation Surrounding Dying," 49.
19. Lawton, "Dying Process," 171.
20. Crandall and Crandall, *Borders of Time*, 99.
21. Bradford, "Waiting to Die, Dying to Live," 77
22. Ibid., 86.
23. Altman, "Waiting Syndrome."
24. Berman, "Todeserwartung Syndrome," 192.
25. Coontz, "Women Under Sentence of Death," 90.
26. Johnson, "Under Sentence of Death," 185–86.
27. R. Levine, "Waiting Is a Power Game."
28. Wright, "Relationships with Death," 450–51.

29. Noyes, "Journey into Alzheimer's," 96.
30. Brodkey, *This Wild Darkness*, 26.
31. Ibid., 99.
32. Ibid., 152.
33. Ibid., 176.
34. Ibid., 69.
35. Ibid., 163.

9. Review and Reminiscence — Remembering

1. Coleman, "Creating a Life Story."
2. Barnhart, *Chambers Dictionary of Etymology*, 1072.
3. Barnard et al., *Crossing Over*.
4. Butler, "Life Review."
5. Ibid., 2:364.
6. Ibid., 2:354.
7. Freeman, *Hindsight*.
8. D. K. Miller, "The Last Post," *Penmachine.com* (blog), May 4, 2011, http://www.penmachine.com/2011/05/the-last-post, accessed June 28, 2013
9. Ibid.
10. DeBaggio, *Losing My Mind*, 113.
11. Ibid.
12. Zaleski, *Otherworld Journeys*.
13. Ibid., 69–74, 128–31.
14. Lorimer, *Whole in One*.
15. Sabom, *Recollections of Death*, 50.
16. Zaleski, *Otherworld Journeys*, 131.
17. Frankl, *Man's Search for Meaning*, 38.
18. Jung, *Undiscovered Self*, 43–44.
19. Coleman, "Creating a Life Story," 138.
20. Lindemann, "Symptomatology and Management of Acute Grief. See also Aldrich, "Dying Patient's Grief."
21. Kellehear and Lewin, "Farewells by the Dying."
22. Worden, *Grief Counseling and Grief Therapy*, 201–206.
23. Webster and Haight, "Memory Lane Milestones"; Cappeliez and O'Rourke, "Profiles of Reminiscence Among Older Adults." See also Molinari and Reichlin, "Life Review Reminiscence in the Elderly."
24. Webster and Haight, "Memory Lane Milestones."
25. Frankl, *Man's Search for Meaning*, 71–72.
26. Darwish, *In the Presence of Absence*, 46–47.

27. Wallace, "Reconsidering the Life Review." See also Merriam, "Butler's Life Review."
28. Coleman, Creating a Life Story."
29. McLuhan and Fiore, *Medium Is the Massage.*
30. Lawton, *Dying Process*, 100.
31. Ibid., 68–69, 99–100.
32. E. F. Diamond, "Brain-based Determination of Death Revisited."
33. Rose, *Love's Work*, 120.
34. Ibid.
35. From H. R. Moody, "Reminiscence and the Recovery of the Public World," quoted in Coleman, "Creating a Life Story," 138.

10. Aloneness — Disconnection

1. McGraw, "Loneliness, Its Nature and Forms." See also Tillich, "Loneliness and Solitude."
2. Ettema, Derksen, and van Leeuwen, "Existential Loneliness and End of Life Care," 156.
3. Ibid.
4. Butler, "Life Review," 353.
5. United Kingdom, Department of Health, *End of Life Care Strategy.*
6. Elias, *Loneliness of Dying*, 85. Note that Elias is using *solitude* here in the negative sense of loneliness.
7. Ibid., 59.
8. Ibid., 70–71.
9. Trillin, "Of Dragons and Garden Peas," 699.
10. G. Chow, "Dying, Day 3," *Dying Is . . .* (blog), November 24, 2004, http://dyingis.blogspot.com, accessed July 10, 2012.
11. Elias, *Loneliness of Dying*, 89.
12. Ibid., 65.
13. Sand and Strang, "Existential Loneliness."
14. Ibid., 1381.
15. Ibid., 1382.
16. Chow, "Dying, Day 3."
17. Fromm-Reichmann, "On Loneliness."
18. Leslie, *Desperate Journeys, Abandoned Souls*, 115–18.
19. Ibid., 121.
20. Ibid., 354.
21. Licence, *Hermits and Recluses in English Society*, 11.
22. Ibid., 139.

23. Zaleski, *Otherworld Journeys.*
24. Kellehear, "Near-Death Experience as Status Passage."
25. Suedfeld, "Aloneness as a Healing Experience," 59–60.
26. Klein, "On the Sense of Loneliness," 549.
27. Merton, *Silent Life,* 38.
28. Tillich, "Loneliness and Solitude," 553.
29. Suedfeld, "Aloneness as a Healing Experience," 64.
30. See Kübler-Ross, *On Death and Dying.*
31. B. Howdle, "Dying Is Lonely," *Dying Man's Daily Journal* (blog), November 24, 2011, http://hudds53.wordpress.com/2011/11/24/dying-mans-daily-journal-dying-is-lonely, accessed July 10, 2012.
32. Kellehear, "Dying Old and *Preferably* Alone?"
33. Howse, *Deaths of People Alone,* 22.
34. Kellehear, "Dying Old and *Preferably* Alone?"
35. Richards, "Fight-to-Die."
36. Huxley, *Doors of Perception.*
37. Muthumana et al., "Deathbed Visions from India"; Kellehear et al., "Family Care of the Dying." For a discussion of why these prevalence rates are much lower in Western industrialized societies such as the United Kingdom or United States, see also Fountain and Kellehear, "On Prevalence Disparities."
38. Cruz, "ALONE/December/Night," 247–48.

11. Transformation — Change, Change, Change

1. Barnard et al., *Crossing Over,* 33.
2. Ibid., 116.
3. Johnson, "Under Sentence of Death," 173.
4. Aminoff and Adunsky, "Dying Dementia Patients."
5. See Muthumana et al., "Deathbed Visions from India"; Kellehear et al., "Family Care of the Dying." On rates in Western industrialized societies see Fountain and Kellehear, "On Prevalence Disparities."
6. *Oxford Illustrated Dictionary,* 902.
7. "Startling Reality of Things," 147.
8. Wright, "Relationships with Death," 443.
9. Small, Froggatt, and Downs, "Living and Dying with Dementia," 201.
10. Yedidia and McGregor, "Confronting the Prospect of Dying," 815.
11. Crane, "I Saw a Man."
12. Toynbee, *End of a Journey,* 345.
13. Hinton, *Dying,* 77.
14. Kellehear et al., *Care of the Dying.*

15. For a review of the hazards of diagnosis and misdiagnosis of persistent vegetative states, brain death, and other forms of coma, see Kellehear, "Dying as a Social Relationship." For a discussion of intriguing cases of persistent consciousness in clinical circumstances where this should not be the case, see Kelly, Greyson, and Kelly, "Unusual Experiences Near Death."

16. See the dozens of medical and psychological studies of near-death experiences conducted since the 1970s. For a good review of the key work in this field see Holden, Greyson, and James, *Handbook of Near-Death Experiences.*

17. See note 5.

18. Fountain and Kellehear, "On Prevalence Disparities."

19. Kellehear et al., "Deathbed Visions from the Republic of Moldova," 311.

20. Muthumana et al., "Deathbed Visions from India," 105

21. Barrett, *Death-bed Visions*, 68–69.

22. Thomas, "Dying as Failure," 3.

23. See note 16.

24. Brown et al., "Waiting for a Liver Transplant," 126.

25. Moody, *Reflections on Life After Life*, 15–16.

26. Elder, *And When I Die*, 36–39.

27. Kellehear, *Experiences near Death.*

28. Saint-Exupéry, *Little Prince*, 99.

29. Quoted in Leslie, *Desperate Journeys, Abandoned Souls*, 366. Emphasis added.

30. Brodkey, *This Wild Darkness*, 177.

31. Noyes, "Journey into Alzheimer's," 96.

32. Darwish, *In the Presence of Absence*, 96.

12. Some Final Reflections

1. Lindquist, *Rowing Without Oars*, 87.

2. Chomin, "One Year and a Half," 78.

Bibliography

Abrahams, R. D. "Storytelling Events: Wake Amusements and the Structure of Nonsense on St. Vincent." *Journal of American Folklore* 95, no. 378 (1982): 389–414.

Aldrich, C. K. "The Dying Patient's Grief." *Journal of the American Medical Association* 184 (1963): 329–31.

Altman, L. L. "The Waiting Syndrome." *Psychoanalytic Quarterly* 26 (1957): 508–18.

Alvarez, A. *The Savage God: A Study of Suicide*. New York: Bantam, 1971.

Amato, J. "Politics of Suffering." *International Social Sciences Review* 69 (1994): 23–30.

Aminoff, B. Z., and A. Adunsky. "Dying Dementia Patients: Too Much Suffering, Too Little Palliation." *American Journal of Alzheimer's Disease and Other Dementias* 19, no. 4 (2004): 243–47.

Arriens, J., ed. *Welcome to Hell: Letters and Writings from Death Row*. Boston: Northeastern University Press, 2005.

Atkins, S. E., ed. *The 9/11 Encyclopedia*. Vol. 1. Westport, Conn.: Praeger Security International, 2008.

Averill, J. R., and E. P. Nunley, "Grief as an Emotion and as a Disease: A Social Constructionist Perspective." *Journal of Social Issues* 44, no. 3 (1988): 79–95.

Baehrecke, E. H. "How Death Shapes Life During Development." *Nature Reviews Molecular Cell Biology* 3 (2002): 779–87.

Barak, Y., A. Achiron, Z. Rotstein, A. Elizur, and S. Noy. "Stress Associated with Asbestosis: The Trauma of Waiting for Death." *Psycho-oncology* 7 (1998): 126–28.

Barbato, M. *Caring for the Dying*. Sydney: McGraw-Hill Australia, 2002.

Barnard, D., A. Towers, P. Boston, and Y. Lambrinidou. *Crossing Over: Narratives of Palliative Care*. New York: Oxford University Press, 2000.

Barnhart, R. K., ed. *Chambers Dictionary of Etymology*. New York: Chambers Harrap, 1988.

Barrett, W. *Death-bed Visions*. 1926. Wellingborough, UK: Aquarian Press, 1986.

Bassett, J. "Facing Mortality: A First-Person Account." In A. Kellehear, ed., *Death and Dying in Australia*, 223–39. Melbourne: Oxford University Press, 2000.

Bauby, J. D. *The Diving Bell and the Butterfly*. London: Fourth Estate, 1997.

Berkowitz, L., and E. Harmon-Jones. "Toward an Understanding of the Determinants of Anger." *Emotion* 4, no. 2 (2004): 107–30.

Berman, M. L. "The Todeserwartung Syndrome." *Geriatrics* (May 1966): 187–92.

Blazer, D. G. "Depression in Late Life: Review and Commentary." *Journal of Gerontology: Medical Sciences* 58A, no. 3 (2003): 249–65.

Block, S. "Psychological Considerations, Growth, and Transcendence at the End of Life: The Art of the Possible." *Journal of the American Medical Association* 285, no. 22 (2001): 2898–2906.

Boer, M. F., R. M. de Ryckman, J. F. A. Pruyn, and H. W. Van den Borne. "Psychosocial Correlates of Cancer Relapse and Survival: A Literature Review." *Patient Education and Counseling* 37 (1999): 215–30.

Boston, P. "Klara Bergman: Burdens from the Past." In D. Barnard, A Towers, P. Boston, and Y. Lambrinidou, *Crossing Over: Narratives of Palliative Care*, 59–78. New York: Oxford University Press, 2000.

Bourdieu, P. *The Weight of the World: Social Suffering in Contemporary Society.* Cambridge, UK: Polity Press, 1999.

Bourke, J. *Fear: A Cultural History.* Emeryville, CA: Shoemaker & Hoard, 2005.

Bowker, J. W. *Problems of Suffering in Religions of the World.* Cambridge, UK: Cambridge University Press, 1970.

Bowlby, J. *Loss: Sadness and Depression.* London: Pimlico, 1998.

Bracha, H. S. "Freeze, Flight, Fight, Fright, Faint: Adaptionist Perspectives on the Acute Stress Response Spectrum." *CNS Spectrums* 9 (2004): 679–85.

Bradford, C. D. "Waiting to Die, Dying to Live." *Interdisciplinary Journal of Human Rights Law* 5, no. 1 (2010–11): 77–96.

Brodkey, H. *This Wild Darkness: The Story of My Death.* New York: Metropolitan Books. 1996.

Brown, J., J. H. Sorrell, J. McClaren, and J. W. Creswell. "Waiting for a Liver Transplant." *Qualitative Health Research* 16, no. 1 (2006): 119–36.

Bruce, S. *God Is Dead: Secularization in the West.* Oxford: Blackwell, 2002.

Butler, R. N. "The Life Review: An Interpretation of Reminiscence in the Aged." *Psychiatry* 26 (1963): 65–76. Reprinted in K. Doka, ed., *Death, Dying and Bereavement.* New York: Routledge, 2007, 2:350–68.

Byrne, A., J. Ellershaw, C. Holcombe, and P. Salmon. "Patients' Experience of Cancer: Evidence of the Role of 'Fighting' in Collusive Clinical Communication." *Patient Education and Counseling* 48 (2002): 15–21.

Bytheway, B. *Unmasking Age: The Significance of Age for Social Research.* Bristol, UK: Policy Press, 2011.

Cappeliez, P., and N. O'Rourke. "Profiles of Reminiscence Among Older Adults: Perceived Stress, Life Attitudes, and Personality Variables." *International Journal of Aging and Human Development* 54, no. 4 (2002): 255–66.

Carr, J. P., and J. P. Fogarty. "Families at the Bedside: An Ethnographic Study of Vigilance." *Journal of Family Practice* 48, no. 6 (1999): 433–38.

Carroll, L. *Alice's Adventures in Wonderland.* New York: Airmont, 1965.

Carson, H. J., and R. Fiester. Letter to the editor. *Canadian Journal of Psychiatry*. December 2004.

Cassell, E. J. *The Nature of Suffering and the Goals of Medicine*. New York: Oxford University Press, 2004.

Cassidy, S. "Emotional Distress in Terminal Cancer." *Journal of the Royal Society of Medicine*, 79 (1986): 717–20.

Casson, J. H. *Dying: The Greatest Adventure of My Life*. London: Christian Medical Fellowship, 1980.

Chochinov, H. M. "Depression in Cancer Patients." *Lancet* 2 (2001): 499–505.

———. "Dying, Dignity, and New Horizons in Palliative End of Life Care." *CA: A Cancer Journal for Clinicians* 56, no. 2 (2006): 84–103.

Chomin, N. "One Year and a Half." Translated by Robert Jay Lifton, Shuichi Kato, and Michael R. Reich. In D. J. Enright, ed., *The Oxford Book of Death*, 78. Oxford: Oxford University Press, 1987.

Clarke, J. "Cancer Meanings in the Media: Implications for Physicians." *Studies in Communications* 3 (1986): 175–215.

Coleman, P. G. "Creating a Life Story: The Task of Reconciliation." *Gerontologist* 39, no. 2 (1999): 134.

Conway, S., and J. Hockey. "Resisting the 'Mask' of Old Age? The Social Meaning of Lay Health Beliefs in Later Life." *Ageing & Society* 18 (1998): 469–94.

Cook, H. T., and T. F. Cook. *Japan at War: An Oral History*. New York: New Press, 1992.

Coontz, P. D. "Women Under Sentence of Death: The Social Organization of Waiting to Die." *Prison Journal* 63 (1983): 88–98.

Cowan, M. A., and R. P. McQuellon. "Turning Toward Death Together." *Furrow* 51, no. 7/8 (2000): 395–402.

Craib, I. "Fear, Death and Sociology." *Mortality* 8, no. 3 (2003): 285–95.

Crandall, R., and W. H. Crandall. *Borders of Time: Life in a Nursing Home*. New York: Springer, 1990.

Crane, S. "I Saw a Man." In Dore, *Premier Book of Major Poets*, 278.

Cruz, V. "ALONE/December/night." In Dore, *Premier Book of Major Poets*, 247–48.

Darwish, M. *In the Presence of Absence*. Translated by Sinan Antoon. New York: Archipelago Books, 2011.

Das, V. "Suffering, Theocidies, Disciplinary Practices, Appropriations." *International Social Sciences Journal* 49 (1997): 563–72.

DeBaggio, T. *Losing My Mind: An Intimate Look at Life with Alzheimer's*. New York: Free Press, 2002.

Dhabhar, F. S. "A Hassle a Day May Keep the Pathogens Away: The Fight-or-Flight Stress Response and the Augmentation of Immune Function." *Integrative & Comparative Biology* 49, no. 3 (2009): 215–36.

Diamond, E. F. "Brain-based Determination of Death Revisited." *Linacre Quarterly* 65, no. 4 (1998): 71–80.

Diamond, J. C: *Because Cowards Get Cancer Too*. London: Vermillion, 1998.

Donaldson, N., and B. Donaldson. *How Did They Die?* New York: Greenwich House, 1983.

Donnelly, S. "Traditions Associated with Dying in the West of Scotland." *Journal of Palliative Care* 15, no. 4 (1999): 64–69.

Donnelly, S. M., and C. N. Donnelly. "The Experience of the Moment of Death in a Specialist Palliative Care Unit." *Irish Medical Journal* 102, no. 5 (2009): 143–49.

Donnelly, S. M., N. Michael, and C. Donnelly. "Experience of the Moment of Death at Home." *Mortality* 11, no. 4 (2005): 352–67.

Dore, A., ed. *The Premier Book of Major Poets*. New York: Fawcett Columbine, 1970.

Doyle, D. *Caring for a Dying Relative: A Guide for Families*. Oxford: Oxford University Press. 1994.

Edinger, A. L., and C. B. Thompson. "Death by Design: Apoptosis, Necrosis and Autophagy." *Current Opinion in Cell Biology* 16, (2004): 663–69.

Eilam, D. "Die Hard: A Blend of Freezing and Fleeing as a Dynamic Defense — Implications for the Control of Defensive Behavior." *Neuroscience & Biobehavioral Reviews* 29 (2005): 1181–91.

Elder, B., ed. *And When I Die, Will I Be Dead?* Sydney: Australian Broadcasting Corporation, 1987.

Elias, N. *The Loneliness of the Dying*. Oxford: Basil Blackwell, 1985.

Eliot, T. S. *The Waste Land and Other Poems*. London: Faber & Faber, 1940.

Eliott, J. A., and I. N. Olver. "Hope and Hoping in the Talk of Dying Cancer Patients." *Social Science & Medicine* 64 (2007): 138–49.

Ellis, C. *Final Negotiations: A Story of Love, Loss and Chronic Illness*. Philadelphia: Temple University Press, 1995.

Engel, G. L. "Psychogenic Pain and the Pain-Prone Patient." *American Journal of Medicine* 26 (1959): 899.

Ettema, E. J., L. D. Derksen, and E. van Leeuwen. "Existential Loneliness and End of Life Care: A Systematic Review." *Theoretical Medicine & Bioethics* 31, no. 2 (2010): 141–69.

Faust, D. G. *This Republic of Suffering: Death and the American Civil War*. New York: Alfred A. Knopf, 2008.

Feifel, H., J. Freilich, and L. J. Hermann. "Death Fear in Dying Heart and Cancer Patients." *Journal of Psychosomatic Research* 17 (1973): 161–66.

Felder, B. E. "Hoping and Coping in Patients with Cancer Diagnosis." *Cancer Nursing* 27, no. 4 (2004): 320–24.

"'Fighting Spirit' After Cancer Diagnosis Does Not Improve Outcome." Editorial. *British Medical Journal* 330 (2005): 865.

Ford, J. K. B., and R. R. Reeves. "Fight or Flight: Anti-Predator Strategies of Baleen Whales." *Mammal Review* 38, no. 1 (2008): 50–86.

Fountain, A., and A. Kellehear. "On Prevalence Disparities in Recent Empirical Studies of Deathbed Visions." *Journal of Palliative Care* 28, no. 2 (2012): 49–51.

Frank, A. "Can We Research Suffering?" *Qualitative Health Research* 11 (2001): 353–62.

Frankl, V. E. *The Doctor and the Soul.* Harmondsworth, UK: Penguin, 1963.

——. *Man's Search for Meaning.* 1946. London: Hodder & Stoughton, 1964.

Freeman, M. *Hindsight: The Promise and Peril of Looking Backward.* New York: Oxford University Press, 2010.

Fridh, I., A. Forsberg, and I. Bergbom. "Close Relatives' Experiences of Caring and of the Physical Environment When a Loved One Dies in an ICU." *Intensive and Critical Care Nursing* 25 (2009): 111–19.

Fromm, E. *The Art of Loving.* London: Unwin, 1957.

Fromm-Reichmann, F. "On Loneliness." In D. M. Bullard, ed., *Psychoanalysis and Psychotherapy: Selected Papers from Frieda Fromm-Reichmann,* 325–36. Chicago: University of Chicago Press, 1959.

Gardner, H., ed. *The New Oxford Book of Verse.* Oxford: Clarendon, 1972.

Gardner, I. R. "Not Dying a Victim: Living with AIDS." In Kellehear and Ritchie, *Seven Dying Australians,* 41–59.

Geertz, C. *Interpretation of Culture.* New York: Basic Books, 1977.

Georgers, J. J., B. D. Onwateaka-Philipsen, A. van der Heide, G. van der Wal, and P. J. van der Maas. "Symptoms, Treatment and 'Dying Peacefully' in Terminally Ill Cancer Patients: A Prospective Study." *Supportive Care Cancer* 13 (2005): 160–68.

Gibson, G. C. *Wake Rites.* Gainesville: University Press of Florida, 2005.

Gilbert, P., and J. Gilbert. "Entrapment and Arrested Fight and Flight in Depression: An Exploration Using Focus Groups." *Psychology and Psychotherapy: Theory, Research and Practice* 76 (2003): 173–88.

Gill, R., C. K. Hadaway, and P. L. Marler. "Is Religious Belief Declining in Britain?" *Journal of the Scientific Study of Religion* 37 (1998): 507–16.

Glaser, B., and A. Strauss. *Status Passage.* Chicago: Aldine, 1968.

Goodall, J. "Personal View: Doctors Fighting, Fleeing, or Facing Up to Death." *British Medical Journal* 317 (1998): 355–56.

Greenberg, J. T. "Programmed Cell Death: A Way of Life for Plants." *Proceedings of the National Academy of Sciences for the USA* 93, no. 22 (1996): 12094–97.

Greenwood, K. A., R. Thurston, M. Rumble, S. T. Waters, and F. J. Keefe. "Anger and Persistent Pain: Current Status and Future Directions." *Pain* 103 (2003): 1–5.

Gregory, D. M., and C. K. Russell, eds. *Cancer Stories: On Life and Suffering.* Montreal: McGill-Queens University Press, 1999.

Gum, A., and C. R. Snyder. "Coping with Terminal Illness: The Role of Hopeful Thinking." *Journal of Palliative Medicine* 5, no. 6 (2002): 883–94.

Hackett, J. T. *My Commonplace Book.* London: Macmillan, 1923.

Hartog, J., J. R. Audy, and Y. A. Cohen, eds. *The Anatomy of Loneliness.* New York: International Universities Press, 1980.

Helm, E. "Fighting Demons, Fighting Cancer." *Eukaryon* 4 (March 2008). http://legacy.lakeforest.edu/images/userImages/eukaryon/Page_7190/Microsoft%20Word%20-%20EthanHelmMemoir.pdf. Accessed August 25, 2011.

Henderson, J. L., and M. Oakes. *The Wisdom of the Serpent: The Myths of Death, Rebirth, and Resurrection.* Princeton, NJ: Princeton University Press, 1990.

Hinton, J. *Dying.* Harmondsworth, UK: Penguin, 1967.

Holden, J., B. Greyson, and D. James, eds. *The Handbook of Near-Death Experiences: Thirty Years of Investigation.* Santa Barbara, CA: ABC-CLIO, 2009.

Horwitz, A. V., and J. C. Wakefield. *The Loss of Sadness: How Psychiatry Transformed Normal Sorrow into Depressive Disorder.* New York: Oxford University Press, 2007.

Houston, R. E. "The Angry Dying Patient." *Primary Care Companion: Journal of Clinical Psychiatry* 1, no. 1 (1999): 5–8.

Howse, K. *Deaths of People Alone.* London: Centre for Policy on Ageing, 1997.

Hu, K. K. "Fighting for a Peaceful Death: A Personal Essay." *Journal of Palliative Medicine* 4, no. 2 (2001): 209–13.

Huxley, A. *The Doors of Perception: Heaven and Hell.* London: Grafton Books, 1977.

Illich, I. *Limits to Medicine/Medical Nemesis: The Expropriation of Health.* Harmondsworth, UK: Penguin, 1977.

Irvin, S. K. "Waiting: Concept Analysis." *Nursing Diagnosis* 12, no. 4 (2001): 128–36.

Jacobson, M. D., M. Weil, and M. C. Raff. "Programmed Cell Death in Animal Development." *Cell* 88 (1997): 347–54.

Jacques, N. D., and B. R. Hasselkus. "The Nature of Occupation Surrounding Dying and Death." *Occupational Therapy Journal of Research* 24, no. 2 (2004): 49.

Jaffe, L., and A. Jaffe. "Terminal Candor and the Coda Syndrome: A Tandem View of Fatal Illness." In H. Feifel, ed., *New Meanings of Death*, 195–211. New York: McGraw-Hill, 1977.

James, W. *The Will to Believe and Human Immortality.* New York: Dover, 1956.

Jarman, D. *Smiling in Slow Motion.* London: Century, 2000.

Johnson, R. "Under Sentence of Death: The Psychology of Death Row Confinement." *Law and Psychology Review* 5 (1979): 185–86.

Jung, C. G. *The Undiscovered Self.* London: Routledge, 1958.

Kaufman, S. R. *And a Time to Die: How American Hospitals Shape the End of Life.* Chicago: University of Chicago Press, 2005.

Keeley, M. P. "Final Conversations: Messages of Love." *Qualitative Research Reports in Communication* 5 (2004): 48–57.

Kellehear, A. *A Social History of Dying.* Cambridge, UK: Cambridge University Press, 2007.

——. *The Book of Gentle Wisdom.* Melbourne: Hill of Content, 2002.

——. "Classics Revisited: Alvarez and the Divisive God." *Mortality* 11, no. 4 (2006): 368–73.

——. "Dying as a Social Relationship: A Sociological Review of Debates on the Determination of Death." *Social Science & Medicine* 66, no. 7 (2008): 1533–44.

——. *Dying of Cancer: The Final Year of Life.* Chur, CH: Harwood Academic, 1990.

——. "Dying Old and *Preferably* Alone? Agency, Resistance, and Dissent at the End of Life." *International Journal of Ageing and Later Life* 4, no. 1 (2009): 5–21.

———. *Eternity and Me: The Everlasting Things in Life and Death.* Melbourne: Hill of Content, 2000.

———. *Experiences near Death: Beyond Medicine and Religion.* New York: Oxford University Press, 1996.

———. Introduction to E. Kübler-Ross, *On Death and Dying,* vii–xviii. 40th anniv. ed. Oxford: Routledge, 2009.

———. "The Near-Death Experience as Status Passage." *Social Science & Medicine* 31, no. 8 (1990): 933–39.

———. "On Dying and Human Suffering." *Palliative Medicine* 23 (2009): 388–97.

———. "The Social Inequality of Dying." In C. Waddell and A. R. Petersen, eds., *Just Health: Inequality in Illness, Care and Prevention,* 181–89. Melbourne: Churchill-Livingstone, 1994.

Kellehear, A., and T. Lewin. "Farewells by the Dying: A Sociological Study." *Omega: Journal of Death & Dying* 19, no. 4 (1988): 275–92.

Kellehear, A., and D. Ritchie, eds. *Seven Dying Australians.* Bendigo, Australia: St. Luke Innovative Resources, 2003.

Kellehear, A., R. Mindruta-Stratan, V. Pogonet, and V. Gorelco. "Family Care of the Dying in the Republic of Moldova: A Qualitative Study." *Journal of Palliative Care* 28, no. 1 (2012): 5–10.

Kellehear, A., V. Pogonet, R. Mindruta-Stratan, and V. Gorelco. *Care of the Dying in the Republic of Moldova.* Chisinau, Moldova: UNESCO, 2011.

———. "Deathbed Visions from the Republic of Moldova: A Content Analysis of Family Observations." *Omega: Journal of Death and Dying* 64, no. 4 (2011–12): 303–17.

Kelly, E. W., B. Greyson, and E. F. Kelly. "Unusual Experiences Near Death and Related Phenomena." In E. F. Kelly, E. W. Kelly, A. Crabtree, A. Gauld, M. Grosso, and B. Greyson, eds., *Irreducible Mind: Toward a Psychology for the 21st Century,* 367–421. Lanham, MD: Rowan & Littlefield, 2007.

Kermode, F. *The Sense of an Ending: Studies in the Theory of Fiction.* New York: Oxford University Press, 2000.

Kierkegaard, S. *Fear and Trembling and the Sickness unto Death.* Princeton, NJ: Princeton University Press, 1941.

Killick, J., and C. Cordonnier. *Openings.* London: Hawker, 2000.

Klein, M. "On the Sense of Loneliness." In Hartog, Audy, and Cohen, *Anatomy of Loneliness,* 547–53.

Kleinman, A. *The Illness Narratives: Suffering, Healing and the Human Condition.* New York: Basic Books, 1988.

———. "Pitch, Picture, Power: The Globalization of Local Suffering and the Transformation of Local Experience." *Ethnos* 60 (1995): 181–91.

Kleinman, A., and J. Kleinman. "Suffering and Its Professional Transformation: Towards an Ethnography of Personal Experience." *Culture, Medicine and Psychiatry* 15 (1991): 257–301.

Knudsen, S. K. "The Dying Animal: A Perspective from Veterinary Medicine." In A. Kellehear, ed., *The Study of Dying*, 27–50. Cambridge, UK: Cambridge University Press, 2009.

Krishnamurti, J. *On Fear.* New York: HarperCollins, 1995.

Kübler-Ross, E. *On Death and Dying.* New York: Macmillan, 1969.

Kylma, J., W. Duggleby, D. Cooper, and G. Molander. "Hope in Palliative Care: An Integrative Review." *Palliative and Supportive Care* 7 (2009): 365–77.

Langner, T. *Choices for Living: Coping with Fear of Dying.* New York: Kluwer, 2002.

Lawton, J. *The Dying Process: Patients' Experiences of Palliative Care.* London: Routledge, 2000.

Leader, D. *Why Do Women Write More Letters Than They Post?* London: Faber & Faber, 1996.

Lederer, S. E. "Dark Victory: Cancer and Popular Hollywood Film." *Bulletin of the History of Medicine* 81, no. 1 (2007): 94–115.

Leslie, E. *Desperate Journeys, Abandoned Souls: True Stories of Castaways and Other Survivors.* London: Macmillan, 1988.

Levertov, D. "Age of Terror." In J. Rothenberg and P. Joris, eds., *Poems for the Millennium: The University of California Book of Modern & Postmodern Poetry.* Vol. 2: *From Postwar to Millennium,* 201. Berkeley: University of California Press, 1998.

Levine, P. A. *In an Unspoken Voice: How the Body Releases Trauma and Restores Goodness.* Berkeley, CA: North Atlantic Books, 2010.

Levine, R. "Waiting Is a Power Game." *Psychology Today* 21, no. 4 (1987): 24–33.

Lewis, C. S. *Surprised by Joy.* London: Collins, 1955.

Licence, T. *Hermits and Recluses in English Society, 950–1200.* Oxford: Oxford University Press, 2011.

Lindemann, E. "The Symptomatology and Management of Acute Grief." *American Journal of Psychiatry* 101 (1944): 141–48.

Lindquist, U. C. *Rowing Without Oars.* London: Viking, 2004.

Lingle, S., and S. M. Pellis. "Fight or Flight? Anti-Predator Behavior and the Escalation of Coyote Encounters with Deer." *Oecologia* 131 (2002): 154–64.

Lloyd-Williams, M., V. Kennedy, A. Sixsmith, and J. Sixsmith. "The End of Life: A Qualitative Study of the Perceptions of People over the Age of 80 on Issues Surrounding Death and Dying." *Journal of Pain and Symptom Management* 34, no. 1 (2007): 60–66.

Locsin, R. C., C. E. Lynn, W. Kongsuwan, and G. Nambozi. "Ugandan Nurses' Experience of Caring for Persons Dying from Ebola Hemorrhagic Fever." *International Journal of Human Caring* 13, no. 4 (2009): 26–32.

Lopez, S. J., H. N. Rusmussen, W. R. Shorupski, K. Koetting, S. E. Petersen, and Y. T. Yang. "Folk Conceptualizations of Courage." In C. L. S. Pury and S. J. Lopez, eds., *The Psychology of Courage: Modern Research on an Ancient Virtue,* 23–45. Washington, DC: American Psychological Association, 2010.

Lorimer, D. *Whole in One: The Near-Death Experience and the Ethic of Interconnectedness.* London: Arkana, 1990.

Lubbock, T. "Tom Lubbock: A Memoir of Living with a Brain Tumour." *Guardian,* November 6, 2010. http://www.guardian.co.uk/books/2010/nov/07/tom-lubbock-brain-tumour-language?INTCMP=SRCH.

MacDonald, B., and C. Rich. *Look Me in the Eye: Old Women, Ageing, and Ageism.* London: Women's Press, 1984.

Marcus, A. D. "The Loneliness of Fighting a Rare Cancer." *Health Matters* 29, no. 1 (2010): 203–206.

Masson, J. Moussaieff, and S. McCarthy. *When Elephants Weep: The Emotional Lives of Animals.* New York: Dell, 1999.

McGraw, J. G. "Loneliness, Its Nature and Forms: An Existential Perspective." *Man and World* 28 (1995): 43–64.

McLuhan, M., and Q. Fiore. *The Medium Is the Massage.* Harmondsworth, UK: Penguin, 1967.

McPherson, C. J., K. G. Wilson, and M. A. Murray. "Feeling Like a Burden: Exploring the Perspectives of Patients at the End of Life." *Social Science & Medicine* 64 (2007): 417–27.

——. "Feeling Like a Burden to Others: A Systematic Review Focusing on the End of Life." *Palliative Medicine* 21 (2007): 115–28.

Merriam, S. B. "Butler's Life Review: How Universal Is It?" *International Journal of Aging and Human Development* 37, no. 3 (1993): 163–75.

Merton, T. *The Silent Life.* New York: Farrar, Straus and Giroux, 1957.

Miller, M. "You Just Shed Life: A Nursing Home Resident Talks About the Future." In Kellehear and Ritchie, *Seven Dying Australians,* 27–37.

Miller, T. "In Many Countries, Cancer Patients Face Stigma, Misperceptions." PBS, June 15, 2011. http://www.pbs.org/newshour/updates/health/jan-june11/cancerstigma_06-15.html.

Mitchell, G. J., F. P. Pilkington, C. Jonas-Simpson, F. Aitkin, M. G. Carson, A. Fisher, and P. Lyon. "Exploring the Lived Experience of Waiting for Persons in Long-Term Care." *Nursing Science Quarterly* 18, no. 2 (2005): 163–70.

Molinari, V., and R. E. Reichlin. "Life Review Reminiscence in the Elderly: A Review of the Literature." *International Journal of Aging and Human Development* 20, no. 2 (1984–85): 81–92.

Moody, H. R. "Reminiscence and the Recovery of the Public World." In M. Kaminsky, ed., *The Uses of Reminiscence: New Ways of Working with Older Adults,* 157–66. New York: Haworth Press, 1984.

Moody, R. A. *Life After Life.* New York: Bantam, 1973.

——. *Reflections on Life After Life.* New York: Bantam, 1977.

Moran, L. *The Anatomy of Courage.* London: Constable, 1945.

Morris, J., and S. C. Adams, eds. *Facing Forward: Poems of Courage.* New York: George Sully, 1925.

Muthumana, S. P., M. Kumari, A. Kellehear, S. Kumar, and F. Moosa. "Deathbed Visions from India: A Study of Family Observations in Northern Kerala." *Omega: Journal of Death & Dying* 62, no. 2 (2010): 95–107.

Nagatsuka, R. *I Was a Kamikaze.* London: Abelard-Schuman, 1972.

Noonan, P. "The Sounds That Still Echo from 9/11." *Wall Street Journal,* September 9, 2006. http://online.wsj.com/article/SB115774704992357920.html. Accessed September 24, 2012.

Noyes, L. "Journey into Alzheimer's." In K. Doka, ed., *Living with Grief: Alzheimer's Disease.* Washington, DC: Hospice Foundation of America, 2004.

Nuland, S. B. *How We Die.* London: Chatto & Windus, 1993.

Ohnuki-Tierney, E. *Kamikaze, Cherry Blossoms, and Nationalisms.* Chicago: University of Chicago Press, 2002.

Oxford Illustrated Dictionary. Oxford: Clarendon, 1975.

Parkes, C. M. "The Dying Patient." *British Medical Journal* 316, no. 7140 (1998): 313.

Pastan, L. *The Five Stages of Grief.* New York: W. W. Norton, 1978.

Patterson, J. *The Dread Disease: Cancer and Modern American Culture.* Cambridge, MA: Harvard University Press, 1987.

Penson, R. T., R. A. Partridge, M. A. Shah, D. Giansiracusa, B. A. Chabner, and T. J. Lynch. "Update: Fear of Death." *Oncologist* 10, no. 1 (2005): 62.

Perera, K. "Faith Keeps Me Going: Living with Motor Neurone Disease." In Kellehear and Ritchie, *Seven Dying Australians,* 85–97.

Pessoa, F. "The Startling Reality of Things." In J. Rothenberg and P. Joris, eds., *Poems for the Millennium: The University of California Book of Modern & Postmodern Poetry.* Vol. 1: *From Fin-de-Siecle to Negritude,* 147. Berkeley: University of California Press, 1998.

Petticrew, M., R. Bell, and D. Hunter. "Influence of Psychological Coping on Survival and Recurrence in People with Cancer: Systematic Review." *British Medical Journal* 325, (2002): 1066–69.

Philip, J., M. Gold, M. Schwarz, and P. Komesaroff. "Anger in Palliative Care: A Clinical Approach." *Internal Medicine Journal* 37 (2007): 49–55.

Pilowsky, I., and N. D. Spence. "Pain, Anger and Illness Behavior." *Journal of Psychosomatic Research* 20 (1976): 411–16.

Plath, S. *Ariel.* London: Faber & Faber, 1965.

Porges, S. W. "Orienting in a Defensive World: Mammalian Modifications of Our Evolutionary Heritage. a Polyvagal Theory." *Psychophysiology* 32 (1995): 301–18.

Pury, C. L. S., and S. J. Lopez, eds. *The Psychology of Courage: Modern Research on an Ancient Virtue.* Washington, DC: American Psychological Association, 2010.

Putman, D. "Philosophical Roots of the Concept of Courage." In Pury and Lopez, *Psychology of Courage,* 9–22.

Rachman, S. *The Meanings of Fear.* Harmondsworth, UK: Penguin, 1974.

Rate, C. R. "Defining the Features of Courage: A Search for Meaning." In Pury and Lopez, *Psychology of Courage*, 47–66.

Ratner, S. C. "Comparative Aspects of Hypnosis." In J. E. Gordon, ed., *Handbook of Clinical and Experimental Hypnosis*, 550–87. New York: Macmillan, 1967.

Rawnsley, M. M. "Recurrence of Cancer: A Crisis of Courage." In A. H. Kutscher, H. B. Haley, and the American Institute of Life-Threatening Illness and Loss, eds. *Living Under the Sword: Psychosocial Aspects of Recurrent and Progressive Life-Threatening Illness*, 161–168. Lanham, MD: Scarecrow, 2004.

Reuter, C. *My Life Is a Weapon: A Modern History of Suicide Bombing.* Princeton, NJ: Princeton University Press, 2004.

Rich, K. R. *The Red Devil: To Hell with Cancer—and Back.* New York:, Crown, 1999.

Richards, N. "The Fight-to-Die: Older People and Death Activism." *International Journal of Ageing and Later Life* 7, no. 1 (2012): 7–32.

Ritchie, D. "Listening and Understanding." In Kellehear and Ritchie, *Seven Dying Australians*, 119–25.

Robins, N. *Living in the Lightning: A Cancer Journal.* New Brunswick, NJ: Rutgers University Press, 1999.

Roget's Thesaurus. Sydney: Maxi Books, 1981.

Rose, G. *Love's Work: A Reckoning with Life.* New York: Schocken, 1995.

Rossi, R. M. *Waiting to Die: Life on Death Row.* London: Vision Books, 2004.

Roth, A. J., and M. J. Massie. "Anxiety and Its Management in Advanced Cancer." *Current Opinion in Supportive and Palliative Care* 1 (2007): 50–56.

Saba, F. "Trying to Be Normal: A Teenager Facing Childhood Cancer." In Kellehear and Ritchie, *Seven Dying Australians.* 9–23.

Sabom, M. *Recollections of Death: A Medical Investigation.* New York: Harper & Row, 1982.

Saint-Exupéry, A. *The Little Prince.* Harmondsworth, UK: Penguin, 1962.

Sand, L., and P. Strang. "Existential Loneliness in a Palliative Home Care Setting." *Journal of Palliative Medicine* 9, no. 6 (2006): 1376–87.

Saunders, C., ed. *Hospice and Palliative Care: An Interdisciplinary Approach.* London: Edward Arnold, 1990.

——. "The Philosophy of Terminal Care." In C. Saunders, ed., *The Management of Malignant Terminal Disease*, 193–202. London: Edward Arnold, 1984.

Savary, L. M., T. J. O'Connor, R. M. Cullen, and D. M. Plummer, eds. *Listen to Love: Reflections on the Seasons of the Year.* New York: Regina Press, 1970.

Scarre, G. *On Courage.* London: Routledge, 2010.

Schwarcz, V. "The Pane of Sorrow: Public Uses of Personal Grief in China." In A. Kleinman, V. Das, and M. Lock, eds., *Social Suffering*, 119–48. Berkeley: University of California Press, 1997.

Seale, C. "Cancer Heroics: A Study of News Reports with Particular Reference to Gender." *Sociology* 36, no. 1 (2002): 107–26.

——. "Sporting Cancer: Struggle Language in News Reports of People with Cancer." *Sociology of Health and Illness* 23, no. 3 (2001): 308–29.

Seligman, M. E. P. "Learned Helplessness." *Annual Review of Medicine* 23 (1972): 407–12.

Seravalli, E. P. "The Dying Patient, the Physician, and the Fear of Death." *New England Journal of Medicine* 319, no. 26 (1988): 1729.

Simmons, L. *The Role of the Aged in Primitive Society.* New Haven, CT: Yale University Press, 1945.

Skott, C. "Expressive Metaphors in Cancer Narratives." *Cancer Nursing* 25, no. 3 (2002): 230–35.

Small, N., K. Froggatt, and M. Downs. *Living and Dying with Dementia: Dialogues About Palliative Care.* Oxford: Oxford University Press, 2007.

Smith, E. N. *Passive Fear: Alternative to Fight or Flight.* New York: iUniverse, 2006.

Sontag, S. *Illness as Metaphor.* London: Penguin, 1991.

Stedman's Medical Dictionary. 22nd ed. Baltimore: Williams and Wilkins, 1972.

Suedfeld, P. "Aloneness as a Healing Experience." In L. A. Peplau and D. Perlman, eds., *Loneliness: A Sourcebook of Current Theory, Research and Therapy,* 54–67. Toronto: John Wiley and Sons, 1982.

Sullivan, M. D. "Hope and Hopelessness at the End of Life." *American Journal of Geriatric Psychiatry* 11, no. 4 (2003): 393–405.

Swensen, C. H., and S. R. Fuller. "Expressions of Love, Marriage Problems, Commitment, and Anticipatory Grief in the Marriages of Cancer Patients." *Journal of Marriage and the Family* 54, no. 1 (1992): 191–96.

Tavris, C. *Anger: The Misunderstood Emotion.* New York: Simon & Schuster, 1989.

Taylor, S. E., L. C. Klein, B. P. Lewis, T. L. Gruenewald, R. A. Gurung, and J. A. Updegraff. . "Biobehavioral Responses to Stress in Females: Tend-and-Befriend, Not Fight-or-Flight." *Psychological Review* 107, no. 3 (2000): 411–29.

Tennyson, A. "Ulysses." In H. Gardner, ed., *The New Oxford Book of Verse,* 644–46. Oxford: Clarendon, 1972.

Thomas, L. "Dying as Failure." *Annals of the American Academy of Political and Social Sciences.* 447 (1980): 1–4.

Thomson, R. "The Concept of Fear." In W. Sluckin, ed., *Fear in Animals and Man,* 1–23. New York: Van Nostrand Reinhold, 1979.

Tillich, P. *The Courage to Be.* New Haven, CT: Yale University Press, 1952.

——. "Loneliness and Solitude." In Hartog, Audy, and Cohen, *Anatomy of Loneliness,* 547–53.

Tolstoy, L. "The Death of Ivan Ilyich." In *The Death of Ivan Ilyich and Other Stories,* 93–152. New York: Signet Classics, 1883/2003.

Toynbee, P. *End of a Journey: An Autobiographical Journal, 1979–1981.* London: Bloomsbury, 1988.

Trillin, A. S. "Of Dragons and Garden Peas." *New England Journal of Medicine* 304, no. 12 (1981): 699–701.

United Kingdom Department of Health. *End of Life Care Strategy*. London: Department of Health, 2008. http://www.dh.gov.uk/en/Publicationsandstatistics/Publications/PublicationsPolicyAndGuidance/DH_086277.

Van Dyke, H. *The Friendly Year*. New York: Charles Scribner's Sons, 1994.

Van Gennep, A. *The Rites of Passage*. London: Routledge & Kegan Paul, 1908.

Wallace, J. B. "Reconsidering the Life Review: The Social Construction of Talk About the Past." *Gerontologist* 32, no. 1 (1992): 120–25.

Walton, D. N. *Courage: A Philosophical Investigation*. Berkeley: University of California Press, 1986.

Warner, M. *Monsters of Our Own Making*. Lexington: University Press of Kentucky, 2007.

Webster, J. D., and B. K. Haight. "Memory Lane Milestones: Progress in Reminiscence Definition and Classification." In B. K. Haight, and J. D. Webster, eds., *The Art and Science of Reminiscence: Theory, Research, Methods and Applications*, 273–86. Washington, DC: Taylor and Francis, 1995.

Wilkinson, I. *Suffering: A Sociological Introduction*. Cambridge, UK: Polity Press, 2000.

Williams, W. C. "The Descent." 1958. Poets.org. http://www.poets.org/viewmedia.php/prmMID/21034.

Wink, P., and J. Scott. "Does Religiousness Buffer Against the Fear of Death and Dying in Late Adulthood? Findings from a Longitudinal Study." *Journal of Gerontology: Psychological Sciences* 60B, no. 4 (2005): 207–14.

Woodhouse, J. "A Personal Reflection on Sitting at the Bedside of a Dying Loved One: The Vigil." *International Journal of Palliative Nursing* 10, no. 11 (2004): 537–41.

Worden, J. W. *Grief Counseling and Grief Therapy: A Handbook for the Mental Health Professional*. 4th ed. New York: Springer, 2009.

Wright, K. "Relationships with Death: The Terminally Ill Talk About Dying." *Journal of Marital and Family Therapy* 29, no. 4 (2003): 450–51.

Yedidia, M. J., and B. McGregor. "Confronting the Prospect of Dying: Reports of Terminally Ill Patients." *Journal of Pain and Symptom Management* 22, no. 4 (2001): 807–19.

Zaleski, C. *Otherworld Journeys: Accounts of Near-Death Experience in Medieval and Modern Times*. New York: Oxford University Press, 1987.

Index

academic and clinical writing on dying: and anger, 101; and depression, 96; focus on sadness and loss in, 12; focus on suffering, 56; limitations of, x–xi, 2, 7, 12; onlooker's perspective as characteristic perspective of, 7; and relationships, 119; and suffering, 16–17; and waiting for death by dying person, 135, 145; and waiting for death by loved ones, 131

acceptance of death, 85–87, 90; controversy surrounding, 85; vs. denial, 86; vs. helplessness, 84; as joint effort with love ones, 90–91; loved ones' difficulty of accepting, 85, 86–87, 88–89, 90–91; and openness to new experience, 208; prevailing "war on disease" paradigm and, 84, 85–86; and resistance to pressure to continue fight, 85, 86, 88–91; Saint-Exupéry on, 178; and social isolation, 173–74; in suicide, 90

Adunsky, Abraham, 189

afterlife: and deathbed visions, reality of as issue, 201–4; possibility of as unknown, 167

aging: dying from, and definition of dying process as issue, 8–9; as slow social death, 78

AIDS patients: acceptance of death in, 86–87; physical suffering in, 18; psychological suffering in, 22; social suffering in, 28–29; stigma attached to, 28; waiting for death in, 132, 143–45, 146

Ainu people of Japan, 133

Alighieri, Dante, 149

aloneness: as condition of modern existential malaise, 169–70; hallucinations in, 176–80; negative perception of, 169–70, 180–81; perception of, as culturally determined, 180–81; protective power of devotion to cause or belief system in, 176

aloneness in dying: and bodily decay, people's aversion to, 174; bystander indifference and, 174; and development of new self, 205–6; difficulty of overcoming, 170; experience of, difficulty of comprehending, 181; and fear, experience of, 48; hallucinations in, 180, 185–86; inability of others to fully empathize and, 172, 173–74, 175, 181, 182–83; individualism of modern culture and, 172; Internet communication with other dying persons as remedy for, 181–84; modern medical care and, 172; at moment of death, fear of, 175, 183; as occasion for transformative experience, 206–7, 212; perception of as negative experience, 169; physical isolation and, 181; positive consequences of, 211;

as, 79–82; and modern medical treatment as "war," 75–77; and morale, 83;
as natural reaction, 39, 89–90; suicide
as, 74–75, 89; time bought by, 74, 82,
83, 213. *See also* courage in dying;
fight response to threat of death
resistance to pressure to fight death, after
acceptance of death, 85, 86, 88–91
Rich, Katherine Russell, 19, 23–24, 29,
30–31, 32, 67–68
Ritchie, David, 43
Rivas, Elizabeth, 66
Robert (cancer patient), 192–93
Robins, Natalie, 99, 106, 125–26, 128
role in life, death as occasion for reevalu-
ation of, 11–12
Ros (elderly person), 78
Rose, Gillian, 87, 113–14, 117–18, 121, 128,
130, 166
Russell, C. K., 27

Saba, Fadia, 25, 99–100
Sabom, Michael, 154
sadness: and anger, as linked emotions, 94, 100–101; in animals, 108–9;
complexity of underlying feelings in,
107–8; *vs.* depression, 94–97; disease
model of, 94–95; etymology and
definition of, 97; family and friends as
support in, 96; focus on in palliative
care literature, 12; hope and love
experienced in context of, 110–11;
hopelessness and, 110; loved ones'
expectations for continuing struggle
and, 100; as normal response to loss,
94–95, 96, 97, 100, 108–9; as occasion
to reevaluate self and social relationships, 111; physical manifestations of,
95; positive consequences of, 211, 213;
psychological pain of loved ones and,
99–100; as self-limiting, 95; thought
of leaving present life and relationships

and, 94, 98–99, 100, 108, 110, 143;
thought of lost future and, 93, 94, 98,
99; thought of past failures and, 100;
thoughts of past losses and, 98; as
under-studied, 96–97
Saint-Exupéry, Antoine de, 15–16, 178,
205, 207
Sand, Lisa, 174–75
Santayana, George, 83
Sarah (cancer patient), 27–28
Sartre, Jean-Paul, 174
Savage-Rumbaugh, E. Sue, 109
Scarre, Geoffrey, 57, 70
Schreiner, Oliver, 93
Schwarcz, Vera, 17
scleroderma, 124–25
sea captains, courage in facing death, 60
self. *See* identity
self-knowledge/self-evaluation: increase
in, through dying journey, 215; Jung
on, 157–58; life story review as means
to, 152–56, 157–59, 160–61, 162,
164–65; and multiplicity of selves, 164.
See also transformation within dying
person
Seligman, Martin, 84
senses, sharpening of, in dying persons,
191–92
separation, as cause of anguish in animals, 95. *See also* aloneness in dying;
relationships of dying persons
September 11th terrorist attacks: courage
of attackers in, 64; courage of Flight
93 passengers, 64–65; courage of
victims of, 64–66
Seravalli, Egilde, 126–27
ships, sinking, captains going down with,
60
shock, painless state experienced in, 6–7
Simmons, Leo, 133
sleep, troubled, 27–28
social isolation: aging as slow process of,